Pastor Horn,
may the Lord continue
to use you to Magnify His Name
and advance His kingdom! 2Cor 5:14-21
Bro. Nick Holden

Ps. 35:27

Magnify the Lord

Ten Reasons to Discover, Declare, and Defend Why Christ Came

Nick Holden

xulon PRESS

Magnify the Lord
Ten Reasons to Discover, Declare, and Defend Why Christ Came
by Nick Holden

Printed in the United States of America

ISBN 978-1-60266-931-4

Unless otherwise indicated, Bible quotations are taken from the
King James Version of the Bible.

www.xulonpress.com

Table of Contents

Acknowledgments

To my bride and best friend, Stephanie, for her unwavering support and dedication to walk with me in the Lord's harvest. To my daughters and arrows, Elizabeth, Lydia, and Lauren, who are so willing to be molded and shaped through the heat of the fire in order to fly straight for the glory of God. To my family, pastor, church, and co-laborers in the Lord's work who have supported me personally and this work by sacrificing their time to intercede, their trust to encourage, and their treasures to grace me with the opportunity to sow in the hearts of men and women everywhere the precious seed of the Word of God. To my teachers over the past eleven years, the servants God has used to invest His ways in my life, who have spent their lives for His glory to preach, teach, write, and sing the Truth. To Xulon Press for their professionalism, diligence, and determination to work with me and to make this material a written witness.

> And God is able to make all grace abound toward you; that ye, always having all sufficiency in all things, may abound to every good work.
>
> 2 Corinthians 9:8

Dedication

To KING JESUS, the Champion of champions, who is raising up men and women to be dangerously strong for His truth on the earth and equipping them with His gospel to impact lives for His Father's glory.

Now unto Him that is able to do exceeding abundantly above all that we ask or think, according to the power that worketh in us, unto Him be glory in the church by Christ Jesus throughout all ages, world without end. Amen.

Ephesians 3:20-21

To the Kingdom Warriors in every generation that were not moved from their course, and who did not take lightly their calling to preach the Gospel with joy, even though their lives were in danger every hour, as they faced suffering, persecution, and death that others may come to know their KING and His eternal message of Truth.

Save that the Holy Ghost witnesseth in every city, saying that bonds and afflictions abide me. But none of these things move me, neither count I my life dear unto myself, so that I might finish my course with joy, and the ministry, which I have received of the Lord Jesus, to testify the gospel of the grace of God.

Acts 20:23-24

Introduction

If we were to walk the streets of our cities and towns and ask one hundred people if they know why Jesus Christ was born, ninety-five percent of them would say, "He came to die on a cross" or "He came to save sinners." They are exactly right. Jesus did come to give His life for the life of sinners. If we took one more step with our question, we would then ask them how was Christ's life any different from ours. We could take it even further and ask them what kind of positional and practical effect Christ has had on those who follow Him. The more specific we got in our questions, the clearer it would become that only a handful out of the hundred would know why Jesus Christ came.

Magnify the Lord is a tool designed to help us discover at least ten reasons why Christ came. It's by no means an exhaustive look at the life of Christ. We will only touch the hem of His garment in this material, but I pray it will help us take hold of Him. As we discover these reasons for His coming, it will encourage us to dig deeper into each one. Why is it important for us to know why He came? The events associated with Christ and His eternal purpose are what make up the gospel. It is absolutely critical for us to discover the gospel! When we know and favor the righteous cause of the Father upon the life of Jesus we will magnify the Lord. King David says, "Let them shout for joy, and be glad, that favor my righteous cause: yea, let them say continually, Let the Lord be magnified, which hath pleasure in the prosperity of His servant" (Psalm 35:27).

The Father takes pleasure in the work and well-being of His Son. The more we know and favor His purpose in coming, the more we'll want to magnify the Lord. The more we discover, the more we will desire to declare His cause and magnify the Lord before a lost and dying world. Disciples of Jesus are people who live a life of declaring what they know about their Master. If we're going to declare a redemptive gospel we must know the central figure of history and the truth, the Lord Jesus Christ.

When we begin to declare the gospel, we'll also have to defend the reasons why Jesus Christ had to die in our place to free us from the power of darkness and deception and put us in a position to love and adore Him and His people. God will put us on the witness stand and demand we testify in defense of His saving grace. I wrote *Magnify the Lord* to glorify God and admonish His people that it is our duty to defend His righteous cause with confidence, conviction, compassion, and clarity.

I must agree with the apostle Paul, who says,

> For I know that this shall turn to my salvation through your prayer, and the supply of the Spirit of Jesus Christ, according to my earnest expectation and my hope, that in nothing I shall be ashamed, but that with all boldness, as always, so now also Christ shall be magnified in my body, whether it be by life, or by death.
>
> Philippians 1:19-20

Join me and let us magnify the Lord together as we discover, declare, and defend the cause of Christ, the gospel of God's grace.

> I will bless the Lord at all times: His praise shall continually be in my mouth. My soul shall make her boast in the Lord: the humble shall hear thereof, and be glad. O Magnify the Lord with me, and let us exalt His name together.
>
> Psalm 34:1-3

Chapter 1

He's Come to Defer

WHAT A NAME

Jesus! There is no name more precious to the children of God than the name Jesus. His name sounds so adoring and attractive to His disciples that it can't be mentioned without them being full of joy unspeakable and glory. Why is His name so special to His people? He Himself is what makes His name so wonderful and amazing. His life and the reasons why He came to the earth are worth more than we have to offer. What do we have to offer Him? All we have is our life. We have nothing more or nothing less. He has given all of Himself to us and requires that we give all of ourselves to Him.

LOSING OUR LIFE TO HIM

Making the point more personal, I must encourage you to give Jesus the life He paid for with His own blood. Give Him your sin, your anger, your hurt, your doubt, your lies, your wounds, your desires, your passion, your plans, your family, your pain, your secrets, your unbelief, your pride, your future, your mind, your heart, your hands, your feet, your strength, your trust, your life—just give Him you! He gave all of Himself in exchange for all of you. His Life for your life! Today is the day of deliverance and salvation. Give Jesus your praise!

When we give our lives to Jesus, we are making a lifelong invest-ment of studying and investigating everything there is to know about the Lover of our souls. There are many reasons why Jesus came to the earth to save sinners. Many of the reasons have such an eternal significance, and only the Godhead can comprehend the fullness of its scope. The Scripture teaches us that it is the glory of God to conceal a matter and the glory of kings to search out a matter.[1] It should be the glory of every blood-bought king to want to search the Word of God to know Jesus more intimately and to learn the reasons for His coming.

A COMPLETELY YIELDED LIFE

The Scriptures reveal many nuggets of truth that will transform our lives regarding the reasons for the coming of Jesus Christ. We're going to take a closer look at ten specific reasons why Jesus Christ came. We must begin with a truth that is somewhat sobering yet, without question, satisfying. Christ has come to defer three things to His Father. He's come to defer all rights, all results, and all rewards to His heavenly Father. These truths are extremely satisfying due to the great comfort they give to a sinner in need of a perfect sacri-fice for sin. The Lord Jesus Christ was found to be without any sin. Therefore, we can rejoice in the fact that at all points Jesus was obedient to the will of His Father. By deferring all things unto His Father's desire, He finished the eternal work of redemption for sinful men. This should bring a divine satisfaction to the hearts and minds of those who have been persuaded that Jesus is the way, the truth, and the life[2] and have entrusted their lives to His redemptive grace.

This is a very satisfying yet sobering thought upon which to meditate. Why is it so sobering? Those who have surrendered their lives unto the Lord Jesus Christ are predestined to be conformed to His image.[3] This would mean that as they subject themselves to the life and love of Jesus, they too would defer all things to their heavenly Father. If Jesus came to defer all, those who belong to Him should also be deferring all. This is a sobering yet satisfying truth that applies to all disciples of the Lord Jesus Christ. All disciples must make every effort to recognize, reflect upon with other disciples, and take on the responsibility of revealing this lifestyle to a world around us.

1. He's Come to Defer All Rights

A MODEL SERVANT

The followers of Christ are people of the Word. And as products of the Word, it will be best if they examine this principle from God's viewpoint, as recorded in the Scriptures, the Bible, God's revelation of Himself. Jesus reveals to His followers on numerous occasions that He only spoke what He heard: "For I have not spoken of Myself; but the Father which sent Me, He gave Me a commandment, what I should say, and what I should speak" (John 12:49). Jesus unashamedly and very clearly stated in the above passage His priority to defer. Jesus delightfully deferred His right to speak on His own authority to His Father.

Jesus is the chosen vessel of the Father, His instrument of redemption. To be and do such a matchless work for God the Father, Jesus had to be totally submissive. Listen to His heart in John 5:30: "I can of Mine own self do nothing: as I hear, I judge: and My judgment is just; because I seek not Mine own will, but the will of the Father which hath sent Me." Wow! Jesus is the perfect and most beautiful manifestation of the proper *disposition, discernment*, and *direction* of an obedient servant. A true servant worth his salt must first defer his rights to his master. Jesus models for His disciples the essence of servanthood.

Throughout the life of Jesus, He exercised the supernatural discernment He had regarding this all-important truth. He knew He did not have the right to speak on His own authority or do anything without first hearing and seeing His Father at work.

May God open our eyes to see this principle and fill our minds with His truth so we can meditate daily upon this eternal reality found in John 5:19: "Then answered Jesus and said unto them, 'Verily, verily, I say unto you, The Son can do nothing of Himself, but what He seeth the Father do: for what things soever He doeth, these also doeth the Son likewise." The life of Jesus is the framework

15

of knowing and doing the Father's will. This fundamental statement, "but what He seeth the Father do," reveals the **priority** and **purpose** of true communion with God that all of His disciples should seek.

CONQUERED BY THE GOSPEL

We, as disciples of Jesus, have a divine obligation to yield our ear to the One who has given us the capacity to hear His voice. When Jesus won our hearts and interrupted our lives, He also enabled us to walk by faith and consequently please our heavenly Father. He opened our hearts to the victory of the gospel over our lives, and our ears to hear His voice so we can do His will. We have been conquered by the King and His glorious message of deliverance to the point where we have learned to live by His decrees.

Now the God of peace, that brought again from the dead our Lord Jesus, that great Shepherd of the sheep, through the blood of the everlasting covenant, make you perfect in every good work to do His will, working in you that which is wellpleasing in His sight, through Jesus Christ; to whom be glory for ever and ever. Amen.

Hebrews 13:20-21

Our Shepherd and King will always lead us for the glory of His Father. Not only do we have a faithful Shepherd but a God of purpose who works in us both to will and to do according to His good pleasure. Why does Jesus shepherd our lives and the Father, through the enabling work of the Holy Spirit, work in us? So we may shine as lights in the midst of a dark world while accomplishing His purpose in the earth. (Phil. 2:12-16)

RUN HIS RACE

Our heavenly Father has chosen a distinct course for us. He has designed us to run a specific path in life. How will He reveal the course to us? He will do this through a lifestyle of intimate fellowship in order to clearly show us the race He has graciously appointed us to run day by day.[4] The cross is not the only factor we need to know about Jesus. The cross is the means by which God establishes us as His sanctified servant for life. Jesus is our salvation and foundation of all the Father plans to do with us. Jesus is the Author and Finisher of our faith, the Captain of our salvation, wisdom, sanctification, redemption, and righteousness! It is His way of living that secures our eternal salvation and supplies our effective sanctification.[5] He is enough!

LOOKING UNTO JESUS

In the book of Isaiah there is a beautiful picture that prophetically describes how Jesus heard from His Father. When Jesus heard the voice of His Father, He would also see what the Father saw. When He saw what the Father saw, He also would know what the Father knew. Jesus had to hear in order to see, know, and have the means necessary to be effective in touching the hearts of those whom His Father would give to Him. How did He help them? He spoke the word He heard from His Father. They also had to hear a word from God in order to see, know, and be helped by Him. This is how Jesus lived His life while on earth.

> The Lord God hath given Me the tongue of the learned, that I should know how to speak a word in season to him that is weary: He wakeneth morning by morning, He wakeneth Mine ear to hear as the learned. The Lord God hath opened Mine ear, and I was not rebellious, neither turned away back. I gave My back to the smiters, and My cheeks to them that plucked off the hair: I hid not My face from shame and spitting.
>
> Isaiah 50:4-6

Jesus said, "He wakeneth morning by morning, He wakeneth Mine ear to hear as the learned." I remember the first time I went "officially" hunting with my dad. The night before I was so excited. I planned and prepared what I was going to wear. I asked him a hundred times what time were we going to get up and leave for the "big woods." I was so excited and anticipated this big day with so much energy that I had a hard time going to sleep. I couldn't wait for morning to come. In the wee hours of the morning, I eventually fell asleep. The neat thing is that I had no problem waking up in the morning. I was awake as soon as I heard my dad stirring in his bedroom. Since those days, there have been many other occasions I anticipated the morning because of some special event or special people I was going to see.

LONGING TO SEE

While I served in the Navy, there were a few times I was really delighted about the dawn of a new day. During my time in the Navy, I was involved in numerous deployments. I had to spend many days away from my wife and daughters. I can remember how sweet a feeling it was the night before I would see my family upon arrival in our home port. The mornings of our arrival were always special. The atmosphere on the ship was full of unexplainable emotions. Anytime we ever pulled in from a cruise, it was not an issue. I never had any problem being drawn out of bed. Why was it not a problem? I had spent days visualizing myself running toward my wife and little girls to embrace them with arms opened wide. I could also see them running toward me with tears in their eyes longing just to sit in my lap, hear my voice, and speak with me face to face.

Can we see the Father longing to meet with His children? Can we picture the Bridegroom desiring to fellowship with His Bride? Can we observe the Spirit brooding over His nest, longing to feed and fellowship with His little ones? God wants to see us running to Him each and every morning.[6]

Jesus always anticipated and was excited about the fact that it was His Father that drew Him out of His sleep each and every day. He was never ashamed to admit that He longed to spend time with His Father. He was never embarrassed over the reality that He survived off what He heard from living in intimacy with Him. He lived to hear and see so He could know what had been assigned for Him to do each and every day.

The Mountain
By Stephanie Holden

Oh how I long for our trips to the Mountain
Where we fellowship sweet with our Lord.
On this mountain we linger. We take our time
And drink from the depths of His Word.

It's here where He teaches the deep things of God.
In His Word we find such delight
The abundance of goodness fills our souls to the depths
And His glory is brought into sight.

Oh that we could stay here forever
As He strengthens our battle worn frames
Each truth He reveals, Each promise He imputes,
Equips for the tasks He has paved.

As He sings over us as we rest in His shadow
We find perfect refuge and peace.
We're renewed. We're restored. We have all that we need.
In Him we are complete.

Oh how we want to stay on this Mountain forever
And never depart from His feet.
Then gently He reminds us the reason He fed us
His riches and precepts so sweet.

It's to go down in the valley where the lost souls are
Who have yet to hear His great pardon.
Beautiful are the feet who bring the Good News
And the time is now before their hearts harden.

There are saints too who are down from the enemies blows
Who need reminding of their Strong Tower
To lead them to the Mountain we so love and desire
So they too can be strengthened in power.

So down we come from the Mountain we love
And oh how we savor each moment passing.
Into the world we go as our Savior instructed,
Armed with truth and filled with passion.

Our trips to the Mountain sustains these old tents
That frame us as were just passing through.
We know why we're here—to take up the cross
And at all cost share His Good News.

SEEK FIRST

The point is we should also be drawn out of our beds by our heavenly Father each day. We ought to be delighted that the God of heaven and earth is actively at work and awaiting our arrival. We should be eternally grateful to Jesus that He has made it possible for us to have an audience and the ear of God Almighty. We must be humbled to know that our covenant-keeping God desires to reveal the secrets of His covenant with us. It could only be the reality of our sin and the manifestation of our flesh that would cause us to look for ways to avoid the secret place of God. We must seek Him with all of our hearts while He still may be found. Jesus, who is our example, did just that.[7]

HE IS THE STANDARD

He's come to defer all rights! He always had a fresh word of life to give away to the weary.[8] What an example to love and follow! What a lifestyle to live! What a Father to listen for and lean on! What a life to emulate! What a One to let live through us!

While we are seeking to discover the reality of this life principle revealed in and through the life of Christ, it will be beneficial for us to examine our lives by the standard of His life. He is God's standard, and He is the life God is using to shape and mold our lives. As we yield our lives to God, the intensity of our passion for His presence will increase, and our longing to hear and discern His voice will not be subdued by our laziness. Why will we overcome the temptations of the flesh that want us to avoid the presence of God? Jesus lives in us through the power of the Holy Spirit, and He is always about the His Father's business. "And He said unto them, How is it that ye sought me? wist ye not that I must be about my Father's business?" (Luke 2:49).

A CHILD IS BORN

It was prophetically spoken that a ruler would come out of Bethlehem who would be supernaturally brought forth and sanctified by the Father for His service.

> But thou, Bethlehem Ephratah, though thou be little among the thousands of Judah, yet out of thee shall He come forth unto Me that is to be Ruler in Israel; Whose goings forth have been from of old, from everlasting.
>
> Micah 5:2

We can discern from what we know of the whole counsel of God's Word that this is a specific reference to Jesus Christ. "Whose goings forth have been from of old, from everlasting," reveals to us the eternal origin and ordained role that Christ was assigned from eternity past. Christ, as the Son of God, has always been. It was when Christ was clothed with flesh in the fullness of time that He became what we have come to know as the historical Jesus or Jesus of Nazareth. Jesus was set apart by God the Father for His specific and perfect will. Micah said this ruler "shall come forth unto Me." The "Me" is none other than the Father.

In the book of Hebrews, we get a snapshot of how proud God the Father was the night Jesus was born: "And again, when He bringeth in the first-begotten into the world, He saith, 'And let all the angels of God worship Him'" (Hebrews 1:6). The writer of Hebrews is proving how Jesus is the express image of the Father and how He is superior to angels by using Old Testament references that should be applied to Jesus. He writes about the night Jesus was born and how the angels were told to worship Him. The word *bringeth* literally means "to introduce." God the Father was so proud of His Son that when Jesus was born, He introduced the angels to Him and told them this child was His Son and they must worship Him: "For unto us a Child is born, unto us a Son is given: and the government shall be upon His shoulder: and His name shall be called Wonderful, Counsellor, The mighty God, The everlasting Father, The Prince of Peace" (Isaiah 9:6). God, as a proud Father, introduced His Son to His ministering spirits and flames of fire (His angels) and said, "Worship Him."

HE IS WORTH CELEBRATING

I have pictures of myself coming out and introducing my daughters to our family and friends. I'm covered in my sanitary hospital garments, holding my very own flesh and blood with a gleam in my eye. I wanted the world to know these little girls were a gift from God and very special to me. I can only imagine how proud God the Father was to introduce Jesus to the world. Every time God births Him in the heart of a new creature, I believe He is proud to announce this new birth in glory. This may be a reason why there is so much celebrating in heaven when a sinner repents and trust Jesus. God today loves to introduce His Son to sinners. What does He say when He does? **"Worship Him!"**

What did the angels do after they were introduced to Jesus that night?

And there were in the same country shepherds abiding in the field, keeping watch over their flock by night. And, lo, the angel of the Lord came upon them, and the glory of the Lord shone round about them: and they were sore afraid. And the angel said unto them, Fear not: for, behold, I bring you good tidings of great joy, which shall be to all people. For unto you is born this day in the city of David a Saviour, which is Christ the Lord. And this shall be a sign unto you; Ye shall find the babe wrapped in swaddling clothes, lying in a manger. And suddenly there was with the angel a multitude

of the heavenly host praising God, and saying, Glory to God
in the highest, and on earth peace, good will toward men.
                                                    Luke 2:8-14

They found someone to tell! They praised and worship the
Savior! They preached Jesus to needy sinners! Why did they do
this? They did it because a proud Father introduced His Son to them
and said, "**Worship Him!**"

As a child, Jesus grew physically, emotionally, intellectually
and spiritually[9:] "And the Child grew, and waxed strong in spirit,
filled with wisdom: and the grace of God was upon Him. And Jesus
increased in wisdom and stature, and in favour with God and man"
(Luke 2:40, 52). This is paramount for us as believers. In order to
grow, Jesus had to be completely subjected to the authority of His
Father. We must subject our rights to His authority if we are going
to grow. Knowing that Jesus increased in every dynamic of His life
through deferring all rights to His Father creates a responsibility for
us to do the same.

INVESTED AUTHORITY

Jesus understood exactly what His authority was and what He
had been authorized to do. He was authorized to give ultimate
authority to His heavenly Father. Authority is an invested right to
authentic representation. It is the permission to embrace, exercise,
and enforce the purpose of the one who has invested this particular
right for true representation. How is authority valued? The value
or quality of authority can always be determined by its origin. The
value of Christ's authority was located in the Father Himself. What
is the vision or aim of authority? The aim of authority is always
authentic representation. To authentically represent His Father, Jesus
had to walk in the authority He had been granted. The authority that
the Father had granted Him was to be submissive to His authority.
Who determines the virtue or potency of authority? The investor is
the one who always determines the degree of potency of authority.
Jesus, at all levels of His life, was subject to His Father's ultimate
authority.

HOW TO GROW

For us to grow in grace we must realize that these principles must be a fundamental part of our lives. If we are going to grow supernaturally, we must give over all rights to the Lord. Believers are not authorized to grow in any other way. There are no other means or possible ways to grow as believers in the grace and knowledge of the Lord without first giving Jesus the right to do as He pleases with our lives.[10]

How does this work? We are exhorted by the apostle Paul in Romans 12:1-2 to give or present ourselves to the Lord as a living sacrifice. What does he mean when he says "as a living sacrifice"? In a previous verse, he helps us understand our mindset when we yield our lives to the Lord. We are to give ourselves to God as those who are dead unto sin and alive unto God. Even Christ died once for all unto sin, but the life He now lives He lives with God. We're also told to live unto God as though being alive from the dead.

KNOW THE TRUTH

What kind of implications does this being alive from the dead have? To be alive from the dead must mean we have died. To die means we have been bought at a price. The price paid was the life of God's Son, Jesus Christ. He paid this price to purchase our lives. The price He paid was His own blood. To shed His blood meant He had to die. He had to die because of our sins. But He died once for all. Therefore, when He paid the price for your sin and died in your stead upon the cross, you also died with Him. Dead men do not have rights. They are dead, and now they have no rights. He was buried, and you were buried with Him. Buried men have no rights. He was resurrected, and you were resurrected with Him. Resurrected men have no rights. Therefore, you are called on by God to present yourself to Him as one who has been bought at a price with no rights of your own. You are His. "And they shall be Mine, saith the Lord of Hosts, in that day when I make up My jewels; and I will spare them, as a man spareth his own son that serveth him" (Malachi 3:17).

WE ARE HIS TREASURE

When God makes us His treasure, we are His. We are His through the life, death, and resurrection of His Son, Jesus Christ. It has been said, "One man's trash is another man's treasure." This may be the case with men on this earth, but it is not so with God. We can't give Him the trash of our lives, thinking He'll take it as a treasure. No! We are His treasure, and we must present ourselves to Him as a resurrected treasure that is at the mercy of its owner. We are His treasure of grace. We are to yield ourselves as men dead to sin, and alive unto God, being holy and acceptable unto Him in Christ Jesus. This is our reasonable service.

Now if we be dead with Christ, we believe that we shall also live with Him: Knowing that Christ being raised from the dead dieth no more; death hath no more dominion over Him. For in that He died, He died unto sin once: but in that He liveth, He liveth unto God. Likewise reckon ye also yourselves to be dead indeed unto sin, but alive unto God through Jesus Christ our Lord. Let not sin therefore reign in your mortal body, that ye should obey it in the lusts thereof. Neither yield ye your members as instruments of unrighteousness unto sin: but yield yourselves unto God, as those that are alive from the dead, and your members as instruments of righteousness unto God.

Romans 6:8-13

A living sacrifice is at the mercy of the One who gave it life. This lifestyle is the only logical way to live as a believer.

GIVING AND GAINING

When we give our rights over to the Lord, we also gain something from Him. We gain a new sense of responsibility to prove His perfect will. Paul described this thought process to the Philippians as being able to approve those things which are excellent:

And this I pray, that your love may abound yet more and more in knowledge and in all judgment; That ye may approve things that are excellent; that ye may be sincere and without offence till the day of Christ; Being filled with the fruits of righteousness, which are by Jesus Christ, unto the glory and praise of God.

Philippians 1:9-11

Paul prayed for their love to increase specifically in knowing the Lord and knowing the Lord's way of doing things, so they too could choose the excellent things and be true representations of His perfect will. To increase, they would have to give themselves and their rights to the Lord and His purpose and pleasure. The result would be that they gain the wisdom of the Lord and, therefore, the accountability and responsibility to choose God's will all the days of their lives.

Peter instructed the church to do the same in 2 Peter 1:5-8:

And beside this, giving all diligence, add to your faith virtue; and to virtue knowledge; And to knowledge temperance; and to temperance patience; and to patience godliness; And to godliness brotherly kindness; and to brotherly kindness charity. For if these things be in you, and abound, they make you that ye shall neither be barren nor unfruitful in the knowledge of our Lord Jesus Christ.

At every phase of the supernatural growth process, we see a principle being applied. If you give, you gain. The result follows the same principle found in Romans 12 and in Philippians 1:9-11. Both Peter and Paul make a great point that we should remember. Believers who continually give themselves to the Lord will always gain from the Lord's knowledge, wisdom, and understanding, and they will receive the discernment necessary to live a productive and eternally fruitful life. They both reveal that we who live this way will never personally be barren of the knowledge of the Lord Jesus Christ, and we'll always have wisdom to give away. The believers who live by these principles not only know Christ and His ways, but they also live to help others know Him and how He works. How did all this happen? Believers gave up their rights to the Lordship of Jesus Christ, and Jesus gave them the responsibility of fulfilling His will.

GROWING SUPERNATURALLY

We must give in order to gain, and we gain in order to grow. Supernatural growth is always twofold. I'll use the word *growth* to illustrate this twofold principle. The first part of the twofold growth principle is based on Romans 12:1: "I beseech you therefore, brethren, by the mercies of God, that ye present your bodies a living sacrifice, holy, acceptable unto God, which is your reasonable service."

G - Giving
R - Rights
O - Over
W - Willfully
T - Trusting
H - Him

This is a loaded principle that is clearly taught throughout the Word of God and exemplified in the life of the Lord Jesus Christ. We who have been effectually graced must give ourselves and our rights over to the Lord all the days of our lives. Growth cannot happen outside this first step of placing our faith in the fact that we died with Christ and our lives are not our own:

For the love of Christ constraineth us; because we thus judge, that if One died for all, then were all dead: And that He died for all, that they which live should not henceforth live unto themselves, but unto Him which died for them, and rose again.

2 Corinthians 5:14-15

We never walk away empty-handed when we give our rights to the Lord. He empowers us to give them over to Him, and He also enables us to carry out His mission.

The second part of the twofold growth principle is based on Romans 12:2: "And be not conformed to this world: but be ye transformed by the renewing of your mind, that ye may prove what is that good, and acceptable, and perfect, will of God."

G - Gaining
R - Responsibility
O - Obediently
W - While
T - Trusting
H - Him

What we see in Romans 12:2 is the fact that we always gain from the Lord when we give Him our rights. Growth can not happen without these two fundamental principles. When we give our rights over to the Lord, we will encounter Him, and He will deposit within us His ways. We must gain His ways and accept His Word as a wise steward. We gain from Him the privilege and responsibility of proving His ways are true. Giving and gaining is God's way of growing and validating His will to us.

We can see that the chief end or aim of authentic worship is to always prove God's perfect will. Worship is the overflow of faith obedience. If we are going to gain an ability to be renewed in mind, and therefore the responsibility to display God's will, we must start by willfully giving our rights over by faith to Him. We do this knowing that God always rewards those who possess His covenant by faith and are persuaded that He longs to feed them.[11] Use the word *growth* to help yourselves and others grow in the Lord.

ROMANS 12:1

G - Giving
R - Rights
O - Over
W - Willfully
T - Trusting
H - Him

ROMANS 12:2

G - Gaining
R - Responsibility
O - Obediently
W - While
T - Trusting
H - Him

BECOMING A WATERER

The liberal soul shall be made fat: and he that watereth shall be watered also himself.

Proverbs 11:25

When you water someone, you encourage them. The more you encourage others to grow in grace, the more the Lord will use others to help you grow. "Give and it shall be given to you, pressed down, shaken together." (Luke 6:38) You can't disregard God's way of doing things. If you're not growing, you're not giving. If you're not being taught the Word, it is because you're not teaching the Word. If you're not being blessed by others, it is because you're not recognizing the blessing; therefore, you are not blessing others. The message is simply this: if you're not gaining responsibility from the Lord, you're not giving your rights over to Him. God's Word is always true. If you water, you will be watered yourself. Amen!

TAKING IT SERIOUSLY

How about your life—could it be described as a life that is yielded to the Lordship of Jesus Christ?

Do you anticipate meeting in the secret place with your heavenly Father day by day?[13]

Has He given you a tongue of the learned and a word for the weary soul?

Have you been obedient to the demands of the Gospel?[14]

Do you really belong to Jesus?

Are you deferring all rights to Him?

What would those who know you best say about each of these questions?

What would Jesus say about your life today?

2. He's Come to Defer All Results

HE TRUSTED THE FATHER

The reason anyone would willfully and joyfully surrender all their rights to someone else is because they have entrusted themselves to their preferred outcome. Jesus gave His rights over purposefully and with pleasure because He trusted His Father with the results. Therefore, when He spoke what He had heard from His Father, He placed His faith in the fact that the Father would accomplish what He desired through the word He spoke.[15] This is why the people acknowledge He (Jesus) taught as one who had authority.[16]

Jesus always deferred the results to His Father. Whenever He taught, touched a sick and diseased-filled person, told a demon to be gone, or transformed a soul, He did it with authority. Why? The results of His actions were in the hands of His Father, the One who "can do exceeding abundantly above all that we ask or think, according to the power that worketh in us, unto Him be glory in the church by Christ Jesus throughout all ages, world without end. Amen" (Ephesians 3:20-21). They saw a Man whose personality was flooded with compassion. They beheld a Preacher whose passion flowed with confidence. They looked upon a Teacher whose purpose was forged with conviction. They observed a Leader whose principles were fortified with clarity. The people marveled at His authority and the uniqueness of His apparent confidence. Why did they stand amazed? Jesus, completely assured of His purpose, deferred the results unto His Father. Was not Jesus able? Yes, He had the power to do as He pleased! But He deferred His rights over to the One He was submissive to in order to be in perfect harmony with His Father's eternal plan of redemption and to provide the framework by which we should live.[17] This is why Jesus simply says the following to those Jews who murmured at Him in John 6:

Jesus therefore answered and said unto them, Murmur not among yourselves. No man can come to Me, except the Father which hath sent Me draw him: and I will raise him up at the last day. It is written in the prophets, And they shall be all taught of God. Every man therefore that hath heard, and hath learned of the Father, cometh unto Me. Not that any man hath seen the Father, save He which is of God, He hath seen the Father. Verily, verily, I say unto you, He that believeth on Me hath everlasting life.

John 6:43-47

He was not threatened when people didn't believe in Him. He knew it took more than knowing facts and information about Him for people to follow His life. Jesus understood what He was called to do and how the Father had to supernaturally move upon the hearts of men before they would be drawn to Him. Jesus was never thwarted or moved off His course because of man's failure to recognize Him as Messiah. He trusted Himself to let God be God and man be man. He knew what was impossible with man was possible with His Father. The Lord clarifies this principle in the gospel of Matthew when He says,

At that time Jesus answered and said, I thank Thee, O Father, Lord of heaven and earth, because Thou hast hid these things from the wise and prudent, and hast revealed them unto babes. Even so, Father: for so it seemed good in Thy sight. All things are delivered unto Me of My Father: and no man knoweth the Son, but the Father; neither knoweth any man the Father, save the Son, and he to whomsoever the Son will reveal Him. Come unto Me, all ye that labour and are heavy laden, and I will give you rest.

Matthew 11:25-28

Jesus, our example, deferred the results of His life to His Father.

HE ENDURED HOSTILITY

Jesus, knowing without question that He was going to be rejected by men according to the Father's will, was not moved off course when sinners mocked His claims because He entrusted Himself to His Father's care.

Looking unto Jesus the author and finisher of our faith; who for the joy that was set before Him endured the cross, despising the shame, and is set down at the right hand of the throne of God. For consider Him that endured such contradiction of sinners against Himself, lest ye be wearied and faint in your minds.

Hebrews 12:2-3

Jesus trusted the intended results of His Father's purpose to the point that "though He were a Son, yet learned He obedience by the things which He suffered; And being made perfect, He became the author of eternal salvation unto all them that obey Him" (Hebrews 5:8-9). He is calling on us to give up our rights and the results of all we do to the pleasure and purpose of a God who loves us and desires to use each of us to manifest His perfect will.

HAVE FAITH IN GOD

When Christ cursed the fig tree while leaving Bethany according to the account given to us in the Gospel of Mark, it would appear that His actions were "out of season" or "they did not make much sense" from a logical standpoint.

And on the morrow, when they were come from Bethany, He was hungry: And seeing a fig tree afar off having leaves, He came, if haply He might find any thing thereon: and when He came to it, He found nothing but leaves; for the time of figs was not yet. And Jesus answered and said unto it, No man eat fruit of thee hereafter for ever. And His disciples heard it.

Mark 11:12-14

It was not the season for figs, so why did He curse the tree? The next day, as they walked past this cursed tree, Peter noticed how the tree was dead and dried up from the roots. He made a spontaneous remark to Jesus about the obvious condition of the dead fig tree:

> And in the morning, as they passed by, they saw the fig tree dried up from the roots. And Peter calling to remembrance saith unto Him, Master, behold, the fig tree which Thou cursedst is withered away. And Jesus answering saith unto them, **Have faith in God**. For verily I say unto you, That whosoever shall say unto this mountain, Be thou removed, and be thou cast into the sea; and shall not doubt in his heart, but shall believe that those things which he saith shall come to pass; he shall have whatsoever he saith. Therefore I say unto you, What things soever ye desire, when ye pray, believe that ye receive them, and ye shall have them.
>
> Mark 11:20-24

EVEN WHEN IT DOESN'T MAKE SENSE

When we surrender our rights to the Lord, there will be times when we are told to do things by Him that seem to be "out of season." He will have us say and do things that just don't make sense to us or to those to whom we are ministering. Joshua was instructed by God to march around a city and shout, and the walls would fall down.[18] Gideon was told to reduce his fighting force down to three hundred men to fight several nations who were as numerous as locusts. He was not only to fight with three hundred men, but he was also commanded to use a strange "weapon" of clay pottery with a candle on the inside to fight with on this dreadful night.[19] It didn't make sense to him nor to any naturally-minded man.[20] Jehoshaphat was led to send out the choir before his army because the battle was not theirs, but the Lord's.[21] All these things are out of season events. None of them logically make any sense. Think about each of these historical accounts and find the four common denominators in each one. We must notice that each account is different. They were all told to do something different to fight. The result was that they all fought differently.

We often will look at a passage like the ones mentioned above and make every effort to emulate what they did. The outcome leaves us frustrated and defeated more often than not.

The four common denominators are:

1. Each leader (individual) heard a Word from God.
2. Each heard an "out of season" word of instruction.
3. Each had to trust God's instruction and obey it even though it was "out of season."
4. Each experienced victory.

FOLLOW HIS EXAMPLE

Jesus did the very same thing in Mark 11, and He instructed Peter and His disciples to live the exact same way. His response to Peter was, "Have faith in God." Keep in mind that Jesus had already unveiled to His disciples that He only spoke what He heard from His Father and did only what He saw His Father do. Therefore, we must agree that Jesus cursed the fig tree because His Father told Him to do so. This is why He told Peter, "Have faith in God." We must put confidence in God's instruction, even when it doesn't make sense to us. When we trust God's Word, we can also trust His response to our obedience. Jesus is our example and our greatest teacher. Our Father is trustworthy, and He is always right.

LISTEN TO JESUS

The Father said of Jesus, "This is My beloved Son, in whom I am well pleased" (Matthew 3:17). He confirmed it to us once again at the Mount of Transfiguration when He said, "...This is my beloved Son, in whom I am well pleased; hear ye Him" (Matthew 17:5). The apostle Peter referred to the Old Testament prophecy concerning a prophet who would come in the last days when he was preaching in Solomon's Portico.[22] The consequences of not hearing this prophet (Jesus) would only result in destruction. Why? Jesus deferred all

His rights and the results of His life over to His heavenly Father's will.

TAKING IT SERIOUSLY

What are you hearing from the Lord?

What are you doing in your own strength?

Are you living or preaching and teaching with a sense of frustration?

Are you puzzled as to why people are not responding to your authority?

Have you deferred all results to a God who is able?

Have you deferred all rights over to Him?

3. He's Come to Defer All Rewards

TO GOD BE THE GLORY

The intent of the heart of our Savior was to glorify His Father. All He did and all He said was to bring glory and honor to His heavenly Father. His obedience was for the Father's glory. His suffering was to glorify His Father. The cross was to glorify His Father. Listen to what He shared with His disciples the night prior to His crucifixion: "But that the world may know that I love the Father; and as the Father gave Me commandment, even so I do. Arise, let us go hence" (John 14:31). The cross is the result of an eternal covenant that Jesus, with pleasure, embraced and endured because through it the Father would be glorified. Jesus knew His disciples had been divinely called and consecrated to bear much fruit to the glory of His Father: "Herein is My Father glorified, that ye bear much fruit; so shall ye be My disciples" (John 15:8). Jesus says it best in John 7:18: "He that speaketh of himself seeketh his own glory: but He that seeketh His glory that sent Him, the same is true, and no unrighteousness is in Him."

Jesus, with all that was in Him, sought to bring glory to the One who sent Him. He knew He "must suffer many things, and be rejected of the elders and chief priests and scribes, and be slain, and be raised the third day"[23] to completely bring glory to our heavenly Father. Jesus deferred all rewards to His Father.

THE FRUIT THAT WOULD FOLLOW

The Old Testament prophesied of these glories in Isaiah 53:10-11:

> Yet it pleased the Lord to bruise Him; He hath put Him to grief: when thou shalt make His soul an offering for sin, He shall see His seed, He shall prolong His days, and the pleasure of the Lord shall prosper in His hand. He shall see of the travail of His soul, and shall be satisfied: by His knowledge shall my righteous servant justify many; for He shall bear their iniquities.

Peter confirms this thought in 1 Peter when he says, "Of which salvation the prophets have enquired and searched diligently, who prophesied of the grace that should come unto you: Searching what, or what manner of time the Spirit of Christ which was in them did signify, when it testified beforehand the sufferings of Christ, and the glory that should follow" (1 Peter 1:10-11). The work of Christ Jesus was a work of glory that honored His Father and provided the means by which His disciples could be delivered from sin and shame.

IT APPLIES TODAY

Each area that Christ deferred to His Father plays a significant part in God's redemptive plan. He did defer all rights, results, and rewards to His Father, and He expects us to do likewise. This is the essence of what it means to put on the mind of Christ.

> Let this mind be in you, which was also in Christ Jesus: Who, being in the form of God, thought it not robbery to be equal with God: But made Himself of no reputation, and took upon Him the form of a servant, and was made in the likeness of men: And being found in fashion as a man, He

humbled Himself, and became obedient unto death, even the death of the cross. Wherefore God also hath highly exalted Him, and given Him a name which is above every name: That at the name of Jesus every knee should bow, of things in heaven, and things in earth, and things under the earth; And that every tongue should confess that Jesus Christ is Lord, to the glory of God the Father.

Philippians 2:5-11

He has and is today deferring all rights, results, and rewards to God the Father. While I write this and while you're currently reading it, Christ is making all things subject to Himself so He can put all things under Himself and turn them all over to His Father for His Father's eternal glory.[24] Amen!

WE MUST ACT ON WHAT WE KNOW

We must settle it right now in our lives. God will not share His glory with us or anyone else. We must defer all rewards to Him for His glory alone. We are responsible for presenting our bodies to Him as a living sacrifice. We need to know that we're alive from the dead, and that we have no rights. We are to cast ourselves upon Jesus and plead with the Lord to cleanse our minds while committing ourselves to walk in the truth concerning His purpose and pleasure. We are obligated to ask Him to fill us with the Holy Spirit and give us unction to prove that good, acceptable, and the perfect will of God. We must grow in grace to be able to choose what is excellent. We have to trust that God longs to feed us and that He'll never let us be in want of His Word.[25] We must be persuaded that we who hunger and thirst for His righteousness will be filled with righteousness by Him.[26] We are accountable to possess what God unveils and cling to what He promises.[27] We are His, and His promises are ours.[28]

Magnify the Lord! He's come to defer!

TAKING IT SERIOUSLY

Why do you do what you do?
What is your motivation in doing what you do for a living?
For whom are you living?
What brings you the single most joy in life?
Is life about you?
Is Jesus truly your life?

Chapter 2

He's Come to Define

IS IT TRUTH?

Seeking God's face on every issue in life is vitally essential for all followers of Christ, and it is especially critical when we are longing to understand truth. Truth cannot be learned without the help of God. It is very important for us to understand and discern that facts and truth are not the same. We can know the facts about something without knowing the truth about it. The reality that many of us live in every day is actually used to suppress the truth. Facts or tangible evidence about this world may be gathered, and information about life may be processed, but it does not mean we have gathered and processed truth. Our own emotions, thoughts, and the reality in which we find ourselves are undeniable facts, yet they are often lies. Just because something is real, tangible, even influential, does not necessarily mean that it is true. Think about it this way. Satan is a reality. He is also an undeniable fact, and his influence has so impacted this world in which we live that we can see and touch the effects of his works daily. Everything the devil and his demons touch and transform is real, but it is also a lie. God describes Satan as a deceiver, a murder, and the father of lies. Satan is nothing but a liar. He is the essence of falsehood, not truth. The only truth about Satan is the truth revealed about him in the Word of God.[29]

GOD MUST REVEAL

Truth must be revealed! If truth is not revealed by God, it can never be known. Jesus has come to define three things about truth that are very important for us to understand: What is truth? Who is truth? What does truth do?

In the previous chapter, a seed of eternal truth was planted whose message will continue to blossom like a spring lily throughout this book. Why will we watch it grow? Would we have planted that seed with no intent that it should grow? Since Christ Jesus was and is the means by which we come to know truth, it was crucial that He be in complete and utter submission to His Father's will. We observed that He deferred all rights, results, and rewards to the desire and glory of His heavenly Father; therefore, if this truth has been revealed to us, we can understand why He said, "… He was born to bear witness to the truth…."[30] Psalm 22 gives an eternal view of the future suffering of Jesus. David, like a captain of a submarine looking through his periscope and seeing something afar, is only describing what he is seeing. It was through the Spirit of God that David recorded the thoughts and meditations of the heart of Jesus while mockers scorned and spitefully misused Him just before His crucifixion.

All they that see Me laugh Me to scorn: they shoot out the lip, they shake the head saying, He trusted on the Lord that He would deliver Him: let Him deliver Him, seeing He delighted in Him. But Thou art He that took Me out of the womb: Thou didst make Me hope when I was upon My mother's breasts. I was cast upon Thee from the womb: Thou art My God from My mother's belly. Be not far from Me; for trouble is near; for there is none to help. Many bulls have compassed Me: strong bulls of Bashan have beset Me round. They gaped upon Me with their mouths, as a ravening and a roaring lion.

Psalm 22:7-13

Jesus, having been supernaturally planted in the womb of the Virgin Mary by the sovereign grace of God Almighty through the

Holy Spirit, was taught to be utterly dependent upon His heavenly Father. This passage unveils to us the uniqueness of Jesus and His virgin birth. It also helps us see why He deferred all rights, results, and rewards to His heavenly Father: so He could be the One to teach us what truth is.

1. He's Come to Define for Us What Is Truth?

WHAT ARE WE GOVERNED BY?

We have all heard a story that goes something like this: A man comes home to his wife of twenty years and tells her he no longer loves her and has fallen in love with another woman. This is a common reality today. Why is it so common and acceptable in society and even in our churches? We have lost an ability to discern the truth. Why have we lost this supernatural gift? We, in general, do not know what truth is. We have lived by our emotions and the facts that surround our lives for so long that we claim these lies as truths that can't be denied. The feelings we may feel toward someone other than our spouses or even the lack of desire for our spouses may be a reality, even undeniable fact, but they are also lies. We and our thoughts, emotions, and actions must be governed by truth, not circumstances.[31]

Homosexuals may have real feelings toward one another, but these emotions and thoughts they are experiencing are deceptive lies. They, like all humanity and unlike Jesus Christ, came out of the womb speaking lies: "The wicked are estranged from the womb: they go astray as soon as they be born, speaking lies. Their poison is like the poison of a serpent: they are like the deaf adder that stoppeth her ear" (Psalm 58:3-4). Truth must be revealed if they're going to understand the depraved nature and sin-sick condition of all humanity outside of Christ Jesus.[32] Humans left to themselves in their inherent condition, no matter if they are heterosexuals or homosexuals, are hostile and rebellious toward God and His everlasting truth. Lost mankind is so self-seeking that in their deception, they will make every effort to discredit the truth by redefining and changing the Lord's ways to fit their sinful lifestyles. The result of this inherited behavior is manifested in the lives of those who "feel" these feelings and claim them as truth when they are actually the result of a fallen and broken nature which only leads to an unapproved lifestyle.[33]

HE WAS SENT TO BEAR WITNESS

Jesus, on the other hand, came to this sin-sick world to define for His sheep what truth is. Pontius Pilate asked Jesus a question on the day He was crucified, and His response will help us in our search to know what truth really is:

> Then Pilate entered into the judgment hall again, and called Jesus, and said unto Him, Art Thou the King of the Jews? Jesus answered him, Sayest thou this thing of thyself, or did others tell it thee of Me? Pilate answered, Am I a Jew? Thine own nation and the chief priests have delivered Thee unto me: what hast Thou done? Jesus answered, My kingdom is not of this world: if My kingdom were of this world, then would My servants fight, that I should not be delivered to the Jews: but now is My kingdom not from hence. Pilate therefore said unto Him, Art Thou a king then? Jesus answered, Thou sayest that I am a king. To this end was I born, and for this cause came I into the world, that I should bear witness unto the truth. Every one that is of the truth heareth My voice. Pilate saith unto Him, What is truth? And when he had said this, he went out again unto the Jews, and saith unto them, I find in Him no fault at all.

John 18:33-38

Pilate himself was confused and confounded concerning the dynamic of what truth is. Today, people outside of Christ are just as puzzled.

In the passage above, we notice that the hearing of the voice of Jesus is based upon being "of the truth." To be "of the truth," one must be of another kingdom. Why do they have to be of another kingdom? Because Jesus is not of this world. He came from outside of this world to bear witness to the truth. This is why Jesus came. To know and understand the truth, one must be part of Christ's kingdom. He also came to reveal that this world and the elements therein are one big lie. The people who are of this world cannot hear or know truth unless the One who came to bear witness to the truth reveals it to them.

UNDER THE INFLUENCE OF SATAN

The world system we now live in is under the legal authority of Satan. Why is it under his influence? When Adam yielded his authority to Satan in the garden, he gave dominion to the enemy of God.[34] God, through the apostle Paul, describes all the children of men in this world as being children of wrath.[35] We were all born as children of wrath, or as "products of the fall of humanity." As a result of this inheritance and the dominion of Satan over us, we lived all our lives prior to being born again in disobedience. The spirit that now influences and controls the lives of those who are still in their sin is none other than the prince of the power of the air, Satan himself.

> And you hath He quickened, who were dead in trespasses and sins; Wherein in time past ye walked according to the course of this world, according to the prince of the power of the air, the spirit that now worketh in the children of disobedience: Among whom also we all had our conversation in times past in the lusts of our flesh, fulfilling the desires of the flesh and of the mind; and were by nature the children of wrath, even as others.
>
> Ephesians 2:1-3

God describes us as being under the influence of the course of this world. Yes, we all live this way and will unless we are interrupted by the Lord and made a new creature in Christ Jesus.[36] Our lifestyles are real and tangible, but they are actually lies. They are real lives being lived out every day, and no one can deny this fact! Our lives are so real that Jesus Christ gave His life on behalf of us.

No matter how real they may be, they are still lifestyles of deception and delusion. Unless they are born again of God and given the ability to hear the voice of Jesus calling on them to follow Him, they cannot know the truth.

IT IS GOOD FOR NOTHING

Jesus understood He was born and sent into this world to reveal the truth to His sheep and expose the works of this world as evil.[37] The world system functions, but it is important to remember it is fallen. The system is broken because it is no longer in its original design; therefore, it has no eternal value. When a drinking glass is shattered on a tile floor, it is discarded because it is no longer useful for its intended purpose. It is thrown away because it is no longer usable and is now good for nothing.

IT IS DECEPTIVE

The New Testament explains on numerous occasions about the devastating effects of any system of learning that is not rooted in and sanctified by God. If it's not to glorify God the Father and to place Christ Jesus at the center of all Spirit-filled living being sanctified by the Word of God and prayer, it should be avoided:[38] "Beware lest any man spoil you through philosophy and vain deceit, after the tradition of men, after the rudiments of the world, and not after Christ" (Colossians 2:8). Paul warned the church at Colosse not to be robbed by the emptiness and vanity of pursuing this world's wisdom. Being fond of the basic principles of the world system is deceitful and deadly. James even shared with his audience that having a fondness with the world is enmity with God.[39]

IN THE NAME OF KNOWLEDGE

Today, many have fallen captive to this satanic scheme. Paul also warned Timothy of this covert effort by the enemy to entice the intellectual seeker who has a weakness for a "well shaped intellect":

O Timothy, keep that which is committed to thy trust, avoiding profane and vain babblings, and oppositions of science falsely so called: Which some professing have erred concerning the faith. Grace be with thee. Amen.

1 Timothy 6:20-21

We can often find our minds so focused on defending the faith against apostate teachers in the church that we miss the fact this also applies to our modern system of education. We may not like this much, but it is a reality. Do our schools and the curriculum used teach our kids to exalt and magnify the Lord Jesus Christ and His gospel? How about our science books? What or who is the core of their authority? Do they heavily promote the God of creation or the theory of evolution? Do they teach the biblical role for us as parents in educating and equipping our children to be champions of God's truth on the earth?

IT'S HAPPENING

Timothy was told to guard the precious truth and the lives that were entrusted to him by not letting empty knowledge cloud his vision of God's glory and truth. The church must be cautious of this travesty happening today. She must sound the alarm. The enemy has infiltrated her strongholds. Statistics show how young adults are fleeing from church houses to the many outhouses of this world. Why wouldn't they go the first chance they have to be on their own? Their sinful natures and appetites have been fed all their lives by a watered-down theology that fits a secular society. We have let our culture shape and conform what they know about an unbiblical god. Why have pastors allowed this to happen? They have done this to be politically correct so they can maintain their jobs in the church and keep their pulpit. Why has this happened? We, as the people of God, have not stood against this great spoiling of the minds of our youth and nation. The church will give an account for not bearing witness to the truth.[40]

45

HISTORY IS REPEATING ITSELF

Micah told the leaders in his day of God's judgment upon their land because they hated good and loved evil.[41] Micah specifically pointed out that both the priest and prophets were teaching for something other than God's glory and the good of the people: "The heads thereof judge for reward, and the priests thereof teach for hire, and the prophets thereof divine for money: yet will they lean upon the Lord, and say, Is not the Lord among us? none evil can come upon us." (Micah 3:11) The prophets gave the verdicts and made their distinctions for silver, not because they heard from God. They loved and wanted money. They told people what they wanted to hear so they could eat and eat some more. Many today, like the prophets of old, love their homes, cars, and all the many things that come with being a "clergyman" in modern times. It is true and it's still a direct promise from the Lord that He'll take care of His own servants. He even says to treat them with double honor if they labor in the Word. This does not mean He gives them permission to preach whatever and however they want to lost people. They were called to be a voice for the Lord and His ways.

THEY HAVE AN UNHEALTHY MOTIVE

The priests, on the other hand, were for hire. They taught for worth, or we should say for success. Power and influence come with success and popularity. Today, people want their pastors to be popular. There is no way a biblical pastor could be popular in the modern day in which we live. It is impossible to be a true man of God in any culture, be popular among a self-indulgent society, and remain true to the Lord and His Word. Many today teach half-truths so they can be successful in a twisted and perverse generation. They usually give up on having a significant impact for God's glory in their community and settle for being successful. Success in a day when vileness is exalted in a culture with wicked people prowling on every side can only come at the expense of truth being compromised. These wicked people learn how to survive among the wolves at the expense of straying from the Shepherd. When pastors/teachers stray from the Chief Shepherd, they lead people into death.[42] Therefore, they'll teach on topics that really appeal to and feed the sinful desires of the flesh. We see preachers who should be anything but a preacher of the Word surviving among the pack of sheep killers.[43]

CAN YOU SEE THE SIGNS?

This type of success-oriented preacher makes light of sound doctrine and the preparation needed to be a teacher of the Word of God. They make their jokes and mock the man of God that is serious about his responsibility as a teacher. The modern preacher has been taught how to keep the system oiled and running well. They are instructed by most, not all, systems of higher learning to "not rock the boat or the denominational built ship in any way." They are led to believe that if they pet the "sheep" even the wolves in sheep's clothing the same will take care of them and everybody will be happy. They are encouraged to stick with the institutionalized church's tradition even if it's not right because in the end it's what the majority favors and if the majority gets upset they could be without a job. The problem with this way of thinking is it's not based on truth. If it's not based on truth, it's not based on Jesus. If it's not based on Jesus, the flock is being led to go the wrong way. We ought to all be for traditions and structure that are rooted and the results of truth. But if it comes down to tradition or truth we must be determined to trade tradition for truth.

WE NEED TRUE PROPHETIC PREACHING

The truth reveals to us that the pastor is assigned by God to take over the aim or vision of the church as His distinct undershepherd. One role the pastor has is to have the superior aim or vision that God desires to give to a local fellowship. This is why it is so crucial to have the man God desires to lead a congregation. Please don't misuse or allow the office of the pastor, what God has ordained for His own glory, to be mocked by ungodly men.

Jokes, humanistic schools, cultural educators, or educations have never set a man free in Christ, and they won't do it today either. The preacher is to preach and teach the Word of God under the authority of God and the anointing of the Holy Spirit. Preaching should never appeal to the flesh, but it should actually call on the sinner to (1) mortify his flesh by denying its cravings (2) turn from known sin (3) trust and follow hard after Jesus. When truth is preached, it should always produce hate for sin in those caught in sin. They will either hate their sin or the servant who has warned them of the consequences of it when truth is preached. Listen to what God instructed Jeremiah to tell His people about the role of the prophetic preacher:[44]

I have not sent these prophets, yet they ran: I have not spoken to them, yet they prophesied. But if they had stood in My counsel, and had caused My people to hear My words, then they should have turned them from their evil way, and from the evil of their doings.

Jeremiah 23:21-22

The prophet is to never fortify and aid the sinner in his rebellion. God sends His prophets with the truth to free the rebellious from their sins. Truth is given by the Lord through His prophets to tell the sinner that God knows where he is and to warn him that there is a consequence for his sin. Because of the grace of God, the prophet is also sent to win the sinner unto repentance through the revelation of truth. God wants to free the sinner from his sin and not aid him in his sin.

DANGEROUSLY STRONG FOR THE TRUTH

Likewise, the same applies for the priests. Malachi is a book that deals with God's disgust over the attitude and actions of the priests in Malachi's day.

For the priest's lips should keep knowledge, and they should seek the law at his mouth: for he is the messenger of the Lord of Hosts. But ye are departed out of the way; ye have caused many to stumble at the law; ye have corrupted the covenant of Levi, saith the Lord of hosts.

Malachi 2:7-8

The priests were called on by God to be His messengers to turn men from their iniquity. They were not called to popularity and fame, but faithfulness to God and His ways.

We are in need of men who will be dangerously strong for the truth on the earth today. Champions of truth are needed in the visible church during this hour. We do not need those who peddle the Word. "Everyone has a price preacher," some might say. That is a fact. The majority will have their price, and the minority accepts the price that has already been paid on Calvary. We have been told things will get worse and worse in the latter days. We are in the latter days. Paul told the church at Corinth that even back then the majority of the preachers were corrupting God's Word for a price. They were retailing the preached Word of God to the highest of bidders: "For we are not as many, which corrupt the word of God: but as of sincerity, but as of God, in the sight of God speak we in Christ" (2 Corinthians 2:17). The word *corrupt* is rooted in the idea of marketing or selling the Word of God. The corruption happened when they distorted it or changed the meaning of the word to fit their listeners' lifestyles. Why did they do it? They wanted to keep their position, make their living, and appear successful. How do they do it today? The exact same way they've done it for centuries.

TAKING IT SERIOUSLY

Are we guilty of converting the truth to fit our lifestyles?

Are we involved with a church that is aiming to be successful at the cost of compromising truth?

How well do we and our churches relate to a functioning but fallen society?

Is there much difference between us and them?

Should there be a difference between the disciples of Jesus and a lost world?

IT'S NOT SUPPOSED TO BE EASY

We have been called to be truth-bearers and to rise up champions for truth. I know how hard it is to do this in a society that functions well and feeds the pleasures of sinful men and women. I've been in the world, and I walked with the emptiness of the culture while being both lost and saved. I know what it's like to have the truth cut deep into my core and shake the very foundations upon which I stand. I've had to deal with deadbeat dads and feminists. I can't stand by and watch the enemy build his strongholds in the minds of my children any longer. I can't stand still while he poisons the minds of so many I care for and love. I can't sit still while a government is making every effort to choke out the voice of God's people. I know this is what lost people do, but I'm not lost, and I don't have the right to conform to their ways and get comfortable in a sin-sick world. I can't be at ease any longer![45]

YOU WILL BE HATED

The world we live in functions because God is not done saving folk from it. There are many things that appear to be good on the surface, and they are used to advance the causes of the functioning society in which we live. The problem is the works it produces have no eternal value. Works that people do in and of themselves are good for nothing eternally. Jesus reveals this when speaking to His half brothers about going up to Jerusalem: "The world cannot hate you; but Me it hateth, because I testify of it, that the works thereof are evil" (John 7:7). Jesus even tells His disciples they will be hated by the world because they are no longer of this world:

If the world hate you, ye know that it hated Me before it hated you. If ye were of the world, the world would love his own: but because ye are not of the world, but I have chosen you out of the world, therefore the world hateth you. Remember the word that I said unto you, The servant is not greater than his lord. If they have persecuted Me, they will also persecute you; if they have kept My saying, they will keep yours also. But all these things will they do unto you for My name's sake, because they know not Him that sent Me.

John 15:18-22

"May God be true and every man a liar!"[46] Truth is really not of this world. Jesus, our King, has come to define for us what truth is.

A TREASURE

God's Word is truth. Jesus, who was sent to bear witness to the truth, said, "Sanctify them through Thy truth: Thy word is truth." (John 17:17) God's Word is truth because He Himself is true. His Word is a special revelation of Himself; therefore, it is a priceless treasure we should cherish and protect. Does this mean that if we open up God's Word and read it we will know the truth? No! Truth must be revealed. If any one nation of people knew what was written in God's Word, it was Israel. The Jews knew what was written in the Pentateuch (the first five books of God's Word), but the majority of them did not know the truth. Jesus told the Jews in His day that the truth was not in them; therefore, they could not receive His Word. Why could they not receive His Word? They were of their father, the devil. If they were of God, they would have loved Jesus and taken hold of His Word to tend to its care with all their heart and might.[47] The problem back then with the Jews and many people in general today is they knew what was written but did not know the truth. Knowing the truth and knowing what is written in God's Word are two different things.

IT IS HIDDEN

In the coming chapters, we will discuss how this can happen. We can know what is written without knowing the truth. The enemy has blinded the world, and there is a veil covering our ability to read the things of God. There is a cover placed over the heart and eyes of every human born in this world. It takes a God who is able to break the curse of this cover and remove it so man can see the truth. Those who are blinded by this covering can know what is written, but not what God is saying. They do not have the supernatural capacity to hear the truth; therefore, they cannot chose to hear what God is saying to His people. A divine result of hearing the truth is seeing the truth.[48]

GOD MUST UNCOVER IT

John the apostle speaks of this in his first letter: "They (lost) are of the world: therefore speak they of the world, and the world heareth them. We are of God: he that knoweth God heareth us; he that is not of God heareth not us. Hereby know we the spirit of truth, and the spirit of error" (1 John 4:5-6). He also says, "In this the children of God are manifest, and the children of the devil: whosoever doeth not righteousness is not of God, neither he that loveth not his brother" (1 John 3:10). The enabling ability to hear, see, know and practice the truth is a distinct result of the grace of God.

God speaks through the Old Testament prophet Malachi and says, "Then shall ye return, and discern between the righteous and the wicked, between him that serveth God and him that serveth him not" (Malachi 3:18). This passage refers to the nation of Israel in a future day, when they as a whole come under the principles of the New Covenant. The application applies to the New Testament believer who is effectually saved by the grace of God today. The reason one serves God is because he is God's; therefore, he is no longer wicked. By the grace of God, he has been made righteous through the all-sufficient and eternally effective work of Jesus. It is the totality of the life of Jesus Christ and His sacrifice upon the cross and resurrection from the grave that ushers in this righteousness by grace.

MUST HAVE THE CAPACITY

The authentic and anointed believer who has been born again can now see and enter the kingdom of God. He also has the capacity to hear the truth and follow the voice of his Shepherd, Jesus Christ.[49] He who has been born again of the Spirit of God has been declared by Him to be righteous on account of Christ's life sacrifice and will now serve the Lord in righteousness.[50] The authentic and anointed believer is now capable of hearing and obeying truth. Why? He is of God. He was brought forth by Him and for Him. "Of His own will begat He us with the word of truth, that we should be a kind of firstfruits of His creatures" (James 1:18). This is a valid description of a believer and the one who ought to give thanks to the Lord for His amazing grace! A believer will forever praise God for such an awesome gift!

HIS WORD IS TRUTH

Truth is what God reveals about a matter. When we come to the knowledge of the truth, it is always clear and bright. Why is it clear? God wants us to know and recognize His works, so He purposefully reveals them to us.[51] If we are going to see the ugliness of personal sin and the uniqueness of the Savior's sacrifice, God must speak truth in us first. If we are going to see how Jesus' sacrifice satisfies the divine and just wrath of Holy God while at the same time supplies the eternal favor of God, truth has to be in us. Redemption can only be experienced and embraced by us when we are of the truth and have it within us:

> If we say that we have no sin, we deceive ourselves, and the truth is not in us. If we confess our sins, He is faithful and just to forgive us our sins, and to cleanse us from all unrighteousness. If we say that we have not sinned, we make Him a liar, and His word is not in us.
>
> 1 John 1:8-10

Notice how God uses John to couple the idea of His truth and His Word as being one and the same. If we say we have no sin or we have not sinned, we are void of the truth, or as John said "His Word." To confess means we are aligned with "another" because we see the same thing, or we are in agreement with "another" because we take the same stand. What is the "other" to which John is referring? It is the truth, which is God's Word. Therefore, the only way to see and stand on the truth about sin and the Savior is to be of the truth. The people of God are people who are of the truth. We who are of the truth are new creatures who have been regenerated and given a nature that can see and stand with the truth and with God.

Seeing ye have purified your souls in obeying the truth through the Spirit unto unfeigned love of the brethren, see that ye love one another with a pure heart fervently: Being born again, not of corruptible seed, but of incorruptible, by the word of God, which liveth and abideth for ever. For all flesh is as grass, and all the glory of man as the flower of grass. The grass withereth, and the flower thereof falleth away: But the word of the Lord endureth for ever. And this is the word which by the gospel is preached unto you.

1 Peter 1:22-25

God uses both Peter and James to affirm we are brought forth or born again by the truth, and this truth is described as the Word of God that lives and remains forever.

TRUTH LOVES THE TRUTH

John gives us the reason why we love those who have been born of God so much in 2 John 1:1-2: "The Elder unto the elect lady and her children, whom I love in the truth; and not I only, but also all they that have known the truth; For the truth's sake, which dwelleth in us, and shall be with us for ever." When we are born of the truth, we will see and stand in agreement with the Lord about our sin and His sacrifice for it, but we will also love His people and will want to fellowship with them because of the truth in us. God's Word is truth, and His Word remains forever. So will those who are born again. Much could be said concerning what truth is, but nothing says it any clearer than Psalm 119:160: "Thy word is true from the beginning: and every one of Thy righteous judgments endureth for ever." He's come to define what truth is.

2. He's Come to Define for Us Who Is Truth

JESUS IS THE TRUTH

"Jesus saith unto him, I am the way, the truth, and the life: no man cometh unto the Father, but by Me" (John 14:6). Our Lord and

Savior Jesus Christ is the truth. Yes, He reveals truth to us, but He Himself is Truth. Jesus is God incarnate. He is the Word, who was, who is, and who will come. He is the very essence of the thoughts and intent of the heart of God manifested.[52] It is because of God the Father, who has chosen us in Him (Christ Jesus), that we have been blessed to know and be part of the truth. When we know Jesus, we know the truth.

> Then said Jesus to those Jews which believed on Him, If ye continue in My word, then are ye My disciples indeed; And ye shall know the truth, and the truth shall make you free. They answered Him, We be Abraham's seed, and were never in bondage to any man: how sayest Thou, Ye shall be made free? Jesus answered them, Verily, verily, I say unto you, Whosoever committeth sin is the servant of sin. And the servant abideth not in the house forever: but the Son abideth ever. If the Son therefore shall make you free, ye shall be free indeed.
>
> John 8:31-36

Here we have a statement by Jesus that binds the idea of freedom to the truth, which is actually Him. Therefore, knowing Jesus means knowing the truth.

We can conclude that knowing the truth means we have eternal life and are of the truth. Jesus reveals to us what eternal life really is in John 17:3: "And this is life eternal, that they might know Thee the only true God, and Jesus Christ, whom Thou hast sent." We glean from this passage that truth is of God. This would mean that truth is also from another kingdom, and the kingdom of this world can not know it or reveal it.

THE HOLY SPIRIT IS TRUTH

The Scripture speaks of the Spirit of truth, and it being none other than the Holy Spirit. "Howbeit when He, the Spirit of truth, is come, He will guide you into all truth: for He shall not speak of Himself; but whatsoever He shall hear, that shall He speak: and He will shew you things to come" (John 16:13). The apostle John helps us to see the Holy Ghost is truth in 1 John 5:6: "This is He that came by water and blood, even Jesus Christ; not by water only, but by water and blood. And it is the Spirit that beareth witness, because the Spirit is truth." As Jesus was sent to bear witness to the truth, we see the role of the Spirit in the life of God's people doing the same thing. God is truth, and only those who are in a personal relationship with Him through the work and life of His only begotten Son and the regenerating and renewing work of the Holy Spirit can know the truth.

GOD IS TRUTH

We know truth because we know the truth, God Himself. We are now considered by God to be the family and fellowship of truth, which is the pillar and foundation of truth today. The blood-bought church of the living God is the means by which God has chosen to support and show forth the strength of His truth today. "But if I tarry long, that thou mayest know how thou oughtest to behave thyself in the house of God, which is the church of the living God, the pillar and ground of the truth" (1 Timothy 3:15). The church, because of its source of life and light and its inherited identity in Christ, is truth today. This is not a reference to the visible church membership of today, but of the called-out assembly of believers who are justified through the blood of Jesus and are being sanctified by the Holy Spirit for good works. They are characteristically and biblically known as disciples of the Lord Jesus Christ. They are zealous about their service upon the earth today and see it as a duty to contend for the faith. They are known as disciples in some parts of the world and "Jesus freaks" in America. They live to be dangerously strong for the truth on the earth because they are of the truth. These are kingdom warriors who live for righteousness and know how and when to repent as needed daily.

PEOPLE OF TRUTH

They are of the truth and in a relationship with the truth, so they know what the truth says about the ugliness of self-centered living and the call of God to die to self daily. They are extremely fond of Jesus. There is within their hearts an appetite and appeal to the nature of Christ Jesus. They truly live with an affection for Jesus and an adoration of Him.[53] They live in His light and know how to deal with personal sin through the blood shed by Jesus.[54] In their position, they are blameless before the throne of God in Christ. In practice, God is willing and working out of them His pleasure. They are His people, people of the God of truth. He has honestly come to define for us who truth is.

3. He's Come to Define for Us What Truth Does

IT SET US FREE

What does truth do for the recipient of it? The truth shall set us free. Set us free from what? Sin and sin-sick thinking! Jesus said, "We shall know the truth and the truth shall makes us free." As truth is revealed, we are continually and graciously set free from thoughts and strongholds that once held us captive. When we are ignorant of God's truth concerning a particular subject, we can only respond in a way that is natural and therefore in a way that is of the world and not of God. Let's look at it this way from 1 Thessalonians 4:13, "But I would not have you to be ignorant, brethren, concerning them which are asleep, that ye sorrow not, even as others which have no hope." Listen to what God is saying here. Their sorrow was in line with those who had no great expectation of eternal truth. They displayed emotions like any natural man would because they were ignorant of truth. They were ignorant which is saying they were "without" or "void" of this divine truth. When we are void of truth on any subject, we can only respond emotionally and mentally like any other natural man. Therefore, their actions revealed that they were not free to expect what God expects and were being held in bondage until this truth was revealed to them. Truth revealed equals freedom from old thoughts, emotions and actions that were contrary to God's perfect will. This is why Paul pleads with the church in Romans 12:1-2, "...by the mercies of God, that ye present your bodies a living sacrifice, holy, acceptable unto God, which is your reasonable service. And be not conformed to this world: but be ye transformed by the renewing of your mind, that ye may prove what is that good, and acceptable, and perfect, will of God." The truth that only God can open to us is the only thing that frees us to prove what is that good, and acceptable and perfect will of God. Never forget that it is Jesus who freed us from ourselves, our sin, our society and the source of our deception and delusion, Satan, himself. He did this to put us in a position to be freed daily by His truth from carnal thinking and living. We are free because of Jesus! It was Jesus who said this in, Matthew 5:21-22, "Ye have heard that it was said by them of old time.., But I say unto you..."

FREE TO BE FREED

We have been set free to be continually freed day by day. We are not free or authorized to let this environment we live in shape our thinking. Jesus came to mold our thinking to His way of thinking. "Commit thy works unto the Lord, and thy thoughts shall be established" (Proverbs 16:3). Do we really want to know what you're authorized to do? We are authorized to surrender our lives to the mercy of God's will, and He will establish and settle our minds on things that are pleasing in His sight. What and how we think shapes who we are. What we commit to is the very thing that will set in place our thought lives.

Blessed is the man that walketh not in the counsel of the ungodly, nor standeth in the way of sinners, nor sitteth in the seat of the scornful. But his delight is in the law of the Lord; and in His law doth he meditate day and night. And he shall be like a tree planted by the rivers of water, that bringeth forth his fruit in his season; his leaf also shall not wither; and whatsoever he doeth shall prosper.

Psalm 1:1-3

VICTORY BEGINS IN THE MIND

Victory or defeat is just one thought away. A thought is the result of only one commitment. Where will we commit our thought lives? "Finally, brethren, whatsoever things are true, whatsoever things are honest, whatsoever things are just, whatsoever things are pure, whatsoever things are lovely, whatsoever things are of good report; if there be any virtue, and if there be any praise, think on these things. Those things, which ye have both learned, and received, and heard, and seen in me, do: and the God of peace shall be with you." (Philippians 4:8-9) Give God your life daily, and He'll daily uncover His truth to you.[55]

WE NEED HELP

It is paramount for us to remember that apart from the unveiling of Jesus, we cannot know the freedom of the truth. "Then opened He (Jesus) their understanding, that they might understand the scriptures..." (Luke 24:45). Jesus opened their understanding after having walked with His disciples for three years. He removed the cover so they could comprehend and understand what was written in the Scriptures. He freed them to follow His teaching while He was not present to physically walk with them. Just prior to doing this, He also expounded on all the Scriptures concerning Himself to the disciples on the road to Emmaus: "And beginning at Moses and all the prophets, He (Jesus) expounded unto them in all the Scriptures the things concerning Himself" (Luke 24:27). The result of this opening of the truth by Jesus freed these men to run back to Jerusalem and bear witness to the resurrection of our Lord. Hours prior to this revelation, they were in bondage to a depressed mindset that held their emotions captive.[56] But the truth freed them to see, stand with, and shout what God knew about this present truth. Wow! Magnify the Lord! He's come to define what truth is, who truth is, and what truth does.

TAKING IT SERIOUSLY

Have you been convinced truth is of another world?

Have you been humbled by this reality?

Do you know the truth?

Will you honor God's ordained role for teachers to teach truth?

Are you seeking a preacher or a teacher who makes you feel good?

Do you want a preacher to teach truth or justify your sin?

Will you be accountable to God for what preaching and teachings you submit to?

Have you thought about the fact you'll give an account of all your thoughts and actions?

Have you been and are you being set free daily?

Are you aligned with and in agreement with God concerning the truth?

Chapter 3

Magnify the Lord
He's Come to Declare

KEEP DIGGING

It is an earnest prayer of mine that God has chosen to make known to you the principles of the previous two chapters. The purpose of Christ coming to die and redeem His people is so deep and rich that we will spend an eternity being taught the fullness of it and its everlasting effect. Each of the ten reasons I will deal with in this book are intended to provoke your interest in exploring each purpose the Bible presents to us. Each purpose can stand alone, yet together they are great pillars that support each other. They are all divinely woven together to create an eternal work of art which is displayed and revealed through the entire counsel of God's Word.

The divine reality that truth must be revealed is a heavenly principle we long to know and understand. Jesus has come to define for us the following: What is truth? Who is truth? What does truth do? He is most qualified to do this. Why is He authorized to define truth? He also came to defer all rights, all results, and all rewards to His heavenly Father. By doing this work, we also see a third reason why He's come. He's come to declare two things specifically: the heart and holiness of God.

1. He's Come to Declare the Heart of God

A DIVINE EXPRESSION

God has used many vessels in times past to communicate His Word to the world. Some of the instruments He chose to use were vessels of wrath fitted for destruction and others were vessels of mercy prepared beforehand for His glory. God has never had a problem with effectively relating His heart's desire to His people. However, He mysteriously hinted about a day when He would open His heart in a way His people had not previously experienced. He would give the world His Son! He would literally give them His heart. "God, who at sundry times and in divers manners spake in time past unto the fathers by the prophets, hath in these last days spoken unto us by His Son, whom He hath appointed heir of all things, by whom also He made the worlds" (Hebrews 1:1-2). Jesus, the Son of God, was sent into this world to declare the heart of His Father through His life, death, and resurrection from the dead. He was on a mission to speak whatever flowed out of the heart of God, His Father. God's Word has taught us that out of the mouth the heart speaks. Jesus, the second Person of the Godhead, is described as being the Word. *Word* means, "The very thoughts and intent of the heart expressed and made known through the means of verbal or visual expression." [57]

KNOWN BY OUR FRUIT

We use our mouths as gateways to verbally express the intent and purpose of our hearts. We're taught by the Lord Jesus Christ that we can specifically know people by the fruit of their lips:

Beware of false prophets, which come to you in sheep's clothing, but inwardly they are ravening wolves. Ye shall know them by their fruits. Do men gather grapes of thorns, or figs of thistles? Even so every good tree bringeth forth good fruit; but a corrupt tree bringeth forth evil fruit. A good tree cannot bring forth evil fruit, neither can a corrupt tree bring forth good fruit. Every tree that bringeth not forth good fruit is hewn down, and cast into the fire. Wherefore by their fruits ye shall know them.

Matthew 7:15-20

Luke's account is more specific in regard to the fruit of the lips:

For a good tree bringeth not forth corrupt fruit; neither doth a corrupt tree bring forth good fruit. For every tree is known by his own fruit. For of thorns men do not gather figs, nor of a bramble bush gather they grapes. A good man out of the good treasure of his heart bringeth forth that which is good; and an evil man out of the evil treasure of his heart bringeth forth that which is evil: for of the abundance of the heart his mouth speaketh.

Luke 6:43-45

HEARTS EXPOSED

The heart of a man or who a man really is can only be seen by what habitually comes out of his mouth and the actions of his life. The way a man lives, which would include the way he talks and walks, is a revelation of the way thinks, and what he thinks he is. "For as he (a man) thinketh in his heart, so is he" (Proverbs 23:7).

In each of us, there is an immaterial part of our lives. It's who we are, and it truly affects what we say and do. The only way to see it is to listen for it as expressed through our words and the actions of our bodies. We communicate verbally and visually to each other.

THE WORD

The Son of God is the Person of the Trinity through which God the Father has expressed Himself to us generally and specifically. We are given a description of the Son of God as the Word. He is and has always been the Word, and He is God. He is how God the Father touches all mankind in a general way through His creation and by

His common grace through the provision of and the sustaining of His creation.[58]

INDESCRIBABLE

God the Father is a Spirit, and the Bible teaches us no man has ever fully and completely seen Him. This is similar to how no man sees our souls except through the expression of it in the way we talk and walk. God the Father's way of physically expressing Himself to His creation is through God the Son (the Word). We must admit there is deep sense of inadequacy within our understanding of the complexity we face in our attempts to perfectly describe the beauty of the Trinity. The complexity is from our perspective, not God's. He is worthy of all we are, even when we can't completely explain Him. Do we have sufficient words to describe Him? These truths are great mysteries we will never fully know and understand.[59] King David can help us with this blessing if we take on God's approach to this indescribable wonder:

> Lord, my heart is not haughty, nor mine eyes lofty: neither do I exercise myself in great matters, or in things too high for me. Surely I have behaved and quieted myself, as a child that is weaned of his mother: my soul is even as a weaned child. Let Israel hope in the Lord from henceforth and for ever.
>
> Psalm 131:1-3

May we in childlike faith rest in the bosom of our Father. He is more than we can ever know. If all of His creation puts everything it knows about Him together, it would be a deficient description. What we do know has been effectually revealed to us in His revelation of Himself by the Holy Spirit and expressed to us through the life of the Son of God, Jesus Christ.[60] What do we know? He is more than enough!

ONE TRUE AND LIVING GOD

We have only one true and living God. He is God; therefore, He is self-existent. Making an all-out effort to explain Him has confused and crippled many of noble character. Why has this happened? Only He can comprehend or understand His essence. He is greater than any possible concept we may have of Him.

He is holy. He is wise. He is true. He is right. He is just. He is love. He is mercy. He is our judge. He is changeless. He is eternal. He is eternity. He is life. He is all-sufficient. He is sovereign. He is infinite. He is infallible. He is certain. He is trustworthy. He is God.

A TRINITY

There are three eternal and divine Persons unveiled in Scripture and make up what we know as the Godhead (or Trinity)—God the Father, God the Son (or the Word), and God the Holy Spirit. They are uniquely one in substance, power, and eternity. They are each fully God, and indivisible, and they work in perfect harmony within the counsel of the Godhead. Each Person of the Trinity is uniquely and personally set apart in Scripture by the work which each One undertakes. The Father planned the method of redemption and provided the means necessary for redemption to be embraced and experienced. The Son is the agent of redemption that has and will carry out the Father's mission to save His lost sheep. The Holy Spirit applies the effectual work of the Son and affirms in the hearts of men the eternal decrees of the Father.

God the Father, God the Son, and God the Holy Spirit are one. God the Son has always existed from eternity past and will forever be. The heart of the Trinity, the Person who cannot be seen by man, is God the Father. The Person of the Trinity who can be seen is God the Son, or the Word. It is true we see the effects of all parts of the Trinity in creation and the power of the Holy Spirit. Christ Jesus is the Word of God who has eternally existed as God. He is the Word, and through Him all that can and cannot be seen was made.[61]

When God the Father encounters mankind, He primarily communicates His heart to them through God the Son. This verbal and visual communication was and is always based on an eternal covenant that was made by the Father and the Son before time ever began. God the Father, in His all-knowing way, knew mankind would sin and be in eternal need of a sacrifice to satisfy the just wrath of a holy God. Therefore, a covenant that the Son of God would be clothed with humanity was made and settled before time. Through the supernatural work of God the Spirit, the Word would become flesh and tabernacle among humanity to rescue them from the fall. The Word, by way of His life and the shedding of His blood through death and His resurrection, would satisfy God's wrath and supply the necessary favor God demanded of His subjects.[62] God the Spirit would be the Person who effectually applied this all-consuming and redeeming work of God the Son. God the Spirit works in harmony with God the Son to fulfill the eternal decrees of God the Father. All three Persons, who are one, execute and administer a perfect salvation upon the eternal state of imperfect sinners. Halleluiah! Praise be unto God in the highest!

GOD'S WAY

God's heart had to be expressed and manifested in such a way that man could relate to the immaterial part of Him, which no man has ever seen. Therefore, we see from the beginning the Father has used God the Son to effectually communicate His heart to the vessels of His mercy who He prepared for His glory.[63]

In the beginning, Adam was the first man to ever encounter God the Son. God the Father fellowshipped with Adam in the garden through the Son of God. If no man has ever seen God the Father, it had to be God the Son who Adam and Eve heard walking in the garden in the cool of the day. "And they heard the voice of the Lord God walking in the garden in the cool of the day: and Adam and his wife hid themselves from the presence of the Lord God amongst the trees of the garden" (Genesis 3:8). How do we know it was God the Son? God the Father is a Spirit. When the Father physically engages men, it is through God the Son. Who was it that killed an innocent sacrifice and clothed Adam and Eve? It was God the Son, declaring the heart of God, who longs to have fellowship with His people, and revealing to us the need to cover over our sin, which is naked and exposed before a holy God. Enoch walked with God the Son for three hundred years and he was taken to be with the Father forever.[64] God the Father has most often expressed His heart to us through God the Son.

IT WAS GOD THE SON

Each encounter is a declaration. Why is that? God never does anything without a purpose. Every time we see God the Son meeting with Abraham, Sarah, Isaac, Jacob, Moses, Joshua, Gideon, David or any other person, His message becomes clearer and clearer. When God invaded time and interrupted His subjects and engaged them physically, it was always through God the Son. He is described in the Bible as the Lord of Hosts, the Angel of the Lord, the Commander of the Army of the Lord, Yahweh, and the Most High God, just to name a few titles. All of these providential meetings were used to declare the Father is upon His throne, and the earth is His footstool.[65] God the Son was unveiling the heart of the Father's redemptive plan for mankind and how He was orchestrating the events in time to carry out this eternal work.

THE PROMISED SEED

God the Son was the prophetic seed that was declared in Genesis 3: "And I will put enmity between thee and the woman, and between thy seed and her Seed; It shall bruise thy head, and thou shalt bruise His heel" (Genesis 3:15). God the Son, speaking on behalf of the Father, declared to Abraham of His coming as a babe when He spoke to him about the seed in his loins that would bless all the nations in a future day:

> By faith Abraham, when he was tried, offered up Isaac: and he that had received the promises offered up his only begotten son, Of whom it was said, That in Isaac shall thy seed be called: Accounting that God was able to raise him up, even from the dead; from whence also he received him in a figure.
> Hebrews 11:17-19

The New Testament confirms this seed is none other than Jesus, God the Son incarnate: "Now to Abraham and his seed were the promises made. He saith not, And to seeds, as of many; but as of one, And to thy seed, which is Christ" (Galatians 3:16).

A GOD THING

God the Son has been promised and talked about from the beginning of time. He is the One who introduced us to the immaterial part of the Godhead and the heart of His plan for man. Jesus, God the Son, in a miraculous and supernatural way, was all man and all God. How all this is worked out is a God thing that the Bible presents to its subjects to believe without having to fully understand. He, God the Son, being the promised seed, invaded time and was given the name of Jesus to declare to us the heart of God. Jesus declared and demonstrated that God's heart was for salvation.

HE HATES SIN

The life of Jesus plainly declares that God will and does not accept what natural and fallen mankind can produce. The product of their lives cannot and will not ever please the heart of God. The fact Jesus came and died to deliver us from ourselves validates that God hates sin. The cross is a vivid declaration of the Father's heart in regard to sin. He hates it! He hates the origin of sin and its outcome so much that He gave us His only begotten Son to declare just how devastating the results of sin are. Jesus declared to us in no uncertain terms through His life and death that sin cannot go without being eternally punished. The heart of the Father must punish sin and sinners.

WE'RE THE PROBLEM

The life-giving and sustaining work of Jesus also reveals to us the problem is not in what we do. The problem is who we are. The problem is us ourselves. We ourselves are sin. The fact God the Son had to take upon flesh to atone for us declares we inherited a nature that is of sin and knows nothing but sinful rebellion and hostility toward God. We all were conceived in sin from the womb. Jesus was conceived in a supernatural and miraculous way, being placed in the womb of the Virgin Mary, because of the divine pleasure and power of God Almighty. This was wrought through the effective work of God the Spirit. Therefore, Jesus is not of the seed of man but of God, and He did not inherit the sin problem as we did.

A PARDON IS NEEDED

It is the decree of the Father and the desire of His heart to eternally change us for His own glory. It's not about what we do, but who we are. Jesus declares to His sheep that our fallen condition is not what the heart of the Father intended for us. God is holy and cannot and will not eternally tolerate sin; therefore, God the Son had to fulfill the righteous requirements of God's standards on our behalf. God could not and will not ever eternally overlook sin. All sin must be punished by death. The just nature of God will not legally allow sin to be pardoned without a just payment. Sin must and will be paid for forever. For the Lord's sheep, sin is paid for in Christ and for the lost goats they will pay for their sin in a place of everlasting torment and separation from the love, life, and light of holy God.

BY JESUS

Our president can legally pardon convicted and guilty criminals before their sentence has been justly fulfilled. He can do this because of a law granting him the authority to release a criminal and give him a clean slate, even though he has not fulfilled the just penalty for such a crime. God cannot do this because He has a binding law which says sins must die. Imagine if the president of the United States pardoned a known serial killer who was completely guilty of known murder and even admitted to all the crimes, yet he (the president) took his death penalty for him that justice could be served. It sounds foolish, doesn't it?[66] This is what Jesus did!

ONLY HE CAN

Remember, Jesus has come to declare the heart of the Father. He is our pardon, He did fulfill the just penalty of our sins, and He dealt with the sin problem, us. This is something a president cannot do. He may stand in the gap for a murderer, but he can't change the nature of the man who he pardoned. Jesus lifts the burden of guilt and shame and goes beyond what we have done and subdues our iniquity. How does He do this? He deals with our problem. What is our problem? It is our hearts. Jesus is the only Person who can conquer our heart's problem and free us to serve His Father.

Who is a God like unto Thee, that pardoneth iniquity, and passeth by the transgression of the remnant of His heritage? He retaineth not His anger forever, because He delighteth in mercy. He will turn again, He will have compassion upon us; He will subdue our iniquities; and thou wilt cast all their sins into the depths of the sea. Thou wilt perform the truth to Jacob, and the mercy to Abraham, which thou hast sworn unto our fathers from the days of old.

Micah 7:18-20

Only Jesus can die in a sinner's place and change their very nature. Jesus died lovingly and legally for His sheep from all nations and in all generations. He's come to declare to man the problem he was born with, the ugly things he loves to do, and how it grieves the heart of His Father. Trust Jesus, my friend. He has truly come to declare the heart of God.

IT CAN HAPPEN

At times on the journey of faith, we can find ourselves serving the church with all our hearts and strength, and essentially be guilty of missing the heart of God. It often happens when we get our priorities out of order. We set out each day to be wholehearted servants rather than wholehearted seekers. The natural tendency all of us have is to revert back to what we know best and what seems to be most convenient and comfortable. The Lord commanded us to seek first the kingdom of God and His righteousness, and all the other things in His service would take their proper place. At times, serving God is easier and more comfortable than seeking with all our heart the face of God. Our service should always be the result of an intimate encounter with the Lord and a revelation of what He warmly embraces.

If we are honest, we can usually catch ourselves with a motivation to serve the Lord, hoping to find Him. The problem with this way of thinking is it is carnal and not supernatural. We want to be in His will, but we do not want to encounter Him. Why do we not want to encounter the Lord? We know there are things in our lives that grieve the heart of God. We can ease the pressure of our conscience by wholeheartedly seeking His will rather than sincerely seeking Him. The flesh always wants to do something in order to get the praise and feed its ego. The carnal element in us has no desire to meet God. God has commanded the flesh be put to death and its influence over our lives be mortified. The flesh and the Spirit of God are at war and directly opposed to each other.[67] When we allow our flesh to influence us in one or more areas of our life, we have backslidden.

BACKSLIDER DEFINED

A backslider is one who has returned to an area of his carnal life to think, feel, and do what he knows naturally and feels most confident and comfortable with, while showing his back to God's Word, wisdom, and ways. The Scriptures teach that backsliders are influenced by their own ways and are not living under the guidance of the Lord. "The backslider in heart shall be filled with his own ways: and a good man shall be satisfied from **outside of** himself" (Proverbs 14:14, emphasis added).The word *filled* speaks of the idea of being controlled and influenced from within and not from above or by the Lord. Therefore, their influence is from a carnal mind which is at war with God.

CARNALITY DEFINED

Carnality is when a believer's thoughts, emotions, and actions are void of God's decree and design; it is common to a natural unregenerate man. Carnal thoughts, feelings, and actions are not characteristic of a disciple of Jesus Christ; therefore, they must be declared as foolish and promptly corrected by the servant of God. Carnal thinking does seem more natural to man, but it only leads to death and destruction: "There is a way that seemeth right unto a man, but the end thereof are the ways of death" (Proverbs 16:25). It does seem more natural to man to serve God will all his strength than to seek Him with his heart. But this way of living is carnal and opposed to God's purpose: "For to be carnally minded is death; but to be spiritually minded is life and peace. Because the carnal mind is enmity against God: for it is not subject to the law of God, neither indeed can be" (Romans 8:6-7).

DON'T TORTURE YOURSELVES

Jesus came to declare that God's heart, His will, is for us to seek Him first. If we place seeking Him among our priorities, we'll find Him first. Then we will embrace His dominion over our lives and His direction for our lives. If we get the order reversed, we'll be torn apart in our minds because of the carnality that will influence our thoughts and actions. We have all tortured our minds enough by pulling them in so many directions. We have heard horror stories of how believers have been tortured and martyred in the past for loving Jesus, His Word, and His people. Many have been torn and ripped in half while being tortured and persecuted for defending the faith. We don't have to torture ourselves any longer, brethren. We do not have to be pulled apart in our minds any longer.[68] We must repent of this kind of thinking/living and seek the Lord as our number one priority in our lives. If we seek Him first, we'll embrace His dominion and experience His direction for our lives. May He grant us repentance so we can see His heart. "But seek ye first the kingdom of God, and His righteousness; and all these things shall be added unto you" (Matthew 6:33).

REPENTANCE DEFINED

Repentance is a gift of God's grace that effectually causes an individual to turn his mind, soul, and body away from a specific sin and accept, affirm, and applaud the deliverance and life found in Christ Jesus. Carnal thinking is sin, and sin must be dealt with through the godly sorrow that leads to repentance. Repentance at conversion or repentance in confessing and forsaking sins as a backslidden believer is the same. It is a supernatural gift of God bestowed upon the recipients of His grace. Repentance is the finished product of godly sorrow. *Repentance* actually means "to think differently afterwards." When godly sorrow has worked genuine repentance, there will be three areas in a believer's life that have been radically altered: First, their hearts are altered from being a conformer to the agenda of this world to being a transformer. Why have they been transformed? Their hearts have been changed to be in agreement with the Lord and are approved for His kingdom work. When believers repent, their hearts are altered and they are truly different people. Repentance alters what they truly are. Second, their attitudes and aptitudes are altered from being self-centered to being single-minded in their personal pursuit of King Jesus. When believers repent of sin, their thoughts and what they treasure encounters a supernatural alteration. Repentance alters what they think. Third, their actions are altered from walking by sight to walking by faith. When believers repent of sin, they place their trust in the promises of God and not in what they physically see and know naturally. Repentance alters how they live.

God desires that our hearts be in agreement with His. He is, therefore, longsuffering, and His kindness and goodness are what lead us to repentance: "Or despisest thou the riches of His goodness and forbearance and longsuffering; not knowing that the goodness of God leadeth thee to repentance?" (Romans 2:4). It's when God brings into view His useful goodness in Christ and how He longs to supply His righteousness in our lives and also take away our iniquities that we are led to repentance. It is through His grace He reveals our complete failure to appropriate and apply His mercy over our personal sins that lead us to repentance. It is through His forbearance that He takes the precious time to unveil to us that our transgressions have been laid upon Jesus at Calvary. This effectual work of grace produces in us a gift of godly sorrow that leads to an altered way of thinking about Jesus, sin, ourselves, and our lives. This altered way of thinking is repentance. "He that covereth his sins shall not prosper: but whoso confesseth and forsaketh them shall have mercy" (Proverbs 28:13).

SEVEN STEPS OF GODLY SORROW

When God shines His light upon our iniquities and we see from His perspective how disgusted He is with our rebellion toward His grace, we are moved toward repentance and motivated by godly sorrow. Godly sorrow works a seven-step process in the lives of all who have experienced grace-granted repentance. The seven steps are as follows:

Step One (SIN'S SERVANT)

By God's grace, godly sorrow allows the sinner to see and know they're a slave to sin (lost man) or a particular sin in their life (back-slider). They thought they were in control of this pleasure until godly sorrow began to reveal to them sin never serves man but man always serves sin: "Jesus answered them, Verily, verily, I say unto you, Whosoever committeth sin is the servant of sin" (John 8:34). "Know ye not, that to whom ye yield yourselves servants to obey, his servants ye are to whom ye obey; whether of sin unto death, or of obedience unto righteousness?" (Romans 6:16).

Step Two (SIN'S STRENGTH)

By God's grace, godly sorrow allows the sinner to see and know the strength of sin is the law. "The sting of death is sin; and the strength of sin is the law" (1 Corinthians 15:56). What does "sin's strength is the law" mean? The law condemns every soul that sins to die. "Behold, all souls are Mine; as the soul of the father, so also the soul of the son is Mine: the soul that sinneth, it shall die" (Ezekiel

18:4). "For the wages of sin is death; but the gift of God is eternal life through Jesus Christ our Lord" (Romans 6:23). The law of God demands all sins be paid for in full.

Step Three (SIN'S SENSE)

By God's grace, godly sorrow allows the sinner to know and recognize the presence of their sin. It allows them to see the ugliness of their sinful heart and the reality of the consequences of their rebellion toward God. "Whosoever committeth sin transgresseth also the law: for sin is the transgression of the law" (1 John 3:4). "And ye know that He was manifested to take away our sins; and in Him is no sin" (1 John 3:5).

Step Four (SIN'S SORROW)

By God's grace, godly sorrow allows the sinner to know and experience the shame and grief they have caused God by allowing sin in their life. "Now we know that what things soever the law saith, it saith to them who are under the law: that every mouth may be stopped, and all the world may become guilty before God. Therefore by the deeds of the law there shall no flesh be justified in His sight: for by the law is the knowledge of sin" (Romans 3:19-20). "Was then that which is good made death unto me? God forbid. But sin, that it might appear sin, working death in me by that which is good; that sin by the commandment might become exceeding sinful" (Romans 7:13). God uses His law when godly sorrow is at work in a sinner's life to produce guilt and shame so their conscience will condemn them.

Step Five (SIN'S SACRIFICE)

By God's grace, godly sorrow reveals to us the purpose of Christ's death on the cross and the desire of God to forgive sins through Christ's shed blood: "And as it is appointed unto men once to die, but after this the judgment: So Christ was once offered to bear the sins of many; and unto them that look for Him shall he appear the second time without sin unto salvation" (Hebrews 9:27-28). "Who hath delivered us from the power of darkness, and hath translated us into the kingdom of His dear Son: In whom we have redemption through His blood, even the forgiveness of sins" (Colossians 1:13-14). "And for this cause He is the mediator of the new testament, that by means of death, for the redemption of the transgressions that were under the first testament, they which are called might receive the promise of eternal inheritance" (Hebrews 9:15). Through godly sorrow, we know our sins are paid in full.

Step Six (SIN SURRENDERED)

By God's grace, godly sorrow compels the sinner to surrender sin, its guilt, and the shame it causes over to Jesus: "If we confess our sins, He is faithful and just to forgive us our sins, and to cleanse us from all unrighteousness" (1 John 1:9). With godly sorrow, God always reveals the truth about ourselves and our sins, causing us to realize that Jesus has already personally paid the wages of our sin. Godly sorrow brings us to the place where we can agree with God about sin and also agree with Him that Jesus must take our sin for us. Thus, we surrender our transgressions and iniquities to our Mediator.

Step Seven (SIN SEVERED)

By God's grace, godly sorrow has brought us to a place where we can walk away from sin with no condemnation of a guilty conscience. Why? We have been severed from that which once held us captive in thought and deed. Godly sorrow has led us to an altered way of thinking called repentance. "How much more shall the blood of Christ, who through the eternal Spirit offered Himself without spot to God, purge your conscience from dead works to serve the living God?" (Hebrews 9:14). "There is therefore now no condemnation to them which are in Christ Jesus, who walk not after the flesh, but after the Spirit." (Romans 8:1) "If the Son therefore shall make you free, ye shall be free indeed" (John 8:36).

LET GODLY SORROW WORK IN YOU

Godly sorrow is sure to work through these seven steps in a most divine and precise way when God graces His people with repentance. Repentance is always the product of God invading sinners with His grace to produce in their lifestyle godly sorrow.

> For godly sorrow worketh repentance to salvation not to be repented of: but the sorrow of the world worketh death. For behold this selfsame thing, that ye sorrowed after a godly sort, what carefulness it (godly sorrow) wrought in you, yea, what clearing of yourselves, yea, what indignation, yea, what fear, yea, what vehement desire, yea, what zeal, yea, what revenge! In all things ye have approved yourselves to be clear in this matter.
>
> 2 Corinthians 7:10-11

Take time to dig deep in this passage and study the effects of godly sorrow which produces genuine repentance. It will produce an altered way of thinking, treasuring, and trusting the deliverance in Christ that we will never regret. This is the heart of God and what Christ came to declare.

2. He's Come to Declare the Holiness of God

NO ONE

God is holy, therefore He demands and grants repentance to bring glory to His name. Our God is completely holy! There is none like Him. God the Son, who was born of a virgin, declares the uniqueness of our God. We have the opportunity to compare ourselves to someone who looks or talks like us. Dads can compare themselves to other dads. A preacher can explain to a young child what he does each week. He can attempt to compare himself to the man who preaches each Sunday in the little boy's own church. The child will be able to recognize how the man is "like" his preacher. We all have something or someone to whom we can compare ourselves. God, on the other hand, does not. This is why He told Moses to tell the people of Israel that "I Am Who I Am" sent him[69] There was no one to whom He could have compared Himself. No one! Our God is unique and stands alone. There is none like Him. He is holy!

Listen to God as He describes Himself through the apostle John: "No man hath seen God at any time; the only begotten Son, which is in the bosom of the Father, he hath declared Him" (John 1:18). No man has ever seen the immaterial part of God the Father but Jesus, God the Son, and He has come to declare He is holy. He also declares all that God does is holy and always right.

> At that time Jesus answered and said, I thank thee, O Father, Lord of heaven and earth, because Thou hast hid these things from the wise and prudent, and hast revealed them unto babes. Even so, Father: for so it seemed good in Thy sight. All things are delivered unto Me of My Father: and no man knoweth the Son, but the Father; neither knoweth any man the Father, save the Son, and he to whomsoever the Son will reveal Him.

> Matthew 11:25-27

INCOMPARABLE

Here we are again, dealing with the reality that truth must always be revealed. If God cannot be compared to anything created, how can that which is created, us, compare Him to anything? Throughout history man has made every effort to do the impossible by attempting to bring God down to a place comparable with things that have been made. God dealt with this issue in the Old Testament. God asked them a serious question we must also ponder. "To whom will ye liken Me, and make Me equal, and compare Me, that we may be like?" (Isaiah 46:5). Notice the automatic tension we find in this question. God speaks in terms that reveal what humanists have always done. What is that? They must bring God down to compare Him to something because there is nothing that can be used to compare Him with.

God cannot be compared to people or to what man fashions in his mind. We, by way of teaching certain qualities about the Lord, will refer to Him as a Father. I have done this in this book over and over again. But there has never been a father who could even remotely be compared to Him. He is the Father, yet He is also the Redeemer. He is the Redeemer, yet He is also the Judge. He is the Judge, yet He is also the Advocate. He is the Advocate, yet He is also without sin. He is without sin, yet He is also the Sin Bearer. He is the Sin Bearer, yet He is also the Propitiation. He is the Propitiation, yet He is also the Shepherd. He is the Shepherd, yet He is also the Lamb. Glory be to God in the highest! Who can be compared to our great God? No one and nothing has a standing chance to be compared to God. Amen!

HUMANISTIC EFFORTS

Our secular culture with its humanistic nature will make every effort to shape its version of our God for us. There are five stages outlined and revealed in Isaiah 46:5 that the humanist takes when he attempts to defend his rights and effortlessly vilifies the character of God. I will paraphrase this passage with some added emphasis to explain some of the wording, and we'll see each of the stages as they unfold. "To whom do you consider I resemble, having already adjusted Me to your level, by comparing and agreeing that our dominion and authority is the same, having made us altogether and completely comparable?"

We will begin with stage five, or where the humanist lives his life. It's a place he has settled in and which all humanists consider 'their god.'

STAGE FIVE

"Having made us altogether and completely comparable." This speaks of what they are currently doing—they are living with a twisted mind and distorted view of God. They are settled and living with this view of God and will be content in the image they have formed and fashioned. They know others may have their own opinion, but this is theirs.

STAGE FOUR

"Having already adjusted Me to their level." This speaks of how they have actually done this—they have found a perverted landmark and brought God down to its level and made Him altogether comparable to it so they can live in a way that fits their personality, pleasure, and purpose for living.

STAGE THREE

"To whom do you consider I resemble?" This speaks of why they have done this—they consider Him as resembling something of their liking in order to limit His authority over them and elevate their rights. This is the motivation of a humanist to reduce the friction of his conscience. All sinners in their lost condition are humanist by default. Therefore, humans by nature must find a way of justifying their authority to live a certain way to ease their conscience.

STAGE TWO

"To whom?" This speaks of what they have willfully done—they have fashioned an idol and are living as idolaters. All sinners are idolaters by nature. Lost humanity is self-centered in all its thoughts and actions (Genesis 6:5).

STAGE ONE

"Consider, adjusted, comparing, and made." This speaks of man's ineffectiveness to even think properly of God or about Him without a divine revelation of Him. When humanists consult among themselves on any subject, and in particular things concerning God, the product of their sinful minds will always be sin!

MAN WILL ALWAYS MISS

To know and understand God, sinners must turn to Jesus, not man. Fallen man will not ever be able to declare the heart or the holiness of God. Man will always miss the mark and misrepresent the purpose and pleasure of God in his efforts to explain His dealings in creation and with the sons of men. Turn from sin and man's opinions to Jesus if you want to know the heart and holiness of God.

GO TO THE SOURCE

Why do we turn to people when tragedy or death comes our way? Why do we go to the one who can't help when we're in need of help? Why are we seeking answers about life among the dead? Take the advice of Jacob when you find yourself searching for life. Quit looking to one another and look to Jesus. "Now when Jacob saw that there was corn in Egypt, Jacob said unto his sons, Why do ye look one upon another?" (Genesis 42:1). In Jacob's day, God had sent a man ahead of His people to meet their needs during the times of a drought. In our day, God has already sent Jesus ahead of His people to declare His heart. We need to get to Jesus.

Why Do You Look at One Another?
By Nick Holden

We dare not trust the sweetest frame
But wholly lean on Jesus' name.
Words we sing through out the land,
Until the time sin binds our hand.
We find our gaze upon our brother,
When trouble comes to only smother.
Looking to our neighbor for his thought,
Going against all we've ever been taught.
Blaming everyone else for our daily loss,
Seeking answers, weighing the cost.
Why is it, that we look at one another,
When famine comes to uncover?
Why do we seek answers from a man,
When despair takes its stand?
We are convinced in what we can do,
Rejoicing to hear who else knew.

Just another lie we seem to trust.
"Like man's freedom is a must!"
When a spiritual famine comes near,
Always tune in with a humble ear.
God desires to meet your need,
His purpose and plan only heed.
He sent a Man ahead of you,
Go to Him for He is ever true.
Though you rejected Him in the past,
He'll give you bread that will forever last.
Stop looking to those who can not provide,
Go to Jesus, His arms are open wide.
Dare not trust the sweetest frame,
Just wholly lean on Jesus' name.

Now when Jacob saw that there was grain in Egypt,
Jacob said to his sons, "Why do you look at one another?"
(Genesis 42:1).

Jesus, God the Son, came to this earth to reveal that God is holy and man is messed up. Man can not help man; therefore, the Son of Man came, as all man and all God, to reveal and declare what we need to know and understand the most: we need to know the heart and holiness of God. How? Coming to know Jesus. "And this is life eternal, that they might know Thee the only true God, and Jesus Christ, whom Thou hast sent." (John 17:3)

Jesus is the exclusive and only sure way of knowing God the Father. Magnify the Lord! He's come to declare the heart of God to His people. Throughout time, God the Son, through His unique birth, life, sacrifice, death, and resurrection, has declared that God is holy. Stop looking to man for the answer and find God's answer to man: Jesus!

TAKING IT SERIOUSLY

Do you know God the Father?
Has Jesus declared to you the Father's heart?

Have you embraced and are you experiencing the holiness of God?

Have you been pardoned by Jesus?

Has the guilt and shame of your sin been dealt with?

Have your iniquities been subdued by King Jesus?

Who is shaping and molding what you know about Him?

Has the culture been your greatest teacher?

How is the Holy Spirit applying the decree of God the Father and the death of God the Son to your life?

Chapter 4

Magnify the Lord
He's Come to Demonstrate

WE'RE GUILTY

Would it be an accurate statement if I were to say that love has been declared more often than demonstrated in most of our lives? We're probably guilty of declaring our great love for others without clearly making a display of it. Our lives can be so full of empty expressions at times that we learn to function in the lies we're telling and believe we've been told: "The simple believeth every word: but the prudent man looketh well to his going" (Proverbs 14:15). We have a desperate need for a prudent heart and a discerning eye!

SHAPED BY OUR VIEW

One of the most convincing and compelling realities in life is when love has been established through action. Embracing, experiencing, and knowing we are loved has a tremendous effect on everything in our lives. Our attitudes and affections have been literally shaped and molded by who we know does or doesn't love us. Whatever concept we have of love will be revealed in how we live our lives. Love dictates our lives!

Some were told by their parents they loved them, but the actions of their parents established the complete opposite. They knew what their parents said and the way they lived were two totally different realities. Their mom or dad, maybe both of them, were consumed with themselves, so they learned how to look for love in other places. The search for love has driven millions to seek love from people and places that will only hurt them in the end. For some it was friends or systems (schools, sports teams, clubs, gangs, etc.), and for others it was someone who would make every effort to prove by their actions they loved them. What they required and wanted more than anything was proof they were loved. The validation did not necessarily have to be things that were good, godly, healthy, or safe, just as long as it confirmed they were loved. Others felt like they were only loved when they performed or met certain standards others expected. They lived a miserable life because they performed not out of a joy of doing what they loved to do for the glory of God, but their motivation was to gain someone's love. For some it was making good grades, playing sports, and giving themselves away through sexual intercourse. Maybe in order to fit in they used alcohol or drugs, and in some extreme cases even murdered somebody just to gain love. They did these things for people who would not love them for who they were, but only for what they did or could give back in return. There were those, on the other hand, who knew they were loved, period. They didn't have to do anything to gain someone's love because they were loved for who they were and not for what they did. They were told they were loved and the actions of their family proved the reality of their family's confession. Our lives can be interpreted by who, what, why, how, and when we love. Do we know how to be loved?

THEY MUST KNOW

Actions do establish and will validate our love for others, but our actions should never be what we do to gain someone else's love. Our spouses, children, and others we love should know we love them, period. We love them because of who they are, not what they do. They need to know that no matter what they do, good or bad, we love them. Our love for them should be settled in their lives. They should never have to perform for our love.

IT'S TAUGHT

Children must be taught how to love. They are taught by learning how to be loved. If they learn to love without first being loved, they will only hurt others and experience the pain of broken relationships. They have to learn how to be loved before they can choose to love others. "Foolishness is bound in the heart of a child; but the rod of correction shall drive it far from him" (Proverbs 22:15). No one can give what they don't have. We must teach our children how to be loved if we want them to learn how to demonstrate their love for others. Isn't this exactly what our heavenly Father has done with us? We love Him because He taught us how to be loved. "We love Him, because He first loved us" (1 John 4:19). How did He teach us to be loved? He demonstrated His love toward us through His Son, Jesus Christ. "But God commendeth His love toward us, in that, while we were yet sinners, Christ died for us" (Romans 5:8).

HE'S RELENTLESS

Jesus did come to defer, define, and declare as we learned in the previous chapters, but He also came to demonstrate some things to us. He came to demonstrate the **love** of God, His **loyalty** to His people, and the **line** by which He will judge the souls of men. The love of God is demonstrated through the witness and work of our living Redeemer, Jesus Christ. Jesus is the demonstration of God's love. He demonstrated a love that was unfailing and steadfast. "The Lord hath appeared of old unto me, saying, Yea, I have loved thee with an everlasting love: therefore with lovingkindness have I drawn thee" (Jeremiah 31:3). Why is God's love steadfast? His love is an everlasting love. It's a love that has no beginning or ending. And because of His fidelity to keep the covenant, He has filled the objects of His grace with relentless, steadfast, and unfailing mercy in order to demonstrate His unquenchable and undeniable love. His love is rooted in eternity past, manifested in time through Christ, and will be embraced and experienced for an eternity by those who will be saved by His amazing grace.

Nevertheless death reigned from Adam to Moses, even over them that had not sinned after the similitude of Adam's transgression, who is the figure of Him that was to come. But not as the offence, so also is the free gift. For if through the offence of one many be dead, much more the grace of God, and the gift by grace, which is by One Man, Jesus Christ, hath abounded unto many.

Romans 5:14-15

BY GRACE

Notice how grace is spoken of in a two-fold manner in the previous verse. We see the grace of the Father and the grace of the Son. Jesus, God the Son, gave His life as a gift of grace. His life was a gift given through the grace of God the Father. "But we see Jesus, who was made a little lower than the angels for the suffering of death, crowned with glory and honour; that He (Jesus) by the grace of God should taste death for every man" (Hebrews 2:9). Jesus lived and died by the grace of God the Father. Yet Jesus Himself gave His life as a gift of grace that resulted in the divine gift of righteousness that is imparted on all who believe. The grace of God the Father has produced the life of His Son, Jesus. The gift (Christ's righteousness) comes through the life of Jesus (the grace of the One Man), which He laid down for God's people. God's people are actually saved because of the eternal grace of God the Father through the death of Jesus.

Jesus Christ came to manifest His Father's grace and finish His work. He came to accomplish the eternal purpose and decree of His heavenly Father. Paul teaches that Christ was sent to accomplish a work that was "...according to the eternal purpose which He (the Father) purposed in Christ Jesus our Lord..." (Ephesians 3:11). This heavenly work of grace has now been effectually applied to the eternal vessels of God's mercy through the life of Christ.[70] By way of the gospel, they were made aware of their call to salvation through the sanctifying work of the Holy Ghost because of the grace of God the Father (in Christ).[71] God's work of eternal grace and the gift of grace by Jesus (His death) have now been made known to His disciples through the regenerating work of God the Holy Spirit.[72] The results of Christ Jesus laying down His life are forever rooted in the eternal grace of God the Father. This is why Jesus said in John 17 He had finished the Father's work. He wanted the world to know He loved His Father and He had been sent to accomplish His Father's pleasure and purpose. "But that the world may know that I love the Father; and as the Father gave Me commandment, even so I do. Arise, let us go hence" (John 14:31). "I have glorified Thee on the earth: I have finished the work which Thou gavest Me to do" (John 17:4). "When Jesus therefore had received the vinegar, He said, It is finished: and He bowed His head, and gave up the ghost" (John 19:30). He finished the work by laying down His life in order to become sin on our behalf so His righteousness could be imparted to us. This was a work that demonstrated the eternal and redemptive love of God. It was the work of grace by the One Man, Jesus, which allowed for the righteousness of God to be eternally conferred in time upon those who would believe the life witness of Jesus.

> Be not thou therefore ashamed of the testimony of our Lord, nor of me His prisoner: but be thou partaker of the afflictions of the gospel according to the power of God; Who hath saved us, and called us with an holy calling, not according to our works, but according to His own purpose and grace, which was given us in Christ Jesus before the world began, But is now made manifest by the appearing of our Saviour Jesus Christ, Who hath abolished death, and hath brought life and immortality to light through the gospel.
>
> 2 Timothy 1:8-10

SAVED BY IT

No one will ever be saved apart from the gospel. Why is it that no one will ever be saved apart from the gospel? God has chosen the method of preaching and the message of the cross to save sinners. The gospel is the power of God unto salvation—or it could be said:

The **means** by which God has chosen to reveal His eternal desire to reconcile sinners unto Himself through the righteousness of His Son, Jesus Christ. God made Jesus, who knew no sin, SIN for His glory. Jesus never sinned at any time before He was placed on the cross or while He was on the cross. God made Him become SIN or imputed all of our sins upon Him while on the cross. God poured out His wrath upon Him and punished Him for our sins so that we could be *forgiven*. On the cross Jesus was made SIN so that His righteousness could be imputed upon us in order to reconcile us unto God. God made us who knew no righteousness, RIGHTEOUS for His glory.[73]

The gospel is a revelation of God's will to use His Son's life to freely forgive, reconcile, and rescue sinners for His own glory. "In Whom (Christ)…having heard the word of truth, the gospel of your salvation…" (Ephesians 1:13). A close examination of the previous verse will clarify the point on this matter. Ephesians 1 helps believers understand we are who we are because of the grace of God in Christ Jesus. "In Whom" takes us back to verses three and four to reveal the blessings we are now experiencing are rooted in an eternal choice of God the Father. It speaks of the fact we were chosen in Christ, and it says because we are in Him, we were given the blessing of hearing the word of truth, the good news of our salvation. How did we come to hear the word of truth, the good news of our salvation in Christ? We hear the truth through God's method (preaching) and the message (the gospel of Christ and our salvation in Him) He's given his servants to preach. We must know and realize we are not saved by the gospel in and of itself. Why are we not saved by the gospel alone? Because we are saved by grace, not the gospel. "For by grace are ye saved through faith; and that not of yourselves: it is the gift of God" (Ephesians 2:8).

IT'S A SIGNIFICANT PART

The gospel is part of the grace of God, but not the whole of the grace of God. God uses the gospel to open our hearts and understanding to the grace of God. The gospel is the means by which God uses to illuminate our hearts to the truth about (1) His grace (2) Jesus and the shedding of His blood for our sins (3) how we have been made new creatures in Christ through the resurrection of Jesus (4) and as a result of being made a new creature we are now the righteousness of God in Him. We are saved by the grace of God, which will never be void of the Gospel because the grace of God includes the Gospel. Paul told Timothy in 2 Timothy 1:9-11 they were saved by God's eternal grace in Christ. The Gospel was the way God let them know they were saved by the grace of God. Salvation is an eternal work of God, and His grace also includes the following:

1. *Eternal foreknowledge* - it is rooted in the eternal counsel of God. (1 Pet. 1:2 ; Acts 15:18)
2. *Predestination* - it is the result of the good pleasure of His own will. (Eph. 1:11)
3. *Election* - it is to the praise of the glory of His grace. (Eph. 1:3-14 ; Rom 9:11-13)
4. *Calling* - it is through the gospel message effectually applied by the Holy Spirit via a God-sent preacher for the purpose of calling on us as sinners to repent of our sin; to place our trust in Jesus, our Mediator and Lord; and to take our life and lead it for His glory. (2 Thes. 2:14 ; Romans 1:16-17 ; Romans 10 ; 1 Cor. 1:18-25)
5. *Regeneration* - it is the work of the Holy Spirit that makes us a new creature and gives us a supernatural affection and fondness for Jesus Christ. (Titus 3:4-7 ; Eph. 2:5 ; John 3:3-8)
6. *Conversion* - it happens as a distinct result of the new birth when we, as new creatures in Christ, respond to the demands of the gospel to repent and turn from self-centered living and the sin we once naturally embraced in order to entrust our lives to Jesus and His truth to be a reconciled servant of God the Father. (1 Thes. 1:9-10 ; Col. 1:3-23 ; Acts 26:18-20)
7. *Justification* - it happens simultaneously at the new birth when we, as new creatures in Christ, place our faith in the finished work of Jesus and the forgiveness of our sins

through the shedding of His blood; and now, being reconciled through His life, we are legally declared righteous by God on Christ's behalf. (Romans 3 - 5)

8. *Adoption* - it happens simultaneously at the new birth and results in us being made an heir of God and a joint heir with Jesus for eternity. (Ephesians 1:3-6 ; Romans 8:15-17)

9. *Sanctification* - it happens simultaneously at the new birth when we are set apart in Christ and baptized in and sealed by the Holy Spirit until the day of redemption, and it will progressively continue through the discipleship process of following the Lord of glory. (Hebrews 10:14 ; Acts 20:32 ; Luke 1:74-75)

10. *Glorification* - it will happen in a future day when we are taken home to be with the Lord and He completes what he started in us and we receive our promised glorified bodies. At that time, we will be free from the presence of sin and we'll live for an eternity, being taught by the Lord Himself. (Romans 8:28-30 ; Romans 15)

Let God be true and every man a liar. Our flesh will always reject the truth about God's redemptive grace. If God be for us, who can be against us?

For whom He did foreknow, He also did predestinate to be conformed to the image of His Son, that He might be the firstborn among many brethren. Moreover whom He did predestinate, them He also called: and whom He called, them He also justified: and whom He justified, them He also glorified. What shall we then say to these things? If God be for us, who can be against us?

Romans 8:29-31

Whosoever will be saved will be saved by grace. And that grace is the eternal grace of God the Father which Jesus Christ came to manifest and establish in the hearts of those who were lost and perishing without it.[74] God's grace is more beautiful than we could ever imagine and greater than we will ever fully know. Grace is God cheerfully and delightfully gratifying Himself, for Himself, in the face of deserved wrath through the life of His Son, Jesus Christ.

GOSPEL OF THE KINGDOM

When we put all the emphasis on man's ability to respond properly to the gospel, making the gospel man-centered rather God-centered, we validate that we do not understand the grace of God. If we're going to minister in the grace of God, we must preach the gospel of the kingdom of God and teach those things concerning Lord Jesus Christ. Jesus said the gospel of the kingdom would be preached to all nations before His coming.[75] Paul taught and expounded on the gospel of the kingdom and the things concerning the Lord Jesus Christ.[76] It's the whole counsel of God that we must preach if we are going to establish the grace of God and the truth that God loves sinners and desires to reconcile them unto Himself through Christ.

> And now, behold, I know that ye all, among whom I have gone preaching the kingdom of God, shall see my face no more. Wherefore I take you to record this day, that I am pure from the blood of all men. For I have not shunned to declare unto you all the counsel of God
>
> Acts 20:25-27

Christ came to establish God's love for sinners. How did He come? He came by the grace of God. Why did He come? He came to reconcile sinners for the glory of God.

MEN ARE SINNERS

The fact that Christ actually came validates the truth that men are sinners. Jesus even said, "Had not He come men would be without sin."[77] Yet what did He come to do? He came to demonstrate that God really does love sinners. Why must He come to demonstrate this truth? God has used the life of Jesus to teach us how to be loved. Without the life of Christ and His suffering for sinners, our view of God would be completely distorted. We could not know or understand how a God who is completely just could eternally love those who are utterly unjust. **Without the cross, God's love would be unknowable and untouchable.**

1. He's Come to Demonstrate the Love of God

HE PROVES IT

"But God commendeth His love toward us, in that, while we were yet sinners, Christ died for us." (Romans 5:8) In giving us His Son while we were sinners, God demonstrated just how much He loves us. The idea we see here is that God has established the fact He surely loves us. The life of Christ Jesus proves to us God's love and stands firm as an established truth in which we can place our confidence. Jesus came to establish a foundational truth in our life that God the Father loves us with an unfailing and relentless love, even while we are enemies of the cross and hostile to God's ways. How can He love us with such intensity and determination while we were at war with Him in our fallen condition? How did He give up His Son who was without sin, knowing He would be scorned and mocked by sinners? How could He be willing to establish such a steadfast love toward us knowing we didn't want His love? It is because of Jesus! Christ Jesus is how and why He loves us! Halleluiah!

ROOTED IN ETERNITY

Jesus came to demonstrate an eternal covenant of love between the Father and Himself that would be shared with the future recipients of His eternal mercy. God's redemptive love has been established through the life and death of Christ Jesus while we were still in our sins. The cross manifests a love rooted in eternity between God the Father and God the Son. The Word of God speaks of this love in Romans as God's relentless love toward us in Christ Jesus: "Who shall lay any thing to the charge of God's elect? It is God that justifieth" (Romans 8:33). "For I am persuaded, that neither death, nor life, nor angels, nor principalities, nor powers, nor things present, nor things to come, Nor height, nor depth, nor any other creature, shall be able to separate us from the love of God, which is in Christ Jesus our Lord" (Romans 8:38-39). This kind of inseparable love is completely in and of Christ Jesus. This is an everlasting love. It's a love that has no beginning or ending because it's based upon an eternal love between the Father and the Son.

HE CAME TO SETTLE IT

Jesus has come to establish the fact that God's love toward us is never based on performance but upon a covenant that can never fail. Because of this eternal love between the Father and the Son we were loved in Christ when we were truly unlovable.

> Blessed be the God and Father of our Lord Jesus Christ, who hath blessed us with all spiritual blessings in heavenly places in Christ: According as He hath chosen us in Him before the foundation of the world, that we should be holy and without blame before Him in love: Having predestinated us unto the adoption of children by Jesus Christ to Himself, according to the good pleasure of His will, To the praise of the glory of His grace, wherein He hath made us accepted in the Beloved.
>
> Ephesians 1:3-6

God's love for us is for His own glory. There was nothing in us that made us loveable. God and His Son established this love before Adam fell in the garden. Notice what Romans 5:14 says: "Nevertheless death reigned from Adam to Moses, even over them that had not sinned after the similitude of Adam's transgression, who is the figure of Him that was to come." Adam was a type of Him (Jesus) who was to come. We would conclude then that the Godhead had already determined the effective plan of redeeming fallen man, if Adam was a type of Him who was still yet to come.

Jesus is described in the Word as the Lamb of God who was slain before the foundation of the world. John the Baptist calls Him the Lamb of God: "The next day John seeth Jesus coming unto him, and saith, Behold the Lamb of God, which taketh away the sin of the world" (John 1:29). God also confirms to John that Jesus is the One to be looking for when He says, "And I knew Him not: but He that sent me to baptize with water, the same said unto me, Upon Whom thou shalt see the Spirit descending, and remaining on Him, the same is He which baptizeth with the Holy Ghost" (John 1:33). God even confirms this when He speaks over the life of His Son: "And lo a voice from heaven, saying, This is My beloved Son, in whom I am well pleased" (Matthew 3:17). God is revealing to us that Jesus, the Lamb of God, is His much-loved Son. This Son, who is now wearing flesh, is the Son whom He has loved with an everlasting love. He is the Lamb slain from the foundation of the world: "And all that dwell upon the earth shall worship him, whose names are not written in the Book of Life of the Lamb slain from the foundation of the world" (Revelation 13:8). Wow! We also find in the book of Revelation the fact that the names of His redeemed have been written in the Book of Life of the Lamb from the foundation of the world:

> The beast that thou sawest was, and is not; and shall ascend out of the bottomless pit, and go into perdition: and they that dwell on the earth shall wonder, whose names were not written in the Book of Life from the foundation of the world, when they behold the beast that was, and is not, and yet is.
>
> Revelation 17:8

We are blessed benefactors of this eternal covenant of love between God the Father and God the Son.

IT IS A MYSTERY

There are many truths put forth in God's Word that reveal this divine reality. Many of them are mysteries not yet unveiled to us. Others are great and precious promises that bring us true comfort when we trust the Lord and His redemptive work in our lives. In the high priestly prayer of Jesus, we get a snapshot of this eternal covenant that He shared with His Father:

> And now, O Father, glorify Thou Me with Thine own Self with the glory which I had with Thee before the world was. I

have manifested Thy name unto the men which Thou gavest Me out of the world: Thine they were, and Thou gavest them Me; and they have kept Thy word.

John 17:5-6

And the glory which Thou gavest Me I have given them; that they may be one, even as We are one: I in them, and Thou in Me, that they may be made perfect in one; and that the world may know that Thou hast sent Me, and hast loved them, as Thou hast loved Me.

John 17:22-23

O righteous Father, the world hath not known Thee: but I have known Thee, and these have known that Thou hast sent Me. And I have declared unto them Thy name, and will declare it: that the love wherewith thou hast loved Me may be in them, and I in them.

John 17:25-26

BUT COMFORTING

What a comforting word. He is speaking about a glory and a love they shared before time existed and is now being bestowed upon God's people. Why now? Jesus came to demonstrate and establish the fact that in Him, we were and are loved by God, period. His redemptive love for us is not based on anything in us or anything about us whatsoever. What kind of effect will this have upon a regenerated soul that can now see what Christ has come to do? It will cause him to rejoice in the hope of God's love forevermore. The love of God has been poured out into our hearts by God the Spirit: "And hope maketh not ashamed; because the love of God is shed abroad in our hearts by the Holy Ghost which is given unto us" (Romans 5:5). It has been God the Spirit who has applied this established work of God through His Son, Jesus. This ought to make us want to shout!

God has settled it for all time through Christ Jesus. He has established the truth about His love. His love toward us has never been based on anything about a man. His love is rooted in the love for His Son; therefore, now we know how and why He loves us. We can also know we are loved apart from anything we've done or ever will do. His love toward us is because of Jesus. Glorify Jesus, who will glorify His Father. The attention and the glory is directed upon Him, and not upon us.

HE LOVES HIS ENEMIES

"For God so loved the world, that He gave His only begotten Son, that whosoever believeth in Him should not perish, but have everlasting life" (John 3:16). John 3:16 does not reveal to us the full story of what it means that He gave His only begotten Son. Nicodemus didn't know at the time this meant the cross. We know because we can see from the rest of the counsel of God that Jesus died upon a cruel Roman cross. Nicodemus eventually came to know what Jesus meant, but not that night when he came to Him by the cover of darkness.[78] We also know by the rest of the counsel of God's Word that the love God has for the world is rooted in Christ Jesus. God can love a sin-sick people because of a sinless and spotless Lamb. In Christ Jesus, our Lord, is where God's redemptive love is centered. It is also what caused His Son to come and establish this eternal truth to us. We can also look at the rest of God's counsel and understand that the world referred to in John 3:16 includes Jews and Gentiles. God's Word speaks of these people as being dead in their trespasses and as children of wrath. He describes them as being hostile enemies and rebellious toward His ways. Yet in other places we see them spoken of as sheep, saints, elect, and the church of God. Nicodemus didn't know what Jesus fully meant that night, but the Son of God knew and that was why He shared these things with His disciples.

I am the good shepherd: the good shepherd giveth His life for the sheep.

John 10:11

I am the good shepherd, and know My sheep, and am known of Mine. As the Father knoweth Me, even so know I the Father: and I lay down My life for the sheep. And other sheep I have, which are not of this fold: them also I must bring, and they shall hear My voice; and there shall be one fold, and one shepherd. Therefore doth My Father love Me, because I lay down My life, that I might take it again.

John 10:14-17

Jesus answered them, I told you, and ye believed not: the works that I do in My Father's name, they bear witness of Me. But ye believe not, because ye are not of My sheep, as I said unto you. My sheep hear My voice, and I know them, and they follow Me: And I give unto them eternal life; and they shall never perish, neither shall any man pluck them out of My hand. My Father, which gave them Me, is greater than all; and no man is able to pluck them out of My Father's hand. I and My Father are one."

John 10:25-30

When the Son of Man shall come in His glory, and all the holy angels with Him, then shall He sit upon the throne of His glory: And before Him shall be gathered all nations: and He shall separate them one from another, as a shepherd divideth his sheep from the goats: And He shall set the sheep on His right hand, but the goats on the left. Then shall the King say unto them on His right hand, Come, ye blessed of My Father, inherit the kingdom prepared for you from the foundation of the world...

Matthew 25:31-34

And the King shall answer and say unto them, Verily I say unto you, Inasmuch as ye have done it unto one of the least of these my brethren, ye have done it unto Me.

Matthew 25:40

IT LEADS TO FEAR

These and all the precious promises of God that are given to us in Christ bring great comfort to our souls. When we are established in the fact that God loves us no matter what we do, it will produce a healthy type of fear in our life. It is the fear of God that has been placed in our hearts to keep us from departing from the Lord.[79] There is a difference between fearing God and having the fear of God. Fearing God means that we stand in utter awe of what has been made known to us about God by His grace. When we fear God, we give Him the proper place, priority and purpose in life. The response of our lives giving place to Him will be that we live to praise and glorify His name. This type of fear leads to the fear of God resulting in a supernatural ability to know and understand certain things the way God does. When we have the fear of God, we also have the gateway of wisdom and discernment open to us. "The fear of the Lord is the beginning of wisdom: and the knowledge of the Holy is understanding" (Proverbs 9:10). Our passage didn't say "fear in" or "knowledge in," but the "wisdom of the Lord" and the "knowledge of the Holy One."

GOD FEARS

Did you know there are things that God fears?

I said, I would scatter them into corners, I would make the remembrance of them to cease from among men: Were it not that I feared the wrath of the enemy, lest their adversaries should behave themselves strangely, and lest they should say, Our hand is high, and the Lord hath not done all this.
Deuteronomy 32:26-27

God gave place to or feared the wrath of the enemies of Israel, knowing they would have claimed victory over His people in the wilderness. It's not that God fears any enemy in and of themselves, but He considers the reality that the enemy will take credit for something God did and distort His name and how He works before the world. I recall when God told Moses He was going to destroy the people of Israel and start over with just with him. Moses pleaded with the Lord not to do this for fear of the enemy. What was he afraid of? The enemy would have great occasion to blaspheme or vilify the character of God by saying He was not able to deliver His people. Did Moses come up with this thought on his own? No! Remember, Moses was described as being a humble and meek man who talked face to face with God. The character of God and what He feared was being manifested in Moses. He spoke what God had placed in His heart. God had placed His fear in the heart of Moses, and Moses knew what to do next in that situation—he said what God had already planned to do.[80] Just the opposite is true with king David. He took God lightly, and it resulted in actions that gave the enemies of God occasion to speak perversely about His character.[81] When we have the fear of God, we will also have the wisdom to guard His name!

NO SHAME

I have known all my life that my Mom and Dad loved me. I knew their love for me was based on who I was and never on what I could do. I did fear my Dad's wrath because I knew he meant business when he said he was going to do something. I was never afraid of my Dad because I had a healthy respect for who he was. I stayed away from certain people and particular situations as a kid not because I feared getting caught, but because I feared the reality of bringing shame on my father's name. I also didn't want to hurt my mom and dad. I knew they would love me even if I did hurt them or embarrassed them by doing something I knew I shouldn't be doing. Knowing they would love me no matter what didn't give me permission to do wrong, but it actually prevented me from doing a lot of it. My Dad told me up front what he did and didn't like for me to do, yet I clearly understood the difference between "love" and "like." I received a many a whooping as a child because I did what my Dad didn't like. He told me ahead of time the consequences of doing things he didn't like because he loved me.

I BELIEVE IT

I know God loves me no matter what. I'm not afraid of my heavenly Father, but I do fear I could do something that would vilify His character and He would take His hand of favor off my life. He has settled it before me and I know God loves me no matter what. I just want to bless His name. I have done things my heavenly Father does not like, but because He loves me He will chasten me for it.[82]

GOD MUST DO IT

What's the point of these illustrations? God has sent His Son to settle it in our hearts that He loves us. He sent Him to establish this truth and to teach us how to love. We do need the touch of God's heart and His hand to love Him and others. "And the Lord thy God will circumcise thine heart, and the heart of thy seed, to love the Lord thy God with all thine heart, and with all thy soul, that thou mayest live" (Deuteronomy 30:6). He teaches us how to choose to love. Love is a choice that should be made from within a person, not from without. We must be born again (circumcised in heart by God) to love the way He's shown us to love sacrificially. "This is my commandment, That ye love one another, as I have loved you. Greater love hath no man than this, that a man lay down his life for his friends" (John 15:12-13). God is love; therefore, He does not need anyone to teach Him how to be loved in order to love. We, on the hand, are not love; therefore, we have to be taught by God how to be loved so we can love Him and others the way He does.

> Marvel not, my brethren, if the world hate you. We know that we have passed from death unto life, because we love the brethren. He that loveth not his brother abideth in death. Whosoever hateth his brother is a murderer: and ye know that no murderer hath eternal life abiding in him. Hereby perceive we the love of God, because He laid down His life for us: and we ought to lay down our lives for the brethren.
>
> 1 John 3:13-16

We, through the new birth experience, are enabled by God's grace to supernaturally love His children and our brethren.

Whosoever believeth that Jesus is the Christ is born of God: and every one that loveth Him that begat loveth him also that is begotten of Him. By this we know that we love the children of God, when we love God, and keep His commandments. For this is the love of God, that we keep His commandments: and His commandments are not grievous.

1 John 5:1-3

Why are they not grievous? God has taught us how to be loved through His demonstration of His love toward us in Christ Jesus.

2. He's Come to Demonstrate The Loyalty of God

HE'S COMMITTED

Since God established and settled His love toward us by giving up His Son on our behalf while we were hostile enemies of His, how much more has He established His commitment to us now we are at peace with Him?

Much more then, being now justified by His blood, we shall be saved from wrath through Him. For if, when we were enemies, we were reconciled to God by the death of His Son, much more, being reconciled, we shall be saved by His life.

Romans 5:9-10

Think about this principle truth that has been established through Christ Jesus. Jesus is a demonstration of God's loyalty to initiate, interrupt, invade, and involve Himself in every dynamic of our life. God has committed Himself to us for the advancement of His kingdom and His glory. He's committed to continually delivering us from the snares and pitfalls of the wrath of the sons of disobedience. God has obligated Himself and the integrity of His kingdom to perfect what He started in His saints. "Being confident of this very thing, that He which hath begun a good work in you will perform it until the day of Jesus Christ" (Philippians 1:6). Paul was so confident of the loyalty of God that he said he was persuaded that all authentic believers would endure until they died or were transformed to meet the Lord in the air. "For the which cause I also suffer these things: nevertheless I am not ashamed: for I know whom I have believed, and am persuaded that He is able to keep that which I have committed unto Him against that day" (2 Timothy 1:12). He knew if God commenced His own work of salvation in us, He would have to also be the One to continue and complete it.

PERSUADED

Living life without wavering in regards to the trustworthiness of our God is founded upon our persuasion of the gospel of the Lord Jesus Christ. When God opens the eyes of our understanding and shines the light of the gospel in the recesses of our regenerated soul, we are awakened to the truth of the loyalty of God. True, we do grow in grace and knowledge of our Lord, but there is given to us a supernatural endowment of faith to trust God's faithfulness. "If ye continue in the faith grounded and settled, and be not moved away from the hope of the gospel, which ye have heard, and which was preached to every creature which is under heaven; whereof I Paul am made a minister" (Colossians 1:23). We are taught by the gospel seed itself a living hope is reserved for us in heaven. "For the hope which is laid up for you in heaven, whereof ye heard before in the word of the truth of the gospel" (Colossians 1:5). We, as believers, have been persuaded of the reality of God's loyalty to fulfill His Word. If He proved His love for us when we were enemies, we know He'll take care of us who are now in love with Him and His people. Notice how the Spirit inspired Peter to affirm and equip the church concerning these things.

Blessed be the God and Father of our Lord Jesus Christ, which according to His abundant mercy hath begotten us again unto a lively hope by the resurrection of Jesus Christ from the dead, to an inheritance incorruptible, and undefiled, and that fadeth not away, reserved in heaven for you, who are kept by the power of God through faith unto salvation ready to be revealed in the last time. Wherein ye greatly rejoice, though now for a season, if need be, ye are in heaviness through manifold temptations: That the trial of your faith, being much more precious than of gold that perisheth, though it be tried with fire, might be found unto praise and honour and glory at the appearing of Jesus Christ: Whom having not seen, ye love; in whom, though now ye see Him not, yet believing, ye rejoice with joy unspeakable and full of glory: Receiving the end of your faith, even the salvation of your souls.

1 Peter 1:3-9

This is the life of authentic discipleship from the point of being born again to living with joy unspeakable and full of glory. It's a life that knows how to suffer for the glory of God, and live looking for the return of Christ. Why is this so? The power of the effectual grace of God has saved to the uttermost. Amen!

HE'S LOYAL

God is a loyal Father, and knowing He loves us enough to save us and deliver us from wrath to come, we also know He is going chasten and scourge our life to produce out of us the fruit He desires.[83] He is faithful, and we can trust Him to do His work in and through our life.

I thank my God always on your behalf, for the grace of God which is given you by Jesus Christ; That in every thing ye are enriched by Him, in all utterance, and in all knowledge; Even as the testimony of Christ was confirmed in you: So that ye come behind in no gift; waiting for the coming of our Lord Jesus Christ: Who shall also confirm you unto the end, that ye may be blameless in the day of our Lord Jesus Christ. God is faithful, by whom ye were called unto the fellowship of His Son Jesus Christ our Lord.

1 Corinthians 1:4-9

God is faithful, and He has promised to confirm and prove we are His unto the end.

IT'S TRUE

The Scripture speaks of this unwavering spirit of looking for Jesus that resides in and is manifested in all persuaded believers. Let's examine this thought in the New Testament:

We were saved in a hope

And not only they (creation), but ourselves also, which have the firstfruits of the Spirit, even we ourselves groan within ourselves, waiting for the adoption, to wit, the redemption of our body. For we are saved by (in this) hope: but hope that is seen is not hope: for what a man seeth, why doth he yet hope for? But if we hope for that we see not, then do we with patience wait for it.

Romans 8:23-25

God has so worked in His people that they long for more of heaven

For we know that if our earthly house of this tabernacle were dissolved, we have a building of God, an house not made with hands, eternal in the heavens. For in this we groan, earnestly desiring to be clothed upon with our house which is from heaven: If so be that being clothed we shall not be found naked. For we that are in this tabernacle do groan, being burdened: not for that we would be unclothed, but clothed upon, that mortality might be swallowed up of life. Now He (God) that hath wrought us for the selfsame thing is God, who also hath given unto us the earnest of the Spirit.

2 Corinthians 5:1-5

His people know they do not belong here on earth and live differently

For our conversation is in heaven; from whence also we look for the Saviour, the Lord Jesus Christ: Who shall change our vile body, that it may be fashioned like unto His glorious body, according to the working whereby He is able even to subdue all things unto Himself.

Philippians 3:20-21

Their turning away from the culture while waiting for Jesus is stunning

For they themselves shew of us what manner of entering in we had unto you, and how ye turned to God from idols to serve the living and true God; And to wait for His Son from heaven, whom He raised from the dead, even Jesus, which delivered us from the wrath to come.

1 Thessalonians 1:9-10

The day of the Lord Jesus is a sure thing and so is sanctification

And the very God of peace sanctify you wholly; and I pray God your whole spirit and soul and body be preserved blameless unto the coming of our Lord Jesus Christ. Faithful is He that calleth you, who also will do it.

1 Thessalonians 5:23-24

Because of grace we are taught how to live and look for Jesus

For the grace of God that bringeth salvation hath appeared to all men, Teaching us that, denying ungodliness and worldly lusts, we should live soberly, righteously, and godly, in this present world; Looking for that blessed hope, and the glorious appearing of the great God and our Saviour Jesus Christ; Who gave Himself for us, that He might redeem us from all iniquity, and purify unto Himself a peculiar people, zealous of good works.

Titus 2:11-14

He is going to crown His people who have obeyed His instruction of grace

Henceforth there is laid up for me a crown of righteousness, which the Lord, the righteous judge, shall give me at that day: and not to me only, but unto all them also that love His appearing.

2 Timothy 4:8

He is only coming for those who are eagerly waiting for Him

So Christ was once offered to bear the sins of many; and unto them that look for Him shall He appear the second time without sin unto salvation.

Hebrews 9:28

God is faithful to do this in our life, for it is He who has prepared us for it

Wherefore, beloved, seeing that ye look for such things, be diligent that ye may be found of Him in peace, without spot, and blameless.

2 Peter 3:14

WHAT A WORK

God has done such a marvelous work in the hearts of those who once lived in direct rebellion to Him; now they live looking for His coming. Why do they live this way? The life, death, resurrection and intercession of Jesus have established two things in their life. First, His love is eternal and not based upon their performance. Second, He is loyal to His subjects; therefore, He will provide and protect them both now and forever.

When a believer is living at peace with a holy God through Christ's blood they know God is faithful to His Word. They live a life that convinces others to trust God's love and loyalty. They are witnesses to the reality that God is not ashamed to be called their God.

> These all died in faith, not having received the promises, but having seen them afar off, and were persuaded of them, and embraced them, and confessed that they were strangers and pilgrims on the earth. For they (anyone persuaded of God's faithfulness) that say such things declare plainly that they seek a country. And truly, if they had been mindful of that country from whence they came out, they might have had opportunity to have returned. But now they desire a better country, that is, an heavenly: wherefore God is not ashamed to be called their God: for He hath prepared for them a city.
>
> Hebrews 11:13-16

They embrace and confess because they are sure they no longer belong in this world, and they're excited to let the world know they are only passing through. To God be the glory!

3. He's Come to Demonstrate the Line of God

A STANDARD

Prior to laying a foundation or a building being framed, a measuring line is usually run as a standard point of reference. A plumb line is a sure way to have a standard of measurement that goes beyond the judgment of a professional's eye. The human eye can be deceptive. Something may look level or even straight to the naked eye yet actually be several feet off center. Therefore, carpenters use certain tools when building to help them determine a standard of measure.

Jesus came to demonstrate that God has a standard of measure. His standard will be used to measure all people. The life that Christ Jesus lived is that standard. The standard is not the law of God, but the perfect life of His only begotten Son. The spotless life of Jesus will be the life by which every man will be measured.

A COVENANT

God initiated a covenant of works with man in the Garden of Eden. This covenant was based on the terms of each one fulfilling their part of the agreement. God committed to Adam the responsibility and accountability of maintaining and multiplying. Adam was given the duty to maintain the creation God had given him. God made all things subject to Adam. He put all things under his feet and gave him dominion over His creation.

O Lord, our Lord, how excellent is thy name in all the earth! who hast set thy glory above the heavens. Out of the mouth of babes and sucklings hast thou ordained strength because of thine enemies, that thou mightest still the enemy and the avenger. When I consider Thy heavens, the work of Thy fingers, the moon and the stars, which thou hast ordained; What is man, that thou art mindful of him? and the son of man, that Thou visitest him? For thou hast made him a little lower than the angels, and hast crowned him with glory and honour. Thou madest him to have dominion over the works of Thy hands; thou hast put all things under his feet: All sheep and oxen, yea, and the beasts of the field; The fowl of the air, and the fish of the sea, and whatsoever passeth through the paths of the seas. O Lord our Lord, how excellent is Thy name in all the earth.

Psalm 8:1-9

All creation was placed under the dominion of Adam. God blessed him and provided all he needed to maintain and multiply in the Garden of Eden. The terms were to work the ground and rule over all of God's creatures. Adam was given permission within the covenant to eat of all the trees of the garden with the exception of one tree.

God warned Adam of the consequences of eating what was forbidden. He told Adam up front he would forfeit his right to live, properly maintain, and multiply if he devalued his responsibility to not follow the covenant completely.[84]

MAN FAILED

Adam failed to fulfill his end of the agreement. The results of his actions are greatly affecting the world in which we live to this day. Sin and death are constant reminders of our inability to do what is necessary to please a covenant-keeping God.[85] Because of Adam's disobedience, we inherited a nature to rebel against God and His covenant.[86]

HIS MERCY

God, in His compassion and mercy, gave the world His law to reveal how off center we have become. Since the days of Adam, man has progressively moved farther and farther away from God's standard. We are taught God's Word is a plumb line we can use to measure our lives by. We need to thank God for His Word and use it as a plumb line in our life.

JESUS IS THE ANSWER

Jesus, the incarnate Word, came to this world to establish another covenant. The covenant He established is in perfect harmony with God's eternal covenant of grace. He also came to fulfill the covenant of works and establish the new covenant in His blood. Jesus did just that in and through His earthly life. He, as God's agent of redemption, unveiled God's eternal covenant of grace to us who believe. He also fulfilled God's covenant of works and became the plumb line by which all people will be judged.

HE'S RIGHTEOUS

It is important to remember the law is for the unrighteous, not the righteous. Jesus had no need for the law because He had never been unrighteous. He was far greater than the law. The law will not be the instrument used to judge lost sinners in the final judgment. The life of Jesus will be the standard by which all lost sinners will be judged. Sinners' actions are judged by the written Word of God, but the man himself will be judged by the life of Jesus.

MEASURED NEXT TO JESUS

God's judgment will be a judgment of righteousness, and the standard He'll use will be His Son, the Lord Jesus Christ.

And the times of this ignorance God winked at; but now commandeth all men every where to repent: Because He hath appointed a day, in the which He will judge the world in righteousness by that Man whom He hath ordained; whereof He hath given assurance unto all men, in that He hath raised Him from the dead. And when they heard of the resurrection of the dead, some mocked: and others said, We will hear thee again of this matter.

Acts 17:30-32

Every lost soul will be measured up next to the life of Jesus.

BOOKS WILL BE OPENED

On that great and awesome day of judgment, the books will be opened. The record of each life will be given. The sins of all lost men and women and their eternal effects will be brought forth before the Judge of the universe. He will give them a verdict of guilty, and their eternal sentence will be declared. It will be eternal separation in the lake of fire from the love and light of our God. Keep in mind He's a God who delights in granting mercy. Why then this harsh verdict? Will it be because their sin and sinful lifestyle were more damaging and deceptive than ours? No! Will it be because they didn't keep the law? No! Why will they be cast into the lake of fire? Their name will not be found in the Lamb's book of Life. The standard will not be the law or the sins they committed, but the life of Jesus.

WE MUST BE BORN AGAIN

If our life has not been hidden in Christ and recreated by Him through the new covenant He's established, we are without hope. Jesus didn't come into this world to condemn people, but to live a sacrificial and sinless life so the people of this world might be saved. The people outside Christ are already condemned. They need not to be further condemned. Jesus came to demonstrate to the world the standard by which God will use to judge everyone. Magnify the Lord! He has come to demonstrate the love and loyalty of God and that His life is God's line of judgment.

TAKING IT SERIOUSLY

Is your life hidden in Christ?
Have you lost your identity to the Lordship of Jesus Christ?
Are you being conformed to the image of Jesus Christ?
Are you more concerned with keeping the law or being consumed with Christ?
Is Christ your life?

Chapter 5

He's Come to Destroy

OUR GOD REIGNS

"He's come to destroy?" "Yes, He has come to destroy!" "Was it Jesus who came to demonstrate the love of His Father?" "Yes!" "Praise the Lord for His coming!"

Jesus did come to destroy some specific things in this world. Knowing God is love helps us to understand He also hates. God hates sin, Satan, and demons. As we look in the unparalleled Word of God, we find Jesus was sent by His Father to do a unique work. This particular work would include destroying the works of the devil and the power of darkness with which he used to blind us. Satan and every other everlasting enemy of God is a defeated foe who is reserved under the wrath of God for everlasting destruction in the lake of fire and brimstone:

> And the angels which kept not their first estate, but left their own habitation, He hath reserved in everlasting chains under darkness unto the judgment of the great day.
>
> Jude 1:6

These (sinners/enemies of God who die in their sins) are wells without water, clouds that are carried with a tempest; to whom the mist of darkness is reserved for ever.

2 Peter 2:17

And the devil that deceived them was cast into the lake of fire and brimstone, where the beast and the false prophet are, and shall be tormented day and night for ever and ever.

Revelation 20:10

Our God and King reigns both now and forever!

Now unto Him that is able to keep you from falling, and to present you faultless before the presence of His glory with exceeding joy, to the only wise God our Saviour, be glory and majesty, dominion and power, both now and ever. Amen.

Jude 1:24-25

We must surrender our allegiance and our lives to King Jesus!

WE CAN'T FORGET

We must keep in mind it is impossible for us to know and comprehend the truth revealed in God's Word unless God opens our understanding. It will always be in our best interest to do whatever it takes to position ourselves humbly before God's throne in order to receive truth when He's ready to reveal it. Therefore, it would be wise for us to ask God to teach us why He came to destroy the devil and the power of darkness.

1. He's Come to Destroy the Works of the Devil

HE'S ALL ABOUT SIN

God used John the beloved to explain to His people one of the main reasons for Christ's coming to the earth:

He that committeth sin (habitually practices known sin with no victory or passion to overcome sin in Christ's sacrifice) is of the devil; for the devil sinneth from the beginning. For this purpose the Son of God was manifested, that He might destroy the works of the devil. Whosoever is born of God doth not commit sin (habitually practice known sin); for His seed (Christ nature/DNA) remaineth in him: and he cannot sin (continue to willfully rebel because of his new nature), because he is born of God (bears the identity of His Father).

1 John 3:8-9

This passage shows us the nature of the enemy and his primary work. His primary work is sin. The person who has not been born again lives and breathes sin. Every intent and motive to do good is sinful because it's not of God or for His glory. "An high look, and a proud heart, and the plowing of the wicked, is sin" (Proverbs 21:4).

GOOD CAN BE A SIN

Humanity, outside of being in a relationship with God the Father through the life sacrifice of His Son, is completely and totally tainted with sin. The good they do is sin before God because it proceeded out of an evil heart. "If ye then, being evil, know how to give good gifts unto your children, how much more shall your Father which is in heaven give good things to them that ask Him?" (Matthew 7:11). Jesus described them as being evil yet they knew how to give a good gift. Even a mother's love that is expressed and demonstrated is sinful if she is lost. If a mother dies lost in her sins, the love she shared, as sincere as it may have been, will have no heavenly value when she is cast into the lake of fire and brimstone for eternity. Why is this so? Everything a lost person does is rooted in the devil's primary purpose—to distort the things of God and prompt them to receive glory for themselves. Satan cannot ever hit the mark of God's standard. It is impossible for him to ever be right. He is the essence of sin, and all the world is under his persuasion.

MUST BE BORN AGAIN

The essential need for the new birth is the only means available to destroy the works of the devil that have gripped the very nature of fallen humanity. Being made a new creature in Christ Jesus is the only possible way anyone can be set free from the curse of original sin that we received as an inheritance from Adam. We can only be living by and for one source today. We are either of the devil or of the Lord Jesus. If we are of the devil, we are under the curse of our father Adam. If we are of the Lord, we are under the blessings of our heavenly Father and His kingdom agenda.[87] Scripture is clear about the difference in the righteous and the wicked.

JESUS MAKES THE DIFFERENCE

Jesus, in His sinless and sacrificial life and death, made it possible for the Holy Spirit to apply His works to our lives. Therefore, this reveals God the Father is completely satisfied with the work of His Son and chose to impart our sins on Jesus while He was on the cross, and to impart His righteousness on our lives when we believe. His redemptive work provided the means necessary to regenerate our lives. The effects of this recreation and reconciliation have produced a supernatural appeal and affection for the things of God.[88] "Therefore if any man be in Christ, he is a new creature: old things are passed away; behold, all things are become new" (2 Corinthians 5:17).

CAPTIVITY-LED CAPTIVE

The idea we see in 1 John 3 is that Jesus came to loosen the toil of the taskmaster who had legal authority over our life prior to being born again. When we were lost and perishing in our own sin, we were bound under the restraint of a cruel master who held us under chains of deception and delusion. The only way to be free from Satan's service is to be freed by the Father, who subjected us to Satan's authority through Adam's fall. His payment is too high for us to buy our own freedom, so His Son gave His lifeblood to purchase us for His Father's service. When we are birthed into the kingdom of God and eternally sealed by the Holy Ghost, we who once were in captivity to Satan and his demonic plan to thwart God's purpose have now been taken captive by King Jesus to walk worthy of His gospel.[89] Jesus, through the cross, paid our ransom. He justly fulfilled the eternal obligation set by His Father to rightfully own our lives and open our eyes.

EYES WIDE OPEN

We, once we're born of God, can now see the deception behind the devil's agenda. The devil uses two works to hold his slaves in bondage. First, he blinds them. Second, he uses the deception of darkness to hold them in fear of the unknown. This error and corruption of darkness is what keeps men in their sin.

HE BLINDS

Blindness is the means by which the enemy of God kept his subjects from seeing the glorious gospel of Jesus Christ:

> But if our gospel be hid, it is hid to them that are lost: In whom the god of this world hath blinded the minds of them which believe not, lest the light of the glorious gospel of Christ, who is the image of God, should shine unto them. For we preach not ourselves, but Christ Jesus the Lord; and ourselves your servants for Jesus' sake. For God, who commanded the light to shine out of darkness, hath shined in our hearts, to give the light of the knowledge of the glory of God in the face of Jesus Christ.
>
> 2 Corinthians 4:3-6

From this passage we can see those who are described as lost are those who are not persuaded about the gospel; therefore, they do not obey the gospel's demands. We also see why this is and who is behind their inability to see the glory of God in the face of Jesus Christ. The god of this age has blinded them so they cannot see the purpose, power, and pleasure of the gospel of our Lord Jesus Christ.

BORN BLIND

This blindness is the direct result of Adam's sin in the Garden of Eden. We all were born blind to the gospel. This blindness is specific to the gospel. The enemy, through the deceitfulness of sin, has caused an obscurity of vision in the understanding of those who are perishing.

PERISHING

When someone is lost in a vast wilderness with no means of getting themselves out, they are perishing. Man outside of Christ is perishing. We, by nature, have an appeal toward sin that cannot be altered, curved, or satisfied by sin itself. The pleasure they pursue is only temporary. The more they are involved in sin, the greater the degree of intensity and longing they'll have for it.

ONE HOPE

The only hope for man is the new birth brought about by God Himself. "Of His own will begat He us with the word of truth, that we should be a kind of firstfruits of His creatures" (James 1:18). Being born again is the work of a sovereign God who uses a vessel of His mercy to preach His Good News of our redemption through Christ. The gospel is the power of God unto salvation or the means by which He has ordained to birth us into His kingdom. The problem with men is they are blinded to this gospel until God shines in their hearts and gives them the light needed to see and know Him through the life of His Son, Jesus. Who is it who effectually applies this work of God? The Holy Spirit does this awesome work of regeneration, birthing us into God's kingdom. This is why God told Nicodemus no one could see or enter into the kingdom of God without first being born again.

Jesus answered and said unto him, Verily, verily, I say unto thee, Except a man be born again, he cannot see the kingdom of God.

John 3:3

Jesus answered, Verily, verily, I say unto thee, Except a man be born of water and of the Spirit, he cannot enter into the kingdom of God.

John 3:5

DO THEY LIKE JESUS?

The new birth is how Jesus loosens the works of the devil over our life. Paul speaks of those who don't have an affection or appeal for Christ as being still under the curse of the fall: "If any man love not the Lord Jesus Christ, let him be Anathema Maranatha" (1 Corinthians 16:22). If any man is not fond of Christ with that same natural appeal we develop toward a close friend, he is lost and perishing. This type of love is the kind of love you have when you meet someone for the first time and you really like them even though you don't know them. You are naturally drawn to them with an appeal that cannot be denied. David and Jonathan were drawn to each other this way. "Then Jonathan and David made a covenant, because he loved him as his own soul" (1 Samuel 18:3). They embraced and enjoyed a natural friendship that was born the moment they met. If you've been born again, you will not only love Jesus Christ, but you will also forever like Him.[90] Do you really like Jesus?

Paul wants us to see the distinct result and power of the new birth. Prior to being born again, we may have been fond of a false Jesus we let our secular culture shape for us, but not the Jesus who demanded all of our lives. Not a Jesus who calls on us to die to ourselves and reveals there is nothing beneficial in our flesh. Why has our culture shaped a Jesus who is not described in the Bible? It is because of an enemy who has clouded their vision of who Jesus is and has led them also to shape Jesus to their own liking.

121

HE WILL LOVE HIM

Moreover, when a man is born again by the Spirit of the living God, he will not only love the authentic historical Jesus revealed in the Scriptures, but he will also like Jesus. He, because of his new nature, will have an unquenchable appeal for Jesus. He will have an undeniable adoration and an unconditional appreciation for Jesus Christ, who has forgiven him of so many sins and made him into a new creature. He acts on this *unquenchable appeal* and makes a well thought out choice to love God based on a truth that will be continually revealed to him. On the other hand, if a man is not drawn to Christ with an overwhelming fondness because he likes Jesus, he'll never chose to love Him for what He's done. His claims of loving Jesus do not match his affections and actions.

MARKED BY THE NEW BIRTH

What is the difference between the man who is fond of Jesus and the one who's not? Jesus Himself is the difference. The eternal purpose of the new birth is what has made the difference effective.

But we are bound to give thanks always to God for you, brethren beloved of the Lord, because God hath from the beginning chosen you to salvation through sanctification of the Spirit and belief of the truth: Whereunto He called you by our gospel, to the obtaining of the glory of our Lord Jesus Christ.

2 Thessalonians 2:13-14

The difference maker is God, and the difference that He's made is a new creation. He freely and forever forgives, reconciles, and rescues His subjects through Christ, to the praise and glory of His grace. Praise Him for this indescribable gift.

NO BIRTHMARK

Before we move on from this thought, I want to help you see what Paul is saying when he says, "Let be accursed," in regards to those who profess Christ as their Savior but show no evidence they like Him or His people. This doesn't mean you leave him there and move on. He is teaching us to not claim someone is saved when they're not. If you have a spouse, children, other family members, or friends who are not absolutely fond of Jesus, pray to God He'll deliver them for His own glory. "Even with those who claim to be saved?" "Yes!" Even those who go to church with you but show no affection and adoration for Jesus.

WHAT DO THEY TREASURE?

Men can fake many things and get away with it most of the time. But they cannot fake what they like and what they treasure. New creatures that have been saved by the grace of God will treasure and like the Lord Jesus Christ. Listen to those you know when they talk about what they treasure and like the most, and see if you can discern the presence of God in their thoughts. "The wicked, through the pride of his countenance, will not seek after God: God is not in all his thoughts" (Psalm 10:4). We all seek what we treasure and talk about what we like. God's presence is not discernable or evident in guiding all the thoughts of the wicked. If we were to read the whole psalm, we would see the wicked think about God, but God is not involved in initiating or instructing the thoughts of the wicked. Why not? God has not established His thoughts. Why has He not established His thoughts? The wicked has not surrendered His life unto the Lord. "Commit thy works unto the Lord, and thy thoughts shall be established" (Proverbs 16:3). We commit ourselves to what we treasure, and we trust what we treasure. We will always be found talking the most about three things: (1) what we treasure (2) what we like (3) what we know the most about. If it's not Jesus, we're lost and perishing in our sins!

PRAY FOR THEM

When we know others don't like Jesus, pray God will shine in their hearts so they can see and know Him through the gospel of Jesus Christ. They will never have an appeal for the authentic Jesus until they are born again. Pray for light to shine in them for God's glory. Salvation is about God's glory. Men become better people when they are saved, but this is not the reason we should pray for them to be saved. Salvation is not so we'll go to church and enjoy it more, but it is completely for the glory of God.

TO GOD BE THE GLORY!

Men can not glorify God the way He deserves to be glorified while in a lost condition. It is impossible for a lost man to be humble and bring honor and glory to our great God and King. Therefore, if you want to touch the heart of God, ask Him to save those you know are not fond of Him for His own glory. Do this not so they will escape hell and go to heaven, but so another soul will be loosened from the works of the enemy through Christ Jesus and be able to glorify our King. Bless the Lord His way, and He'll bless you with people who will glorify His name with you.

2. He's Come to Destroy the Power of Darkness

TURN THEM

The second way the devil works through the fallen system of this world is darkness.

When the apostle Paul shared his life witness with King Agrippa, he bore witness to the commission the Lord gave him on the road to Damascus:

But rise, and stand upon thy feet: for I have appeared unto thee for this purpose, to make thee a minister and a witness both of these things which thou hast seen, and of those things in the which I will appear unto thee; Delivering thee from the people, and from the Gentiles, unto whom now I send thee, to open their eyes, and to turn them from darkness to light, and from the power of Satan unto God, that they may receive forgiveness of sins, and inheritance among them which are sanctified by faith that is in Me.

Acts 26:16-18

Paul was an instrument God was going to use to open their eyes so they could turn from Satan and his darkness to God and His light. This darkness is understood to be a life of error and falsehood. Satan had the authority to hold them under this error until God opened their eyes to see the truth and flee to God Himself. This is important to keep in mind. We have, by way of our position in Christ, escaped the error of this world, but we often find ourselves in error. Jesus has made it possible for us to be continually set free from the darkness of the lies we once believed. We were under the dominion of darkness while we were dead in our trespasses and sins. We had no clue of this until our eyes were opened and our heart and ears were circumcised to hear and know the Lord and His truth.

EYES MUST BE OPENED

God reveals this to us through the Israelites in the Book of Deuteronomy: "The great temptations which thine eyes have seen, the signs, and those great miracles: Yet the Lord hath not given you an heart to perceive, and eyes to see, and ears to hear, unto this day" (Deuteronomy 29:3-4). God must decree our eyes, ears, and hearts be opened supernaturally before we can know Him and His ways. "And the Lord thy God will circumcise thine heart, and the heart of thy seed, to love the Lord thy God with all thine heart, and with all thy soul, that thou mayest live" (Deuteronomy 30:6). This is what we know as the new birth, the opening and circumcision of our hearts and ears to hear, see, and know the Lord. This is a transfer from living in error and darkness to living in truth and light. "Light is sown for the righteous, and gladness for the upright in heart" (Psalm 97:11). The Jews saw the signs and wonders with an eye that was full of darkness. God had not given them what was needed to see the light or truth. "Take heed therefore that the light which is in thee be not darkness" (Luke 11:35).

TRANSLATED

God the Father has done such a work through birthing us into His kingdom; He moved us from the kingdom or dominion of darkness to the kingdom of the love of His precious Son. When we are born again through God, we are simultaneously moved from the legal authority of Satan to our eternal destination, the authority of King Jesus over our lives. "Who hath delivered us from the power of darkness, and hath translated us into the kingdom of His dear Son" (Colossians 1:13). Satan, who had rulership over us, was dealt a blow through the death of Jesus upon the cross. His mouth was stopped and he was rendered helpless concerning our new position in Christ. God struck the roaring lion on the cheekbone and crushed his teeth, rendering his bite harmless.[91] Satan's main tool he used was the law of God. God's law condemned the soul that sinned to death. He used this to his advantage over us. He has, since the beginning, kept men in bondage and terrified of death and its outcome. Jesus, however, overcame death and the grave. He frees men of the error concerning death that Satan used to hold his captives in bondage with. Jesus also took the law out of the way and rendered Satan powerless over us when He fulfilled the righteous requirements of the law of God on our behalf.

Through the eternal work of Jesus and the blessings of the new birth experience He accomplished on the cross, we can truly say He came to destroy the work of the devil. He has let the air out of his deception and nullified the power of darkness he used over our life. This is why John says, "This then is the message which we have heard of Him, and declare unto you, that God is light, and in Him is no darkness at all. If we say that we have fellowship with Him, and walk in darkness, we lie, and do not the truth" (1 John 1:5-6). John reveals to us what Jesus Himself says in regard to this issue of walking in error and corruption: "Then spake Jesus again unto them, saying, I am the Light of the world: he that followeth Me shall not walk in darkness, but shall have the light of life" (John 8:12). This is possible because of the new birth, and because God has transferred us from one kingdom to another.

What happened when God spoke His truth in us? Darkness itself had to flee. "Again, a new commandment I write unto you, which thing is true in Him and in you: because the darkness is past, and the true light now shineth" (1 John 2:8). The words "darkness is past" speak of darkness itself personally going away because of the true light that shines in its place. Darkness had to pack up and move out. Why did it leave? Something stronger had come in to bind it up, kick it out, and move in forever:

> When a strong man armed keepeth his palace, his goods are in peace: But when a stronger than he shall come upon him, and overcome him, he taketh from him all his armour wherein he trusted, and divideth his spoils. He that is not with Me is against Me: and he that gathereth not with Me scattered.
>
> Luke 11:21-23

The darkness in the beginning of creation could not overcome the light when God said, "Let there be light…," and darkness cannot overcome the light of the gospel in the hearts of men either. "For God, who commanded the light to shine out of darkness, hath shined in our hearts, to give the light of the knowledge of the glory of God in the face of Jesus Christ" (2 Corinthians 4:6).

WHAT A HARVEST

Light is sown for the righteous, and gladness for the upright in heart (Psalm 97:11). When most anything is sown in the right soul under the right conditions, a harvest is sure to come. It will always be like seed (same kind); it will always come later than when it was sown, longer than when it was sown, more lovely than when it was sown, and larger than what was sown. The same applies when God sows light and gladness in the hearts of His people. He is the One who gives the increase and is worthy of our praise. "I have planted, Apollos watered; but God gave the increase. So then neither is he

127

that planteth any thing, neither he that watereth; but God that giveth the increase" (1 Corinthians 3:6-7). The seed is the Word and light of God: "Thy Word is a lamp unto my feet, and a light unto my path" (Psalm 119:105). "... The seed is the Word of God" (Luke 8:11). The soil is the hearts of the righteous: "But that on the good ground are they, which in an honest and good heart, having heard the word, keep it, and bring forth fruit with patience" (Luke 8:15). God uses His people to sow His seed for a distinct and intentional harvest.[92] The light sown in the hearts of the righteous will yield a harvest like the seed that was sown. Light will be what shines in and out of the life of the righteous—more light than what was originally sown! The harvest lasts longer and will be larger than what was sown at first. In each harvest there will be more seed for future sowing. This may be why Jesus, who is the light, said we would do greater works than He.[93] Think about it.

VICTORY IS OURS

Knowing that God, through Christ Jesus, destroyed the works of the devil and the power of darkness is only the beginning of victory for believers. We must also trust the Lord has a place of refuge designed for His people even though He has cast out the darkness and destroyed the power of Satan over their lives. Satan is alive and still at work in the world. Believers can still be taken captive by him to do his will. We have the victory in Christ, but we must also trust the place of refuge God has designed and position ourselves in it to experience the fullness of Christ's triumph over Satan.

STAY IN POSITION

With the idea of being positioned in the right place I'm reminded of a proverb that instructs us to stay in our proper place. When we get out of our place, we compromise our protection and forfeit our provision: "As a bird that wandereth from her nest, so is a man that wandereth from his place" (Proverbs 27:8). Have you ever found a tiny bird that has fallen out of the nest? When we come across a baby bird that has fallen from its nest, we find them in one of three conditions: they're either dying, dead, or decomposing. The moment a helpless bird falls from the protection of its nest, it is dying. Its lifespan has just drastically shortened because it is no longer in the protection of its designed place. The poor little thing can't fly, and with no one to pick it up, it's dying.

HELPLESS

A defenseless bird is a cat's greatest delight. The bird can't fight back, and the cat knows he has an easy meal laid out before him. The Bible describes Satan as a roaring lion: "Be sober, be vigilant; because your adversary the devil, as a roaring lion, walketh about, seeking whom he may devour: Whom resist stedfast in the faith, knowing that the same afflictions are accomplished in your brethren that are in the world" (1 Peter 5:8-9). Notice, if you will, there is a place designed by God for us to be if we're going to oppose this "big cat." We oppose him by being in our place. Even though God has rendered him powerless over our lives, we are ordered to be positioned in the nest designed by the Lord if we're going to oppose the enemy.

DEAD

I have come across little birds that have just died. The elements of this world were just too strong for unprotected birds to make it. Without proper protection and provision, we all will die: "The man that wandereth out of the way of understanding shall remain in the congregation of the dead" (Proverbs 21:16). The enemy uses the lust of the world and its philosophies to draw people from their proper place. God has fashioned His believers in such a way that they can't survive outside of being in intimate fellowship with Him and His people. We are taught it is impossible to understand the fullness of God's love independently of ourselves. God uses His people collectively to teach each other the depth of His love:

That Christ may dwell in your hearts by faith; that ye, being rooted and grounded in love, May be able to comprehend with all saints what is the breadth, and length, and depth, and height; And to know the love of Christ, which passeth knowledge, that ye might be filled with all the fullness of God.

Ephesians 3:17-19

REAL OR FAKE?

Thinking along the lines of being provided for and protected while in our proper position, have you ever noticed how an artificial plant never wilts? Why not? Unlike a living plant, it doesn't need good soil, water, or sunlight. On the other hand, a living plant must be nourished. So it is with authentic believers and false witnesses. Just like an artificial plant doesn't need the daily nourishment of light and water, neither does a false witness. Yet an authentic believer can't live without being nourished with light and water. The only differences between a disciple of Jesus and a false witness is the fact that all true witnesses have been given a new heart and can't live without the presence of the Son of God and the living water of the Word of God. When a disciple of Jesus forsakes these two things, he will die spiritually. Why? He has left the place of understanding. Is it noticeable? Yes! Doesn't an undernourished and wilting plant stand out? So will a backslidden disciple. He's not in a position to be provided for and protected.

DECAYING

I once found a precious little bird already decaying. It had been dead for some time. Many churches have left their place as a prophetic voice in our day and are decomposing also. Think about the church at Sardis and the one at Laodicea. One had a name that was alive, but Jesus said it was dead.[94] The other thought it was in need of nothing, but the Lord's description of them was otherwise: "Because thou sayest, I am rich, and increased with goods, and have need of nothing; and knowest not that thou art wretched, and miserable, and poor, and blind, and naked" (Revelation 3:17). Why did this happen? They had left their place. The result was horrifying.

God said He would remove them from being a church if they did not repent. You might ask what good repentance would do. Put them in a position to hear and obey the Lord while having a kingdom impact on the earth. How many churches do you know named Laodicea? This church is decomposing before our eyes. We only have the remains of a church of the past. There are many Laodicean churches out there because they will not position themselves under the mighty hand of God's protective care.

A PROMISE MADE

With this in mind, I want to illustrate this thought with an Old Testament example of a king who had everything he needed in the nest with him yet chose to wander away from the promise. King Josiah was a young boy when became king of Judah.[95] God used him to bring about a great religious reform in his day. We are told in his day they recovered the Book of Law, and when it was read, Josiah humbled himself before God Almighty.

> Because thine heart was tender, and thou didst humble thyself before God, when thou heardest his words against this place, and against the inhabitants thereof, and humbledst thyself before Me, and didst rend thy clothes, and weep before me; I have even heard thee also, saith the Lord. Behold, I will gather thee to thy fathers, and thou shalt be gathered to thy grave in peace, neither shall thine eyes see all the evil that I will bring upon this place, and upon the inhabitants of the same. So they brought the king word again.
> 2 Chronicles 34:27-28

God promised to bring destruction upon Judah, but not while Josiah was ruling as king.

LEFT HIS PLACE

For thirteen years we see Josiah following the Lord. He remained in the protection and provision of God's nest. Then, after thirteen years of peace, an Egyptian king came near to Jerusalem as he traveled to make war with another nation. More than likely, at the request of his advisors and military council, Josiah felt the need to look into the activity of the Egyptian king, Necho. We can only imagine how the circumstances, the mounting pressure that came with being king, and the fact that everyone was looking to him for answers began to cloud his God-given vision. From what we know, God never came to Josiah again to remind him of the promise He made regarding the peace Josiah would die under. We are told in the Scriptures that God used the pagan king to warn Josiah to mind his own business.

> After all this, when Josiah had prepared the temple, Necho king of Egypt came up to fight against Charchemish by Euphrates: and Josiah went out against him. But he (Necho) sent ambassadors to him (Josiah), saying, What have I to do with thee, thou king of Judah? I come not against thee this day, but against the house wherewith I have war: for God commanded me to make haste: forbear thee from meddling with God, who is with me, that He destroy thee not. Nevertheless Josiah would not turn his face from him, but disguised himself, that he might fight with him, and hearkened not unto the words of Necho from the mouth of God, and came to fight in the valley of Megiddo.
>
> 2 Chronicles 35:20-22

CLING TO HIS PROMISE

God is not obligated to speak twice concerning His promises. We are responsible for clinging to every word that proceeds out of His mouth and obligated to live by them. I love what David says to the Lord in Psalm 119:49: "Remember the word unto thy servant, upon which thou hast caused me to hope." If only Josiah would have remembered what God had said about His promise to supernaturally protect Judah from war, he would have never gone out to stop Necho. He would have stayed in the nest with the Lord and said, "Lord, the word You gave me thirteen years ago I believe today, even though everything in me and around me says to fight the king.

Lord, Your Word is my hope in the time of trouble and adversity. I know the people want me to fight and my advisors are encouraging me to do something, but You said You would protect me if I stay in the nest. Lord, I'm at Your mercy and I believe Your promise."

GIVEN A WORD

The Lord put me through a similar situation as I prepared for my first staff position in ministry. I was serving in the church as a deacon and also preaching on a regular basis during my first year after surrendering my life to the gospel ministry. The church I was serving in was working on calling me on staff, and for providential reasons at the last minute the Lord shifted our direction. The thing is I had no clue at that time the Lord was moving me into a position to pastor a church. I had been in the Navy for the past nine years and didn't have a house or job waiting for me when I got out. Why? I had been working toward going on staff at our church for the last four months of my time in the Navy. I had met with the pastoral leadership on a Wednesday over lunch to discuss responsibilities, and that night they were going to present this to the personal committee of our church. They met that Wednesday night after church, but I didn't hear back from my pastor until Friday evening at around five o'clock.

On that Thursday evening, I was going into town on my way back to the church for something and God spoke to my heart a life-altering word. It was so clear to me what He said. He said, "I'm testing the heart of the people; I have a place prepared for you."

I had no idea the personal committee and the pastoral leadership decided it just wasn't the right time to bring on another staff member. My pastor called me on Friday evening and said, "Bro. Nick, I have dreaded this phone call for three days now, but I think you need to know it's not going to work out." I was free! I knew God had spoken to me the day before and He had a place for me in which to serve. I was truly free! I had such liberty and joy anticipating what God was going to do. No one understood why I was so delighted over the response of our church.

My wife was hurt by this, and her natural instincts of self-preservation began to be a stronghold for her. She had been asked to sing that following Sunday, and she didn't want to even go. She really felt betrayed. She knew we had no home to move into from base housing, and there were no job prospects at all. She had a hard time with me being so excited about what God was doing.

HE'S FAITHFUL

I believed God when He spoke to me that day. To this day, I still believe the word He spoke to me then was not just for that time, but it was a lifelong word for the ministry He gave me. I heard from God on Thursday, my pastor on Friday, and my first church on Monday morning at around eight o'clock. God in His matchless way gave my name to a member of a pastor search committee. The church was ordaining a deacon that Sunday night, and the young man's mother was a member of our church. She recommended they talk with us. They did, and we started on that church field the day before I was honorably discharged from the Navy. I was discharged on September 20, 1999, and the church called me as their pastor on September 19, 1999. God spoke and I believed Him and positioned myself in the promise.

Remember the word unto thy servant, upon which Thou hast caused me to hope. This is my comfort in my affliction: for Thy word hath quickened me. The proud have had me greatly in derision: yet have I not declined from Thy law. I remembered Thy judgments of old, O Lord; and have comforted myself. Horror hath taken hold upon me because of the wicked that forsake Thy law. Thy statutes have been my songs in the house of my pilgrimage.

Psalm 119:49-54

We must trust the Lord and His nest if we're going to experience the reality of His victory over darkness and deception. The devil has no power to stop God's people from accomplishing God's work. It is our responsibility to stay in the nest so we can be in a position to hear and obey the Lord.

THEY BUILT A NEST

For Mother's Day a couple of years ago I bought my wife a decorative birdhouse for our yard. It was a wooden A-frame birdhouse that stood on a six-foot metal support that was painted a deep forest green. She loved it and placed it in the front yard, hoping some little bird would make her nest in it soon. During spring of the following year, we noticed a pair of eastern blue birds building a nest in this little house. As time went by, we found three very fragile eggs tucked away in a neatly-crafted nest within the house. We enjoyed watching the pair protect their nest with diligence. Both mom and dad would take time to incubate the eggs between their own personal feeding times. We soon started to notice the frequency of their visits back and forth to their nest. As we investigated the situation even closer, we found three little blue birds peeking through the little hole in front of the house, their home and protection. The mom or dad would fly up on a power line and watch over the nest while the other gathered food. When one would fly back to the house, they would land on top of the roof and lean over the edge and go into the little hole in the front. What was so neat to see was the reaction of the little ones. Each time mom or dad would land on the roof of the house, they would begin to squeak and squawk while sticking their little heads out of the hole. They were so hungry and with their mouths wide open they let the world know they needed to be fed. The mom and dad provided and protected their little ones with their lives and a nest they built. All of our family and friends enjoyed sitting on our swing watching God validate His Word to us.[96] My bride loved to take pictures. She had fun photographing this beautiful new family. They eventually grew and left the birdhouse in our yard, but the lessons our family learned while watching these birds are forever etched in our memories.

OPEN YOUR MOUTH

With mouths wide open, mom or dad would put their beak in the babies' mouths, one at a time, to feed each bird. The picture of those wide open mouths is a vivid reminder of that day. Through these birds, God confirmed to me this is exactly what He desires to do with us. He showed us how important it is to stay in His designed nest with a desire to feed on what He gives. He really wants to feed us mouth to mouth. This is how He fed His servant Moses and His Son, Jesus:

My servant Moses is not so, who is faithful in all Mine house. With him will I speak mouth to mouth, even apparently, and not in dark speeches; and the similitude of the Lord shall he behold: wherefore then were ye not afraid to speak against My servant Moses.

Numbers 12:7-8

JUST STAY!

If we stand a chance against this world, Satan, and our flesh, we must abide in our proper place. We can't grow, be what He wants us to be, or do what He's called us to do unless we remain in the nest with mouths wide open for our heavenly Father to feed us. He has promised to nourish and feed His subjects: "The Lord will not suffer the soul of the righteous to famish: but he casteth away the substance of the wicked" (Proverbs 10:3). We are accountable to stay in our "nest," and He is responsible to provide and protect us. He has always desired to feed His people so He might deliver them from the hand of their oppressors.

I am the Lord thy God, which brought thee out of the land of Egypt: open thy mouth wide, and I will fill it. But My people would not hearken to My voice; and Israel would none of Me. So I gave them up unto their own hearts' lust: and they walked in their own counsels. Oh that My people had hearkened unto Me, and Israel had walked in My ways! I should soon have subdued their enemies, and turned My hand against their adversaries. The haters of the Lord should have submitted themselves unto Him: but their time should have endured for ever. He should have fed them also with the finest of the wheat: and with honey out of the rock should I have satisfied thee.

Psalm 81:10-16

God reveals the benefit and blessings of staying in the proper place and in the right position with Him in the previous verses. He promises to supply us with all we need and subdue all our enemies.

Stay in the nest with your mouth wide open and you'll be in a good position to be fed and filled by the Spirit. Magnify the Lord! Christ came to destroy the works of the devil and the power of his darkness over our life. We cannot be ignorant of the fact he is still capable of great delusion and darkness. We can't be naïve of his wiles and his efforts to thwart the plans of God in our lives. We can't fight him from a position of immaturity and expect victory when we know better. He is a real enemy to God and His people, and we can't neglect our responsibility to give him no place in our lives. Stay in the nest and take refuge under the shelter of the wings of God Almighty.[97] Let Him feed you the bread of life.

THANK GOD

Don't ever be afraid to ask God to remember the promise He spoke to you. Let Him hear your heart of gratitude and thankfulness for a lifelong word He has spoken in you. Tell Him He has given you hope and comfort in His promises for your life.

TAKING IT SERIOUSLY

Have you been born again?
Do you like Jesus?
Do you follow His ways?
Is He the light of your life?
Are you still in darkness?
Is God dealing with you about your sinful condition?
Has light been sown in your heart?
Do you really treasure Jesus Christ?
Do you enjoy talking about what He's done in your life?
Are you helping others turn to the light in Christ?

Chapter 6

Magnify the Lord
He's Come to Deliver

FROM SOMETHING TO SOMETHING

Isn't this an awesome thought? He's come to deliver. This is a wonderful truth that brings deep comfort to our souls. Knowing Jesus as the Deliverer helps us to see one of the most significant reasons for His coming. When we ponder and meditate on the very idea of a Redeemer who came to save, we can't get past the fact it speaks of a Deliverer. Why a deliverer?

When deliverance is needed, isn't it always from something that can harm or hurt us? Therefore, deliverance can only take place if we have been delivered from that which is harmful to that which is safe and secure. Christ Jesus, our Lord and Savior, has come to deliver God's people. He's come to deliver us from something to something.

Today, in America, it is common to hear most people make the claim Jesus is their Savior. We must ask them this simple but most serious question: Can Jesus be a personal Savior without being a personal Deliverer? I must say no!

IT'S NOT ABOUT US

On every street corner and in most neighborhoods we often find people who profess to be saved and acknowledge their connection with the "church." The fruit in their life will bear witness against them and reveal they have actually put their personal faith in a specific prayer they prayed, an action they did, a preacher, or even their own faith. The problem with placing faith in these things is that it won't deliver anyone from sin. Faith is only worth the object in which it is put. Faith is valued by God in its origin. If God is not the origin of grace-given faith, it has no eternal usefulness to Him. The modern gospel advocated in America today has taught men they have to do something in order to be saved. The Americanized gospel (which is a false gospel) has been so effectively preached by the masses that when the true gospel of the kingdom of God is preached, it is distinctly rejected by the established church of America. Why is it rejected? America's gospel is universally man-centered. God's gospel is uniquely Christ-centered. This is one of the reasons why the established church in America is having very little effect on the secular culture. There are great claims of salvation everywhere we turn, yet there is not much biblical evidence of individuals being called out of this world and set apart by God who are worthy of the gospel. This is exactly the point. Everyone lives out the gospel that they've heard and believed. If it's the Americanized gospel, the marks of it will be upon them. If it's the gospel of the kingdom of God, the life of Christ will be manifested in their life. Everyone is marked by the message they support and promote.

MAN-CENTERED

The American gospel communicates to its converts the need for only a mental or intellectual acknowledgement that Jesus lived, died for sin, was buried and rose again, and now lives to make intercession for the church. He also will come one day and get the church to live with Him forever. The problem with their message is rooted in their focal point. They have made the ministry of reconciling sinners into a global enterprise that promotes the message that sinners are sinners and they can have both God and all the enticements of this world. They have taken the message of reconciliation and made it marketable and profitable to fit what the culture wants, not what they need. Characteristically, the church of America has settled on gaining claims of salvation in its pursuit to look successful and has utterly denounced the power of Jesus Christ to unmistakably deliver a life from the power of darkness into the unparallel service of God the Father.

A CLASSIC EXAMPLE

The northern ten tribes of the divided kingdom of Israel is a perfect example of what has happened in America. For fear of losing their people to the two southern tribes called Judah, they instituted their own way of doing church. They were afraid of preaching and teaching what God required of His people, so they developed a new way to minister to the people and a new message. What they did was incorporate certain elements that identified with God's way of doing things, but for the purpose of comfort and convenience, they altered it in such a way as to appeal to the flesh of all involved. The people bought into it, and for the next two hundred-plus years they taught each new generation how to worship God and live in idolatry.

It started with one leader, a king by the name of Jeroboam, whose personal and fleshly fear led generation after generation to transgress against God's original message. From his life we can see where the foundation of all compromise begins in leading others to worship false gods. It starts when someone makes an effort to keep people involved, interested, and invested in their own special interests. The fear of personal loss dictated and directed his mission, ministry, and message.[98] Jeroboam led Israel away from God for twenty-two years, and most every king that followed after Him for two hundred-plus years is described as doing evil in the sight of the Lord and walking in the way of Jeroboam and his sin (1 Kings 15:26, 34; 1 Kings 16:19, 26, 30-31, 33; 1 Kings 22:52; 2 Kings 3:3; 2 Kings 10:29; 2 Kings 13:2, 11; 2 Kings 14:24; 2 Kings 15:9, 18, 24, 28). The sad thing is it worked for them for two centuries with very little resistance from this false system because it became the norm and it was easy.

The results of this delusional way of thinking led to God's judgment of Israel as a nation. Second Kings 17 reveals the essence of what was being taught and how it affected everything about the nation. God used the Assyrians in 722 B.C. to overthrow Israel and take captive some of her people. The king of Assyria took possession of Samaria and transplanted peoples of other nations there to occupy that territory. They were attacked by lions and felt like the God of the land was angry at them because they did not know His rituals and therefore couldn't practice His ways. What was their answer to this problem? The king of Assyria commanded that a priest be sent to them to teach them the rituals of the God of the land. A priest, a product of Jeroboam's two hundred-plus years of compromise, was sent and taught them what he knew. He taught the people how to fear God. The problem with his message was that it permitted the nations to do what Israel also did, supposedly fear God and serve their idols.[99] This is why Isaiah the prophet said the people drew near to the Lord with their mouths but their hearts were far from Him. How could they do this travesty? They taught them how to fear God according to the commandments of men, not the truth. "Wherefore the Lord said, Forasmuch as this people draw near Me with their mouth, and with their lips do honour Me, but have removed their heart far from Me, and their fear toward Me is taught by the precept of men" (Isaiah 29:13).[100] Jeroboam's compromise to the true message of God was still producing false converts and giving men false hope.

STAINED BY OUR GOSPEL

The unscriptural idea of acknowledging Jesus to be a Savior with the option of submitting to His lordship later is absolutely demonic and a complete compromise to the truth. This thought process and message has its origin in hell and comes from the father of lies. Those who preach this are preaching another gospel. This would mean that they're preaching a corrupt and cursed message. They are following in the footsteps of Jeroboam. The historical/biblical Jesus is anointed by the Lord. He is the Lord Jesus Christ. He's not the Savior who might be our Lord one day. No! He is the Lord who delivers His people into His service. The purpose of His death is for Him to be Lord over the living and the dead: "For to this end Christ both died, and rose, and revived, that He might be Lord both of the dead and living" (Romans 14:9). The gospel we believe is the gospel we will acknowledge and advocate through our attitudes, actions and affirmations. We are all stained by the message that has consumed and marked our lives. All of us are persuaded about a gospel. We have embraced a message or a culmination of messages as being authentic. Is it God's message or man's mission we have given our lives to?[101]

IT'S A PROBLEM

Countless millions have done all they have been told to do. They have been taught to believe more in what they must do than what Christ has already done. Therefore, men have put their faith in their actions, prayers, and more than anything else their own personal faith. They have made every attempt to be "saved" to assure themselves rather than being consumed with the biblical truth that Jesus Christ is God's Deliverer who has come to deliver us from ourselves, sin, society, and Satan. Jesus is God's Deliverer, and He has come to deliver each of us from a carnal way of thinking and to set us free to follow Him. He is our deliverance, and in Him we are eternally safe and secure. What has He come to deliver us from?

1. He's Come to Deliver Us from Something

A. He's Come to Deliver Us from Self

"That we should be saved from our enemies, and from the hand of all that hate us" (Luke 1:71). Salvation from our enemies speaks of a specific place of refuge and safety we would come to know and embrace after we'd been delivered from their hand into the hands of Jesus Christ. The passage above is a prophetic message that Zacharias, John the Baptist's father, is prophesying in regards to the fact that God has come to visit and redeem His people. In particular, he is prophetically speaking of a promised Deliverer, the

Lord Jesus Christ, who at that time was still in the womb of Mary. This prophetic word speaks of a deliverance that would be effectually applied to those whom God would redeem. One aspect of God's promise was the fact they would be delivered from their enemies and the hand of all who hated them. This promise speaks of the faithfulness of God and the power of His Son to truly deliver us. The significance of this deliverance comes when we see that we ourselves are an enemy of the things of God. There can be no salvation from God (safety, refuge, rest) without first being delivered from that place of hostility and rebellion toward the kingdom of God. God has promised to reconcile His people to Himself; therefore, He rescues them from themselves.

OWN WORST ENEMY

Our worst enemy is our self. The nature we were born with was completely and totally an enemy to anything godly. We have already discussed the nature we inherited from Adam. We were bent on sin. Everything about our life was ungodly and a lie. We were corrupt creatures because of the seed of sin passed down to us through the ages. God describes us as unrighteous enemies with a heart set on rebelling against Him. As products of the fall, He called us children of wrath. We were hostile toward Him, and in no way did we seek after Him.

What then? are we better than they? No, in no wise: for we have before proved both Jews and Gentiles, that they are all under sin; As it is written, There is none righteous, no, not one: There is none that understandeth, there is none that seeketh after God. They are all gone out of the way, they are together become unprofitable; there is none that doeth good, no, not one. Their throat is an open sepulchre; with their tongues they have used deceit; the poison of asps is under their lips: Whose mouth is full of cursing and bitterness: Their feet are swift to shed blood: Destruction and misery are in their ways: And the way of peace have they not known: There is no fear of God before their eyes.

Romans 3:9-18

IT IS CRITICAL

The reason men and women do not follow Jesus today is because they have never been delivered from themselves. To follow Jesus, one must first be delivered by Him. As discussed in the previous chapter, one must be born again to escape the blindness of Satan and the power of darkness that all lost men are under. The reason He came to destroy the works of the devil was to ultimately deliver us from his controlling hand. We first had to be delivered from the condition in which we were born. We were born in rebellion. Why were we born this way? We were conceived in iniquity: "Behold, I was shapen in iniquity; and in sin did my mother conceive me" (Psalm 51:5). What is the only natural result of this conception? "Yea, in heart ye work wickedness; ye weigh the violence of your hands in the earth. The wicked are estranged from the womb: they go astray as soon as they be born, speaking lies" (Psalm 58:2-3). From the womb, we are sinners, and we live out our days as sinners. We are our worst enemy. We need to be delivered from ourselves. The things we do that are hostile toward God are the result of who we are in our lost condition inherited from our fathers. "The heart is deceitful above all things, and desperately wicked: who can know it?" (Jeremiah 17:9). As a result of this crooked and perverse heart, we "feel" like we're right and just: "All the ways of a man are clean in his own eyes; but the Lord weigheth the spirits" (Proverbs 16:2). The way we think and the way we do things will always seem right and good to us because "we" are the most deceptive enemy we have.[102] "There is a way that seemeth right unto a man, but the end thereof are the ways of death" (Proverbs 16:25). God's Word is true, and we are messed up people. Who are we going to believe?[103]

THE MEDIATOR

Jesus is the only Mediator between God and rebellious man. Jesus gave Himself, as a substitution, to be a specific payment for sin. Through the shedding of His own blood, He forgave hostile sinners of their rebellion and reconciled us to His Father.[104] It was through this great work of mediation that the problem with our rebellion could be dealt with. Jesus is the only Mediator (go-between) who could declare to us God's heart and holiness while establishing the fact He loved us even while we were in our sins and hostile to His ways. As a go-between, He is the only way possible we could have access to and fellowship with the Father. Jesus is the way, the truth, and the life.

AN OFFENSE

We were an offense to God while in our sins. Therefore, God delivered up His Son upon the cross to deal with our offenses against Him. God placed upon Jesus our sin, making Him become sin so it could be possible for Him to deal with us: "Who (Jesus) was delivered for (on behalf) our offences, and was raised again for our justification" (Romans 4:25). This passage reveals to us the essence of our deliverance in Christ. We were bound to our sinful nature and the offenses that resulted from it until we were born again as a new creature in Christ Jesus. Christ Jesus is our life.[105] When God made us a new creature, we also died with Jesus. This all takes place in the new birth. This is a complete work of God from start to finish. Jesus, by way of His life, death, and resurrection, made it just and legal for God to deal with the problem—"us." When Paul is explaining to the church at Ephesus about these blessings that surround the new birth, he says, "Blessed be the God and Father of our Lord Jesus Christ, who hath blessed us with all spiritual blessings in heavenly places in Christ: According as He hath chosen us in Him before the foundation of the world, that we should be holy and without blame before Him in love" (Ephesians 1:3-4). Paul is glorifying the God and Father of our Lord Jesus Christ who has currently blessed us with every supernatural blessing there is as a direct result of His eternal grace. Grace belongs to God, and He can grant it, bestow, it or release it as He desires. Paul reveals to the church that the new birth is a complete work of God and the eternal benefits of this work are in line with His plans or "just as He planned" since before time began. God is the rightful owner of eternal salvation, which is totally through the work of Christ and utterly of His own grace. What are the supernatural blessings? It is the new birth that comes from above and the glories that follow the redeemed.

GOD AT WORK

God, who brings about the new birth, is the One who also puts us to death in Christ. Why are we put to death? Because we were bound by a law we could not fulfill. His law was like a wall that separated us from Him. His law is a manifestation of how holy He is and just how sinful we really are. God's law was given to show us there is a barrier between God and fallen man, the barrier being the corrupt and sinful nature inherited from Adam. God's law was given so that man could see how exceedingly sinful he is. His law was good and right; therefore, it was opposed to our nature as sinners. His laws as they stand are completely contrary to us and what we have become as humans.

> And you, being dead in your sins and the uncircumcision of your flesh, hath He quickened together with Him, having forgiven you all trespasses; Blotting out the handwriting of ordinances that was against us, which was contrary to us, and took it out of the way, nailing it to His cross.
>
> Colossians 2:13-14

This was His purpose in giving the law to us. "Now we know that what things soever the law saith, it saith to them who are under the law: that every mouth may be stopped, and all the world may become guilty before God. Therefore by the deeds of the law there shall no flesh be justified in His sight: for by the law is the knowledge of sin" (Romans 3:19-20). By design, the law was given to shut us down and to reveal how messed up we are compared to God.

HIS LAW

His law condemned all sinners to death. God's law is the means by which He reveals we are condemned sinners and deserve to be put to death and separated from God for all eternity. The law of God is designed so it cannot convert or pardon the sinner under any circumstances. God's law is forever impartial to its purpose. Every soul that sins is confined to death under the law. This law applies until the sinner dies. "Behold, all souls are Mine; as the soul of the father, so also the soul of the son is Mine: the soul that sinneth, it shall die" (Ezekiel 18:4). We were bound by the law until death: "Wherefore, as by one man sin entered into the world, and death by sin; and so death passed upon all men, for that all have sinned" (Romans 5:12).[106] We were also promised a just hearing after death: "And as it is appointed unto men once to die, but after this the judgment" (Hebrews 9:27).

JUST AS HE

The only way we could be free from this problem as we are, sinners bent on sinning, is in the heart and hands of God. How deep the Father's love is for us! How rich is His work of grace! He accomplished more than we will ever know upon the cross. He has blessed us with every spiritual blessing in heavenly places through Christ Jesus. It is all just as He planned before time ever began. He made us a new creature in Christ Jesus. He put us to death in Him upon the cross and raised us up with Him to sit in the heavenly places together forever. This is entirely His work and we must praise Him because He has dealt with the problem—us.

IT'S A FACT

We were our biggest problem. But thank God for Jesus, who fulfilled God's law and dealt with it for God's glory on a tree called Calvary. God dealt with the problem when He birthed us into His kingdom, and in His sovereign way He put us to death in Christ: "For ye are dead, and your life is hid with Christ in God" (Colossians 3:3). Praise God! He's come to deliver us from our worst enemy: ourselves.

B. He's Come to Deliver Us from Sin

UNTAINTED WORSHIP

What a day it will be when we see Jesus for the first time with eyes that are not tainted by the presence of sin. Can you imagine worshipping the Lord without the presence of sin? This world is defiled and full of death. It is important for us to know we have been delivered from the penalty and power of sin. It is equally important to know we have not been delivered from the presence of sin in this world or the problem of sin's effects. The snow ball effect of sin continues to roll down the mountain of this judged world like an avalanche headed for a valley. Sin has rolled down through the corridors of time and is gaining momentum as it increases in mammoth proportions in these last days. We have all been broadsided at times by this gigantic snowball and will be again and again as long as we're living in this world. We will not be delivered from sin's presence until the new heaven and earth appear and Satan, death, and the grave are made subject to Jesus and cast into the lake of fire and brimstone for eternity. Until then we are called on to endure in the present victory we have over sin's penalty and power.

WE SEE IT

All authentic believers long for that day when mortality will be swallowed up by immortality. The new natures that believers possess are bent on the things of eternal righteousness. There is a craving in the heart of every new creature in Christ to long to be clothed in more of heaven. This is a great indicator of the Spirit of God living within us as new creatures in Christ. It is a birthmark that can be found upon the desire of those who have been persuaded by the grace of God to follow Jesus.

For we (all believers) know that if our earthly house of this tabernacle were dissolved, we have a building of God, an house not made with hands, eternal in the heavens. For in (knowing) this we groan, earnestly desiring to be clothed upon with our house which is from heaven: If so be that being clothed we shall not be found naked. For we that are in this tabernacle do groan, being burdened: not for that we would be unclothed, but clothed upon, that mortality might be swallowed up of life. Now He that hath wrought (fully and permanently worked this in us and accomplished this longing effect in the heart of) us for the selfsame thing is God, who also hath given unto us the earnest of the Spirit. Therefore we are always confident, knowing that, whilst we are at home in the body, we are absent from the Lord.

                                                    2 Corinthians 5:1-6

What a change has be wrought in our heart by God. Remember, as a man thinks in his heart, so is he.[107] The dynamics of the new birth are far reaching within the heart of a believer, and it affects his hands and his feet to reflect the work of God in his heart. One day we will be delivered from sin's presence. Oh, what a day that will be!

WE HATE IT

The problems of sin are also manifested to us daily. Death, disease, destruction, and devastation are a few problems we face daily. All of these are the direct consequences of sin. How many people do we know who have cancer or diabetes? How many people do we know who have experienced a divorce? How many people do we know who have encountered the reality of death in the last month? How many people do we know who knows someone who has been affected by them? Everyone on the planet has felt the impact of this devastating blow in some way or fashion. We will have to face each problem daily for as long as we live. They are the results of the problem with sin. Sin kills! It always has.

PAID IN FULL

One of the greatest blessings for believers is to know we have been delivered from the penalty of sin. We have previously discussed in detail the problem with our nature and God's law condemning us because of our sins. The penalty for sin is death: "For the wages of sin is death; but the gift of God is eternal life through Jesus Christ our Lord" (Romans 6:23). If anyone is going to have life in Christ, they must first die. This death is accomplished supernaturally by God Himself when we are born again. In Christ we die. We were put to death in Christ, and not only did we die to the law, but we also died to sin. Christ paid the penalty for our sins. This was a debt we could not pay.[108] Our sins were placed upon Christ while He was on the cross, and upon the cross God legally judged our sin. Our sins were paid for by the sacrificial Lamb of God. Christ paid our wages and suffered the death of the cross to free us from a debt that was only payable through death. Jesus was the only One who could satisfy the heart of God's wrath by atoning for our sin. He also supplied the favor needed to reconcile us unto His Father.

NOT FOR SIN

All believers will give an account of their life at the judgment seat of Christ, but not for a payment for sin because Christ already paid the wages of death for our sin. We can have confidence and boldness before our God because we are free from the penalty of our sin. Because of His grace, we can enter into God's presence through the torn body of our Champion and Deliverer. He is the veil we must go through to enter into the holy of holies if we're going to have fellowship with the Father. We have peace with God now because our debt has been paid, our sins are forgiven, and we are the righteousness of God through Christ Jesus. Praise Him today because He's come to deliver us from the penalty of our sins.

SIN'S POWER

He's also come to deliver us from sin's power. How did He do this? He did it through the death of the cross. We died to sin upon the cross: "For he that is dead is freed from sin" (Romans 6:7). How have we died? In Christ we died when He died. This is what has been accomplished by God. This is His work, and we are exhorted to believe He put us to death upon the cross and raised us up to newness of life through the resurrection of Jesus.

What shall we say then? Shall we continue in sin, that grace may abound? God forbid. How shall we, that are dead to sin, live any longer therein? Know ye not, that so many of us as were baptized into Jesus Christ were baptized into His death? Therefore we are buried with Him by baptism into death: that like as Christ was raised up from the dead by the glory of the Father, even so we also should walk in newness of life. For if we have been planted together in the likeness of His death, we shall be also in the likeness of His resurrection: Knowing this, that our old man is crucified with Him, that the body of sin might be destroyed, that henceforth we should not serve sin.

Romans 6:1-6

Keep in mind this is what God does in the new birth. You and I are not required to understand all that took place. We are commanded to believe what He said He did and trust the results of this work unto God. We are called to put faith in the fact we died to sin and were raised with newness of life and with victory over the power of sin. Did we die physically? No! We died supernaturally in Christ. How do we die daily? By putting faith in this revealed truth that we are no longer who we used to be. We died with Christ, and the old man inside of us was crucified with Him. We put faith in the truth that our sins are forgiven and we are free from their penalty and power. We put faith in the truth that we're a new creature who has victory in Christ over the power of sin.

For he that is dead is freed from sin. Now if we be dead with Christ, we believe that we shall also live with Him: Knowing that Christ being raised from the dead dieth no more; death hath no more dominion over Him. For in that He died, He died unto sin once: but in that He liveth, He liveth unto God. Likewise reckon ye also yourselves to be dead indeed unto sin, but alive unto God through Jesus Christ our Lord. Let not sin therefore reign in your mortal body, that ye should obey it in the lusts thereof. Neither yield ye your members as instruments of unrighteousness unto sin: but yield yourselves unto God, as those that are alive from the dead, and your members as instruments of righteousness unto God. For sin shall not have dominion over you: for ye are not under the law, but under grace.

Romans 6:7-14

Reckoning means to put faith, trust, and confidence in the truth revealed by God. What is the truth revealed by God? We died with Christ and were raised unto life with Him. How can we have victory over sin? Putting faith in the truth is where our victory over sin is lived out daily.

FAITH

Jesus came to deliver us from our enemies, and sin is an enemy to the throne of God. Be persuaded of the facts that support the truth Jesus has come to deliver you from sin's penalty and power. Walk in His victory today by faith. Redemptive faith is a benefit of God's enabling grace that connects and convinces us to personally possess what God promises. Redemptive faith is the product of God's grace that has persuaded us to take personal ownership in trusting God's faithfulness and His delight and duty to fulfill what He's promised. Redemptive faith is also sustained confidence to live for God's glory as we look for His promises with eager anticipation. Redemptive faith is not only the result of being persuaded, but it's also a persuasive witness to believers and unbelievers. Faith in a Deliverer who truly delivers is also a faith that delivers a persuasive testimony.

POSSESS THE PROMISES

If you have been born again, you have the nature to agree with God's promises. We are not called to fight for victory, but from victory. Jesus has already won the victory. Fight from His triumph over sin, death, and the grave, and you'll be a vessel God can use to be dangerously strong for His truth on the earth. Personally possess the truth as God reveals it to you. Trust Him with what He reveals and He'll free you to take hold of more truth. We overcome sin when we take ownership of God's truth and His promises of victory in Christ. He's come to deliver us from sin. Possess the truth (substance) surrounding a particular principle of truth and take ownership of it as your very own (evidence), even when it can't be physically seen.[109] We'll never possess it until we hear it, believe it, and see it is ours.[110]

C. He's Come to Deliver Us from Society

HEADED FOR DESTRUCTION

"Who gave Himself for our sins, that He might deliver us from this present evil world, according to the will of God and our Father" (Galatians 1:4). We see again in this passage how our sinful nature and our practice of sin had us in bondage with the society in which we lived. Solomon says, "A threefold cord is not easily broken."[111] We were very much a part of this age of hostility. It has already been established in this study that we were rebels with a self-centered motives to exalt our rights above the decrees of God. We were in the flow of an eternally worthless system that would one day come to an abrupt end. This age we now live in and the society governed by its flow will be consumed with fervent heat.[112] The outcome of this evil age is destruction.

NO LEGITIMATE APOLOGY

Christ came to rescue us from this society and the consequences of its dreadful influence. Paul, under the inspiration of the Holy Spirit, described in the book of Romans just how the fall of Adam and Eve affected all of humanity. In the first chapter, he explains how we were all without a legitimate apology. We knew what we were doing as a society, and we had no excuse for it. Apologizing for a rebellion that was deliberate and knowing you enjoyed what you were doing and had the very intent to do it again is inexcusable.

The result of this behavior is God gave our society over to a way of thinking of which He does not approve. The consequence of God's wrath released man to do those things which are not fitting.[113] Secular society overflows with attitudes of ungodliness and acts of unrighteousness, which is proof of God's wrath upon humanity. When anyone is habitually compelled by anything other than the love of Christ and controlled by the excessive desires of their flesh, they are under the wrath of God. They are still in bondage and trapped in an age that is corrupt and bent on sin. Why? They have never been delivered and rescued by Jesus.

MUST BE INTERRUPTED

He came to interrupt the flow of our rebellious lifestyle and put us on a course that honors His righteousness. Jesus told His disciples they were not of this society any longer and the proof of this would be the society's hatred of them. Jesus rescues those whom He delivers from the course of our society and its condemnation. Amen! His grace will continually teach the saints He has delivered to deny this world and what it values while living for God's glory now.[114] Jesus has come to tear us away from the darkness of this world so we might be a light to it. This deliverance is always by force. We were rescued, my friend, from the hand of the enemy and all who hate us. The cross of Christ was a covert invasion of God upon this world. He forcefully defeated the enemy upon the cross and made it possible for us to be rescued from the grip this system had upon His people. We were not looking for the Lord when He interrupted our life. We enjoyed our sin and the lies of sinful people. We were bound together with them in this war. But Jesus broke through our rebellion and rescued us from the grip of sin and this society. Jesus interrupted our agendas and intruded upon our dark hearts when He invaded our lives with His grace. We are rescued sinners who have been freed from this society's influence and instruction.[115]

WE CAN'T BE FRIENDS

God's rescue is personally intentional and forever influential. James warns us of the danger of just wanting to be a friend with this world. It is important to note James did not say we had to be a friend of the world to be an enemy of God. In fact, all we have to do is desire to be a friend of this world and we make ourselves an enemy of God: "Ye adulterers and adulteresses, know ye not that the friendship of the world is enmity with God? Whosoever therefore will be a friend of the world is the enemy of God" (James 4:4). Jesus didn't die for our sins so we could be fond of Him and like the world at the same time. Jeroboam may have preached that message, but not Jesus. He rescued us so we could be transformed by the renewing of our mind and not be conformed to this crooked and perverse world. He gave His life to deliver us from such hostility that we could be His servants shedding light upon a dark and depraved world.[116]

God intentionally rescued our life so the world would no longer be the means by which we were to receive instruction and influence. The world we're living in is passing away. The people who are living under its influence are passing away with it. God has so precisely and perfectly rescued us so He can make us into rescuers also.

If thou forbear to deliver them that are drawn unto death, and those that are ready to be slain; If thou sayest, Behold, we knew it not; doth not He that pondereth the heart consider it? and He that keepeth thy soul, doth not He know it? and shall not He render to every man according to his works?

Proverbs 24:11-12

We have been rescued to ensure we can go forth in the name of the Lord Jesus and rescue the perishing. We have been equipped and called on by God to put our life at risk and even die for His sake to see to it that others may be rescued through the life of His Son: "A true witness delivereth souls: but a deceitful witness speaketh lies" (Proverbs 14:25). Before we can be a rescuer, we have to be rescued by Jesus.

EXAMINE YOURSELF

If you have been marked by America's gospel, you are not a rescuer of the perishing. You are aiding sinners in their rebellion and teaching them how to fear God according to the commandments of men. Have you been rescued from among those who are perishing in the sea of sin? Let God rescue you from yourself and He'll send you on His rescue mission.[117]

D. He's Come to Deliver Us from Satan

We have spent some time looking at how Jesus delivered us from Satan and the darkness he used to blind us with deception and delusion. Through the cross, Jesus rendered the devil powerless over His people. How did He do this? He dealt with their sinful nature and the acts of sin that deserved to be punished by death. He also took care of the problem we faced with the law. The law itself was the tool the enemy used against us and the means by which sin found its strength.[118]

FREE

The devil held men in bondage concerning death and the judgment. Jesus delivered us from this.[119] God delivered us from the authority of Satan, so he must have permission to even touch the saint of God.[120] We are hidden in Christ and free to follow Him all the days of our life. Why are we free? Christ Jesus not only delivered us from those we know hate us, but even those enemies we don't even know are enemies. There are many who would pretend to be friends of God, yet they are an enemy of God's will. Count it as blessing, brethren, you have been delivered from the hand or authority of all God's enemies. "That we should be saved from our enemies, and from the hand of all that hate us" (Luke 1:71). Praise God, we have been delivered from something. Amen!

TAKING IT SERIOUSLY

Have you been rescued from the power that draws and drives this world?

Have you been made a new creature in Christ Jesus?

Have you surrendered and submitted your life to the Lord Jesus Christ?

Have you been delivered from the authority of your enemies?

2. He's Come to Deliver Us to Something

TO BRING GLORY

Praise God, my friend, because if you have been delivered from something, you have also been delivered to something. God's work is always personal, powerful, and purposeful. He has delivered us to unashamed and unadulterated service. Amen! Paul even speaks of this in Romans 1:5 when he says, "By Whom we have received grace and apostleship, for obedience to the faith among all nations, for His name." Through the Lord Jesus Christ, we received the eternal grace of God and His unique and special calling on our life for obedience to the faith. This lifestyle of obedience is to be lived out before the heathens for God's glory. Our lives in Christ have been so designed by the Lord that we can live victoriously in the same environment we once were enslaved to, and all for His glory. This environment of hostility to the things of God now becomes the mission field we have been planted in to serve the Lord. We are delivered to bring glory to our God. God has snatched us right out of the hand of the enemy, and He will use us to see to it others are snatched out of his hand until our dying days.

A. He's Come to Deliver Us to Unashamed Service

GLADHEARTED SERVICE

"That He would grant unto us, that we being delivered out of the hand of our enemies might serve Him without fear, in holiness

158

and righteousness before Him, all the days of our life" (Luke 1:74-75). Having been graciously granted deliverance from ourselves and all others who will oppose us, we have been set free to serve our King without fear. This statement runs deep and wide, and we have already discussed our liberation from the penalty and the power of sin. Therefore, we are going to look at this idea of "without fear" from the standpoint of being unashamed in our service. When we love and especially like someone or something, we're usually not ashamed of them or it. There are occasions when someone loves or likes something that is unacceptable or even immoral, so they will be ashamed to make their relationship to it known. They may not be ready to let the world know of their behavior, but not ashamed enough to stop participating in it.

EVERYTHING IS PROVIDED

We must not forget the truth about our new nature. We were delivered to a place of not only loving Jesus, but also honestly and authentically liking Him. Through the grace of God we have been delivered to a place where we can be taught how to live for Jesus and be obedient to the faith so God may be glorified in our life. We also received the Holy Spirit to empower us to live for and testify about the life of Jesus Christ. We have received everything needed to live life the way God has intended it to be lived. We are His workmanship, and He is working in us to do according to His good pleasure.[121] God has completely and utterly changed us from being antichrists to having a supernatural appeal for Him. Why would anyone be ashamed of a God who has delivered them into such a great salvation? By no means would they be ashamed of Him. Why not? They have been delivered to this particular lifestyle and supplied with all the means to live it out all the days of their life.

A SURE FOUNDATION

This thought is rooted all throughout the Old Testament promises of God in regards to the work God did through Jesus Christ. The picture God painted for the prophet Isaiah is that of a Master Builder who laid a sure foundation and cornerstone for the builders to build upon: "Therefore thus saith the Lord God, Behold, I lay in Zion for a foundation a stone, a tried stone, a precious corner stone, a sure foundation: he that believeth shall not make haste" (Isaiah 28:16). We know the New Testament confirms this stone is the Lord Jesus Christ. God said whoever believes in this stone will align themselves with the stone God laid. He will give up his life to be built, attached to, and placed around the precious stone God gave. He said they would not be ashamed to align their life to the Cornerstone He gave to build His Church around. The word *ashamed* means to be quick to make hast or put on the run. The reason someone would be quick to run away from an object to another object is always based on how they value each object. When we have the nature of God we will value the things He values. When someone is lost they can't appreciate what God considers honorable or agree with Him on what He sees as valuable. God knows that none of His believers would ever want to build their life on or around anything else other than the Foundation He's laid and the Cornerstone He's given in Christ Jesus. Whoever believes in the faithfulness of God and His Choice Stone that He's laid down will never be eager to go to another foundation and build around another cornerstone. Believers do not and will not reject God's proven and perfect Stone.

HE'S PRECIOUS

The reality of God's people affirming, acknowledging, and acting on His Stone is spoken of by Peter in his letter to the elect:

Wherefore also it is contained in the scripture, Behold, I lay in Sion a chief corner stone, elect, precious: and he that believeth on him shall not be confounded. Unto you therefore which believe He is precious: but unto them which be disobedient, the stone which the builders disallowed, the same is made the head of the corner.

1 Peter 2:6-7

Jesus is precious to the Father and precious to us who have been persuaded by Him and believe He is the only life we can be built upon and around. He knew the Lord would not and could not let us down. He is forever faithful. Persuaded believers value the life of Christ with such a high estimation that they give up all other life-style designs to be built upon His life and words.[122] Those who are not persuaded by God and therefore do not believe their life should be influenced by Jesus and identified with Him are described as those who do not obey the words of Jesus and are ashamed of Him: "Whosoever therefore shall be ashamed of Me and of My words in this adulterous and sinful generation; of him also shall the Son of Man be ashamed, when He cometh in the glory of His Father with the holy angels" (Mark 8:38).

When we place such a high value on something that we regard as being very precious to us, it usually becomes something others would recognize as our treasure. Whatever we treasure also has our heart. Wherever we find our treasure is where we'll find our heart: "For where your treasure is, there will your heart be also" (Matthew 6:21). We will give our affection, adoration, and attention to that which we treasure. Why will we do this? It is something or someone who has won our heart. It becomes our highest priority and we give place to it over everything else. It is most precious to us and we will tend to it with all our heart. There is no way to hide it. When we treasure something, we cannot fake it or conceal it. What we treasure we also trust. We are free from other things and give ourselves over to what we trust as its slave. We are a slave to whatever we treasure. Whatever we give ourselves to, we are that thing's slave. Why? It is precious to us. We treasure it. We trust it to meet our most intimate needs. This is why we are not ashamed of it. We have settled it in our hearts that this is what we treasure.[123] What we treasure is what we trust. What we trust we give ourselves over to. What we trust is precious to us. We will not be ashamed of it. We will not be put on the run, but we'll actually stand up and protect what we treasure and trust at the cost of our lives: "And they (saints of God) overcame him (the devil) by the blood of the Lamb, and by the word of their testimony; and they loved not their lives unto the death" (Revelation

12:11). Why are they willing to die for Jesus? He is precious to them!

NOT PUT ON THE RUN

In the book of Joel, we find a prophetic word concerning the great work of deliverance that will come to the people of God: "And it shall come to pass, that whosoever shall call on the name of the Lord shall be delivered: for in mount Zion and in Jerusalem shall be deliverance, as the Lord hath said, and in the remnant whom the Lord shall call" (Joel 2:32). Paul, under the power of the Holy Ghost, grabs this passage from the Old Testament and uses it when he writes to the church at Rome:

> That if thou shalt confess with thy mouth the Lord Jesus, and shalt believe in thine heart that God hath raised Him from the dead, thou shalt be saved. For with the heart man believeth unto righteousness; and with the mouth confession is made unto salvation. For the scripture saith, Whosoever believeth on Him shall not be ashamed. For there is no difference between the Jew and the Greek: for the same Lord over all is rich unto all that call upon Him. For whosoever shall call upon the name of the Lord shall be saved.
>
> Romans 10:9-13

Joel points to a great day of deliverance. He reveals to us the deliverance that God brings will distinctly include a lifestyle of unashamed service. Praise God in the highest. He is worthy of all our life and praise.

LIVING STONES

If anyone—any culture or age—has been delivered from sin by Jesus Christ, they will also treasure Him. Why will they do this? Jesus has delivered and ordained them to take their special place in a precious building that God is constructing today called the church. It is the family of the living God. The church is a called out assembly which has been set apart by God for a specific service.[124] They are not ashamed of this unparalleled work of God, but they rejoice with joy unspeakable and full of glory.[125] They are persuaded and their lifestyle cannot hide the fact they treasure Jesus.

These all died in faith, not having received the promises, but having seen them afar off, and were persuaded of them, and embraced them, and confessed that they were strangers and pilgrims on the earth. For they that say such things declare plainly that they seek a country. And truly, if they had been mindful of that country from whence they came out, they might have had opportunity to have returned. But now they desire a better country, that is, an heavenly: wherefore God is not ashamed to be called their God: for He hath prepared for them a city.

Hebrews 11:13-16

MY PRAYER

God,
Would You speak to us in this evil generation of such a wonderful principle that abides upon those who have been persuaded of You and Your promises? We do embrace and confess we are strangers and pilgrims in this land and that we treasure You, and we are not ashamed to stand up, step out, and speak for Your glory. Your people do treasure You, for you are our King!

B. He's Come to Deliver Us to Unadulterated Service

SOMETHING HAPPENED

"That He would grant unto us, that we being delivered out of the hand of our enemies might serve Him without fear, in holiness and righteousness before Him, all the days of our life" (Luke 1:74-75). When we truly ponder the fact God clothed Himself with humanity so humanity could be clothed with God, we are humbled by this unusual act of humility.[126] Think about this for a moment. Because of being permanently interrupted by Jesus Christ and powerfully invaded by His grace, we went from being one who served ourselves to being a servant of God. Genesis gives the best description of who we were before grace: "And God saw that the wickedness of man was great in the earth, and that every imagination of the thoughts of his heart was only evil continually" (Genesis 6:5). We, by the nature of our character, were unclean. God describes our pre-conversion character as being evil. Our character was good for nothing eternally. The outcome of one's character will be seen by his conduct. The conduct of our life was unrighteous. We lived continually this way until we were interrupted by the deliverance of Jesus. The cross is what made the difference. The power of the cross of Jesus is mighty. We went from having a character that was good for nothing eternally to a character that is now consecrated for God's service. The conduct of our life went from being unrighteous to living and serving God in righteousness. Our character and conduct was changed forever. What a contrast of light and darkness.

APPROVED

The life of Christ was graciously granted to us so we could serve God in holiness and righteousness all the days of our life. Not just all our life, but all day long all the days of our life. "According as He hath chosen us in Him before the foundation of the world, that we should be holy and without blame before Him in love" (Ephesians 1:4). Because of Jesus, we are now approved as a consecrated vessel that can bring glory and honor to our great God. The living King Jesus is the new man which we are admonished to put on in Ephesians: "And that ye put on the new man, which after God is created in righteousness and true holiness" (Ephesians 4:24).

If you have been delivered from the hand of the enemy, you have been delivered to a place of safety and service in Christ, who is your life. Stand up and serve a God who only accepts what He's worked through His own grace. It is by His grace we stand before Him as holy and blameless, without any spot. It is by His grace we can serve Him righteously in this corrupt world. We are His and His alone. We were bought through a means that goes beyond and above the usual purchase. The purchase of our life is incomparable. This is why the Bible describes God's people as peculiar. The means by which we were purchased is so special that the intent and purpose of such a purchase is also above and beyond the normal. Our redemption is special.

PURCHASED FOR SERVICE

We were slaves of sin, and we treasured the life we were living. We gave ourselves to our master and we were free from God in all matters of holiness and righteousness. We did not want a new master, and we were in darkness to His beauty and loveliness. None of these things moved Him. He knew He could change us from being a servant to sin to living and longing to serve righteousness. He knew He could and would make us into a trophy of His matchless grace. He knew that to do this He would have to go farther than any master had ever gone to purchase his subjects. He also knew exactly what each person He would purchase would be doing in His fields. He weighed the cost and paid the price to make His people special. This work has no comparison. It's only for those who have been purchased in such an unusual way by His own blood.

> But ye are a chosen generation, a royal priesthood, an holy nation, a peculiar people; that ye should shew forth the praises of Him who hath called you out of darkness into His marvellous light: Which in time past were not a people, but are now the people of God: which had not obtained mercy, but now have obtained mercy.
>
> 1 Peter 2:9-10

The Lord's people do live a life of service that is unusual, unashamed, and unadulterated even in the midst of a perverse generation. Don't be cheated by the Americanized gospel. Jesus came to deliver us from something to something. Praise God!

1. In Holiness *"...in holiness ...all the days of our lives."*

This helps us see the nature of the character of service. The word *holy* means "to be consecrated for a unique and special purpose." The idea is that of something which has been set apart for God Himself. This is a fundamental truth that reveals the necessity of the sacrifice of Jesus. Apart from the life of Christ, we could not be set apart for God. Christ came to deliver us to a place consecrated only for those who have been washed in His blood and made a new creature. This new creature now has a character acceptable and approved by God for service unto Him. The picture is that of a priest who has been set apart to represent both God and man. The priest was set apart to stand before man on behalf of God and before God on behalf of man. This was an appointed position ordained by God. It was sanctified by God for His service. The book of Revelation tells us how we became a priest before the Lord and therefore consecrated for holy service:

> And from Jesus Christ, who is the faithful witness, and the first begotten of the dead, and the prince of the kings of the earth. Unto Him that loved us, and washed us from our sins in His own blood, and hath made us kings and priests unto God and His Father; to Him be glory and dominion for ever and ever. Amen.
>
> Revelation 1:5-6

CHANGED FROM WITHIN

We have been made kings and priests unto God through the blood of Jesus; therefore, we see that outside of being born again, we cannot be consecrated for holy service. Why? The nature by which the Lord is served must be holy. We had to be made new creatures to serve God in holiness. We had to be changed from the inside.

2. In Righteousness *"...and righteousness all the days of our lives."*

This helps us see the conduct of our service. Now we are in a position to serve the Lord in holiness, we are capable of being in right relationship with the Lord and living out this relationship before the world. Righteousness is being right with God and living out His ways. When we live by God's grace, we live and serve Him in righteousness.

> I am crucified with Christ: nevertheless I live; yet not I, but Christ liveth in me: and the life which I now live in the flesh I live by the faith of the Son of God, who loved me, and gave Himself for me. I do not frustrate the grace of God: for if righteousness come by the law, then Christ is dead in vain.
>
> Galatians 2:20-21

Jesus is the essence of grace. Paul reveals this same principle to us in Corinthians: "But by the grace of God I am what I am: and His grace which was bestowed upon me was not in vain; but I laboured more abundantly than they all: yet not I, but the grace of God which was with me" (1 Corinthians 15:10). It is by His grace we were made a new creature, and through His grace we live out practically what Christ Jesus has done in us. We can see now how our service before the Lord can be unadulterated and undefiled. Magnify the Lord! Jesus has come to deliver us from sin to do His work.

TAKING IT SERIOUSLY

What gospel have you believed?
What gospel has marked your life?
Have you been delivered from sin?
Have you been delivered to service?
Are you following a Deliverer or is your faith in something else?

What a Gift!
By Nick Holden
(Ephesians 1-6)

Has there ever been a gift so treasured,
So precious, so lasting and unmeasured?

A work so priceless it can't be compared,
Thought out and eternally prepared?

A gift that reaches above anything we know,
It keeps giving with an everlasting flow.

Describing it's fullness has driven men mad,
This was not the intent, however so sad.

It is given to please and gratify the Giver,
To also truly free and completely deliver.

A gift that stands alone and indescribable,
One that changes lives and undeniable.

What gift has this kind of power and eternal effect,
To make sinful man complete and perfect?

God called it GRACE before time ever started,
We call it LIFE when it's divinely imparted.

It is a gift greater in power than the sun,
Delivered and imparted by God's only Son.

Without being provoked by our merit He gave,
His Son to seek and gloriously save.

His gift causes a life altering transformation,
It produces a lifestyle of verbal confirmation.

God's amazing GRACE, how sweet the sound,
Freeing the one who is earthly bound.

Has His awesome LIFE set you free?
Give Him yourself, be changed eternally!

Chapter 7

Magnify the Lord
He's Come to Disciple

WILL SHE BE WITH US OR AGAINST US?

Jesus! Is there another name that means so much to believers than the name of Jesus? We are wonderfully blessed if our names are identified with the name of Jesus. There have been many who have stepped in and out of time with unforgettable names, but there is none so great as the name Jesus. The value of a name is found in the quality of the character of the one who possesses it. The Lord referred to a man who was great and the fact that many came from the ends of the earth to hear his wisdom and behold his beauty. Solomon was his name, and he was in a league of his own until God unveiled His Son unto the world. The Lord spoke of Solomon and his greatness, and He said in the judgment of the souls of men there would be a woman who would stand and condemn the world for not being taken with the beauty of God's Son: "The queen of the South shall rise up in the judgment with this generation, and condemn it, for she came from the ends of the earth to hear the wisdom of Solomon; and indeed a greater than Solomon is here" (Matthew 12:42). The woman would be the queen of Sheba.

JESUS TESTIFIED

The Lord shared this heart-gripping reality while speaking to an evil and adulterous crowd of people who were listening to Him only to get something. They did come to Him because of the quality of His character, but also to glean that which appealed to their /flesh. When He spoke about the attitude and actions of the queen of the South, He also reminded them of the Ninevites. These people were hardened sinners who accepted God's message of judgment and His messenger, a Jew. The nation turned at the rebuke of the Lord and experienced a revival. They did repent when God sent a word of life and death through the preaching of His prophet, Jonah. Therefore, the response of the Ninevites and the queen of the South are historical landmarks that will testify against the insufficient reaction of those who fail to embrace the person and preaching of Jesus Christ.

WE NEED TO LOOK

I thought it would be wise for us to investigate her response to Solomon, so I turned to 1 Kings 10 and searched the Scriptures. I discovered some startling facts about the queen's affection for the king of Israel. She was literally moved in a tremendous way after she encountered King Solomon. Her reply forced me to go back and look at what Jesus said about this particular time in history. Remember, it was Jesus who said, "A greater than Solomon is here." In light of this revealed truth, we must consider the fact she was struck with amazement after seeing and spending time with King Solomon.

SHOULD BE NO COMPARISON

Why should we give any attention to her witness? Because Jesus said her reaction to Solomon should really pale in comparison to our response to Him. Why should it pale in comparison? Solomon was great, but he isn't even on the same scale with the greatness of Jesus. She will also stand in the judgment when the souls of ungodly men are being judged, to specifically testify against them for not being absolutely taken by the majesty and splendor of Jesus. The queen's witness for king Solomon should in no way outshine our witness for King Jesus: "The stone (Jesus) which the builders refused is become the head stone of the corner. This is the Lord's doing; it is marvelous in our eyes (believers)" (Psalm 118:22-23). We must not forget it was Jesus who said many would say to Him in the judgment, "Lord, Lord, but I will say, 'Depart from Me you worker of iniquity.'" (Mat. 7:21-23)

WHAT DID SHE DO?

How did she act when she saw the wisdom of Solomon and the witness of his splendor that affected his entire kingdom?

> And when the queen of Sheba had seen all Solomon's wisdom, and the house that he had built, And the meat of his table, and the sitting of his servants, and the attendance of his ministers, and their apparel, and his cupbearers, and his ascent by which he went up unto the house of the Lord; there was no more spirit in her.
>
> 1 Kings 10:4-5

She was utterly breathless after seeing the glory of God's presence upon Solomon. Her dignity as queen of the South dissipated within her when she first saw his glory. She was absolutely consumed with the fullness of Solomon's presence. Her spirit of doubt vanished when she finally saw the beauty and blessing of his wisdom. Others had told her about Solomon and his wisdom, but it appears she questioned some of what she had been told until she had seen it with her own eyes. All her doubts and unbelief were put away when she personally saw it:

> And she said to the king, It was a true report that I heard in mine own land of thy acts and of thy wisdom. Howbeit I believed not the words, until I came, and mine eyes had seen it: and, behold, the half was not told me: thy wisdom and prosperity exceedeth the fame which I heard.
>
> 1 Kings 10:6-7

SIDE BY SIDE

I want to point out five distinctions from the queen of Sheba's personal witness that will be used by her to condemn men in the judgment. First of all, she was breathless! Her breath (spirit) was taken away at what she saw and heard: "And when the queen of Sheba had seen all Solomon's wisdom, and the house that he had built...there was no more spirit in her" (1 Kings 10:4, 5). She had a personal encounter with greatness and couldn't help but embrace his God-given wisdom. He answered all her questions with no difficulty, and this forever impressed her. How about us? When we encounter Jesus are we left breathless? Once we met Jesus, did we say the reports we heard about Him were true, but in reality He was so much greater than anything anyone ever told us about Him?[127] Have we been taken by the wonder of Jesus Christ?

Secondly, she was broken! Her spirit was broken before the majesty of Solomon. Her dignity fled away and her pride left as she stood in awe of all she had witnessed. She was truly humbled by his glory. How about us? Have we been broken and crushed before the Lord of glory?[128] Are we vessels that are being poured out and asking God to fill our lives with Himself?[129]

Thirdly, she was blessed! She was blessed by Solomon's presence, possessions, perception, and prosperity. She was blessed by the attitude of those who served him. She was also blown away by the food, their garments, and the overwhelming abundance of everything. How about us? When it comes to Jesus and His church, are we blessed by His presence and with His servants in the body of Christ who live for His glory and who are clothed in His righteousness?[130] Do we serve God through the righteousness of Christ?

Fourth, she was bought! She was bought by his splendor, and no one would ever convince her otherwise. She would stand on the foundation of this new relationship all the days of her life. Have we been sold on the precious blood of Jesus? Have we been convinced of His unfailing love that you can't be put on the run from the solid foundation of Christ Jesus? Do we live as slaves of righteousness, knowing our rightful owner paid for our lives with His own blood?

Fifth, she was believable! Her witness was convincing and believable.[131] Her actions validate and affirm her witness about this man. Her actions and attitude reveal a true confidence in her experience with Solomon. Her gifts prove her allegiance to this new friendship.

GREATER THAN HE

We must keep in mind that Solomon convinced her of his wisdom when he spoke to her about God's ways, truth, and life, but Solomon himself is not the way, the truth, and the life. She was sold on a creature, not the Creator. How about us? Can the Lord bear witness to the fact we are convinced of His wisdom and convinced His Word is our life? Let's suppose Solomon won her heart when he talked about God's redemption, but Solomon himself is not the Redeemer. How about us? Has Jesus, God's Redeemer, won our heart? I imagine he taught her the realities of life when he discussed the certainties of death with her, but Solomon himself never died for her or any other. How about us? Have we considered the fact Jesus died for us? He is greater than Solomon ever wished to be, even with all the wisdom he had.

A SAD DAY

Can we see Jesus is much greater than Solomon? Our responses to Jesus should be far greater than the queen's response to Solomon. This woman will stand in the judgment and testify against the lifestyles of those who are not believable about the fact they know the Lord. She will condemn those who reveal by their actions they have never been won over or bought by Jesus. Who is this evil generation of which Jesus was speaking? They are those who have manifested very little interest in the beauty of God's Son and are not blessed by His splendor. They do not live a life of humble adoration and brokenness before King Jesus. And they, without question, are not breathless over His work of redeeming grace. They are people who are not dangerously strong for the truth on the earth: "And they bend their tongues like their bow for lies: but they are not valiant for the truth upon the earth; for they proceed from evil to evil, and they know not me, saith the Lord" (Jeremiah 9:3). Those who are not champions for God's truth now do not know the God of truth and will not spend eternity with Him.

MY AIM

I really think Jesus believed His Father radically changed a life forever when He made a new creature in Christ. I felt led to use the testimony of the queen of Sheba to challenge you at this point as you seek to discover the reasons why Christ came to this earth. It's not my objective to talk you out of anything. It is my objective to point you to the truth of God's Word. It all comes down to this; if I can talk you out of something, which is not my objective as I have already said, you never had it to begin with. No one can convince me I'm not married and in love with my wife. No matter what they say, I know she is my wife and has been for nineteen years now and that I love her. Can I love her more? Yes, and I desire to grow more in love with her. No one could convince me my wife doesn't love me, no matter what they say or do. I know she is my wife and she loves me. There is so much evidence that bears witness to the fact she loves me and we're also the best of friends. No one could make me question these facts. Should our relationship be growing? Yes! I know my love for her will increase more and more as we both grow in the Lord together. I not only love my wife, but I also like her. She knows I like her. I know she likes me. The relationship my wife and I have has been designed by God to mirror the relationship between the Lord and His disciple.[132] I want to help you know why Christ came, but even more than that, I want you to be confident you know Jesus and are compelled by what you know about Him.[133]

EXAMINE YOURSELF

Today, if you know the Spirit of God is convicting and convincing you of unbelief and drawing you to Jesus Christ, I encourage you to repent of your sin, turn from unbelief and doubt, and trust Jesus with your life. The problem is not what you do. It's not what you've done. You are the problem. You are sin and need a radical transformation by the grace of God. God has expressed and settled two facts about you: He loves you, and you're a sinner. He proved these two facts when He made Him (Jesus) who knew no sin to become sin on the cross in order to forgive you of your sins and reconcile you unto Himself. The wages of sin is death, and Jesus paid your debt. Will you embrace His gift and answer His call to abandon your life to Jesus? You will not be saved by things you can do for God, but by what Christ has already done on your behalf. God was in Christ, reconciling sinners unto Himself through the forgiveness of sins, which is in His blood. Salvation is by the eternal grace of God the Father, and it is released through the grace gift of the Lord Jesus Christ. Both grace and faith are God's gift to those who believe the life witness of Jesus and answer His call to follow Him. Grace is God cheerfully and delightfully gratifying Himself through Jesus Christ in our lives. Repent and receive God's grace with gladness and follow Jesus by faith today. The Lord Jesus Christ is a Deliverer who came to set you free to love and follow Him as His own disciple. Never forget, Jesus is much greater than Solomon (Matthew 12:42) and He is worth following!

A DISCIPLE

What is a disciple? The basic or ground level concept of a disciple is the idea of an individual who is consumed with learning everything they can about another person. In essence, a disciple is a committed learner who lives to know the love, longing, and life of a particular individual. Authentic disciples are life learners. The life they want to learn is someone else's life. A learner must be a follower. A disciple follows to learn and learns to follow. Jesus came and lived to make followers. The followers Jesus makes are the products of His Father: "For we are His (the Father's) workmanship, created in Christ Jesus unto good works, which God hath before ordained that we should walk in them" (Ephesians 2:10). When God made us new creatures, He made us into disciples. We must walk behind or along with someone if we're going to follow them. *Walking* is a word used in the Bible to speak of the way someone lives. Life is spoken of in a figurative sense in the Bible as the way someone walks. God has made us His trophies of grace (His workmanship or disciples) so we can follow Christ in order to be obedient to the faith. We're the artwork of God, and He wants to use us to display His amazing grace. How will we display His grace? We will display His work of grace when we are obedient to the faith. Can we be obedient to what we don't know? No! We must follow Jesus if we're going to display God's grace before the world.

DISPLAYS OF GRACE

The apostle Paul referred to this principle on two occasions when writing to the church at Rome. In the opening of his letter to them, he says,

By whom (Jesus) we have received grace and apostleship, <u>for</u> obedience to the faith among (before) all nations (heathens), for His (God's) name sake." (Romans 1:5) He also closed the letter by saying, "Now to Him (God) that is of power to stablish you according to my gospel, and the preaching of Jesus Christ, according to the revelation of the mystery, which was kept secret since the world began, but now is made manifest, and by the scriptures of the prophets, according to the commandment of the everlasting God, made known to all nations <u>for</u> the obedience of faith: To God only wise, be glory through Jesus Christ for ever. Amen.
Romans 16:25-27

We received grace for obedience to the faith in order to establish a witness before the world. What is the result of this grace obedience? God is glorified! It takes the grace of God and the Word of His grace by which we are sanctified to be obedient: "And now, brethren, I commend you to God, and to the word of His grace, which is able to build you up, and to give you an inheritance among all them which are sanctified" (Acts 20:32). Disciples are the trophies of God's grace that He uses to display His glory and majesty before the world.

REPENTING IS GOD'S WILL

Does this mean His disciples will be found sinless in this life? No! The disciples of the Lord Jesus will stumble and act out of character at times, but they will still be used by God to display His grace. Repentance is a gift of grace, and it has to be graciously granted by the Lord if we are going to experience the continual presence of the Lord. Why will we need to repent? Because we are going to miss God's mark daily. Therefore, as disciples, confessing and forsaking sin is part of God's will and part of the evidence of His grace upon our lives.

A HEART AFTER GOD

King David is a great example of a man who loved God enough to follow Him and repent when he sinned. The New Testament confirms what we are told about him in the Old Testament and his desire to seek the Lord, yet he did much wrong. David committed adultery, murdered, lied, and disobeyed God regarding a census, and the consequences of his disobedience resulted in thousands of deaths. I imagine there are other things he did that were not recorded in Scripture. The New Testament describes him as a man after God's own heart, one who would do all the will of God and serve his generation by the will of God: "And when he had removed him, he raised up unto them David to be their king; to whom also He gave testimony, and said, I have found David the son of Jesse, a man after mine own heart, which shall fulfill all my will. For David, after he had served his own generation by the will of God..." (Acts 13:22, 36). This is how God described his habitual character.

KING DAVID

David was a man who God supernaturally brought forward for a sovereign purpose. He also was a trophy of the grace of God. I'm not going to point out every detail, but I strongly encourage everyone to take the evidence I present concerning the life king David and use it for future study. His life very much applies to us as disciples.

We are introduced to God's plan for David in a time when God told the prophet Samuel He had found a man to replace Israel's current king. King Saul was exactly what a carnal nation wanted to rule over them. God gave Israel what they wanted to show them it's exactly what they didn't need. Saul failed the Lord, himself, and the people. He had made three terrible mistakes before God, and God told Samuel He had a man ready to replace him. God, who speaks those things which are not as though they are, spoke in the present tense to King Saul as though He had already commanded David to take the lead: "But now thy kingdom shall not continue: the Lord hath sought Him a man after His own heart, and the Lord hath commanded him to be captain over His people, because thou hast not kept that which the Lord commanded thee" (1 Samuel 13:14). Please don't miss this. When God shared this message with Saul, David, at that time, had not been born yet. David would not be born for another eight years. Wow! God spoke as though he was alive, yet it would be eight years before Jesse would hear the cry of his youngest son. God said he would be a man "after" or according to His own heart. The New Testament said he would be a man who would fulfill all God's will and serve his generation by the will of God. David's life was the product of grace. He was the workmanship of God. Halleluiah!

SEARCH IT OUT

I encourage you to find out the age of Saul and David when they both became king. How long had Saul been king before God revealed to him His heart about another man He had found? The Bible will support what I just shared with you. Think about what David said in Psalm 139 when he referred to the fact all his days were written in God's book before the first one.

For Thou hast possessed my reins: Thou hast covered me in my mother's womb. I will praise Thee; for I am fearfully and wonderfully made: marvellous are Thy works; and that my soul knoweth right well. My substance was not hid from Thee, when I was made in secret, and curiously wrought in the lowest parts of the earth. Thine eyes did see my substance, yet being unperfect; and in Thy book all my members were written, which in continuance were fashioned, when as yet there was none of them. How precious also are Thy thoughts unto me, O God! how great is the sum of them!

Psalm 139:13-17

The following passages will help you trace out the timeline: 1 Samuel 13:1 (Saul's second year on the throne), Acts 13:21 (Saul reigned over Israel for forty years), 1 Samuel 13:1-15 (Saul had thirty-eight more years to rule Israel), 1 Samuel 14:49 and 2 Samuel 2:8-11 (Only three of Saul's sons were mentioned because Ishbosheth had not been born. He was forty years old when he reigned over Israel after the deaths of his father and three brothers.), and 2 Samuel 5:4 (David was thirty years old when he began to reign in Hebron after the death of Saul.). May these passages bless you!

IT'S HELPFUL

How is this beneficial for disciples today? Remember how God described David? In the Old Testament, He says, "...sought Him a man after His heart..." The New Testament says, "I have found...a man after Mine own heart..." What does it mean to be "after the heart of God?" Let's think about another man God spoke to while using this same phrase. God told Abraham He would establish His covenant between Himself, Abraham, and his descendants after him: "And I will establish My covenant between me and Thee and thy seed after thee in their generations for an everlasting covenant, to be a God unto thee, and to thy seed after thee" (Genesis 17:7). God could have easily said to him "your seed," but He didn't. He said He would establish His covenant with the seed that was "after" or according to the same kind of seed of Abraham. He's not refer-ring to their physical nature or lineage, but their spiritual lineage as a covenant people of faith. He's talking about grace.[134]

181

WHAT DOES IT MEAN?

In the Book of Jeremiah, God tells the people if they return to Him in repentance, He will bless them with teachers according to His heart: "And I will give you pastors according to Mine heart, which shall feed you with knowledge and understanding" (Jeremiah 3:15). The phrase "according to Mine heart" is the same one used when He described David before he was born in 1 Samuel 13:14. The words *according* and *after* are the same Hebrew words in all three verses at which we've looked. It means to have a heart like God's heart, a heart in line with what God wants to do. This can only happen at the mercy of God. David and Abraham are two men who had been blessed by the grace of God in order to be obedient to the faith. "For I know him (Abraham), that he will command his children and his household after him, and they shall keep the way of the Lord, to do justice and judgment; that the Lord may bring upon Abraham that which He hath spoken of him (father of many nations)" (Genesis 18:19). Praise be unto God! David is a seed after the same kind of Abraham. God told Samuel what he would do with David and his seed in future generations.[135] Take some time to read Psalm 89:24-37 and you'll be blessed by God's promise of security in His eternal covenant. Read what David said about these things: "For Thy word's sake (eternal promise), and according to Thine own heart, hast Thou done all these great things, to make Thy servant know them" (2 Samuel 7:21). These men are trophies of God's grace. They are His workmanship even today because God is not the God of the dead, but of the living.[136]

WE MUST

We must have a heart like God's heart if we're going to follow Him in discipleship and be obedient to the faith before the nations. The psalms David wrote help us see the life of pursuing the Lord with a heart of praise. The book of Psalms allows us to see the highs and lows of discipleship and encourages us to look to the hills from whence comes our salvation. I'm reminded of Psalm 143, when David asks the Lord to speak to him or he'll be as useless as a dead man: "Hear me speedily, O Lord: my spirit faileth: hide not Thy face from me, lest I be like unto them that go down into the pit. Cause me to hear Thy lovingkindness in the morning; for in thee do I trust: cause me to know the way wherein I should walk; for I lift up my soul unto Thee" (Psalm 143:7-8). David, a man who had a heart in tune and in line with God's heart, knew he was powerless and utterly useless without hearing God's covenant or knowing the path God had chosen for Him to walk that day. This is the heart of a disciple in harmony with God. He had the wisdom to know what to do next. He sought God's face early and understood that God had to cause His voice to be heard and His path to be made known. He's asking God to disciple him. He wants the Lord to teach, lead, guide, instruct, and direct his life. Why or how could he know to ask for such a thing? He had a heart according to the heart of God.

IT MADE THE DIFFERENCE

There were several things David knew that drove Him to seek the Lord and lift up his soul unto God. Watch how this fits together. He knew the eye of the Lord was on those who feared Him. Who are those who fear the Lord? They are those who trust the Lord.[137] "Behold, the eye of the Lord is upon them that fear Him, upon them that hope in His mercy" (Psalm 33:18). The words *mercy* and *lovingkindness* are the same word in Hebrew. It's a covenant word that speaks of God's unfailing eternal promises and His steadfast love and faithfulness to fulfill them. Why is God's eye on them? Because He takes pleasure in those who fear Him: "The Lord taketh pleasure in them that fear Him, in those that hope in His mercy" (Psalm 147:11). Now we know why David wanted to hear God's lovingkindness in the morning. He knew he couldn't hope for what he didn't have. He couldn't anticipate with eagerness that which he had not heard. "It is a good thing to give thanks unto the Lord, and to sing praises unto Thy name, O most High: To shew forth Thy lovingkindness in the morning, and Thy faithfulness every night" (Psalm 92:1-2). He also knew how beautiful it was to the Lord when His disciples took what they heard and declared it right away. He knew how precious it was to give God thanks in the evening for

His faithfulness to keep us on His course throughout the day. God had kept him from the path of the destroyer and used him to honor His name. How did He keep him from the path of the destroyer? "Concerning the words of men, by the word of Thy lips I have kept me from the paths of the destroyer" (Psalm 17:4). Having a heart in sync with God's heart is what kept David from destruction. David knew the works and words of men, which were void of God's truth, were of the destroyer. How did he know this? He heard from God! This is the life of a disciple! They live to hear and follow the voice of their Master.

EVEN TODAY

Jesus says, "My sheep hear My voice, and I know them and they follow Me." (John 10:27) This is His view of a disciple. The concept of being a disciple was not a foreign way of thinking to the men and women Jesus taught. Disciples had been around since the beginning of time. Learners have followed their respected teachers throughout history. In every culture there are teachers and learners and masters and followers. Jesus affirmed this when He taught the principle law concerning disciples and their masters: "The disciple is not above his master: but every one that is perfect shall be as his master" (Luke 6:40).[138] There are certain principles that govern the master/disciple relationship. These dynamics are true for the disciples of Jesus today. There are seven principal laws that can help us see if we are really a disciple of Jesus:

Seven Principal Laws of Discipleship
(Luke 6:40; Matthew 10:24, 25)

Principal Law #1 - There must be a willing teacher/master, a teacher who is willing to invest his life and love into a follower.
Principal Law #2 - There must be a submissive pupil/follower, a student willing to give up his life to learn and live the way of his master.

Principal Law #3 - There must be a common nature. They must be likeminded in nature, with a desire to invest in each other.

Principal Law #4 - There must be a personal relationship, a connection that relates emotionally, mentally, physically, and spiritually.

Principal Law #5 - There must be clear communication that comes through an intimate knowledge of each other's purpose.

Principal Law #6 - There must be life-altering instruction, a specific doctrine/truth in which they believe.

Principal Law #7 - There must be lifestyle affirmation and allegiance. A disciple is not to be above his teacher, but like his teacher.

A CLOSER LOOK

Principal Law #1 - There must be a willing teacher/master. There must be an individual who will make every effort to invest what they know and how they live into a follower or a group of followers. This individual is seeking a follower who will allow him to pour his very life into them. There is no discipleship without a willing teacher. He opens up his heart, head, hands, and home to a learner who makes himself his subject.

Principal Law #2 - There must be a submissive pupil/follower. Without a follower, there can be no discipleship. A follower must be willing to make himself subject to a master. The reason they do this is because they want to consume everything their teacher knows. They want to be like their teacher. They give up their life to follow the light, life, and love of their master. They forsake all previous ambitions so they can give themselves to their new master.

Principal Law #3 - There must be a common nature. Without a common nature, there is not a willingness to be likeminded. Followers of other men have a likeminded nature and desire to be like their teacher. People followed a rabbi's teaching in Jesus' day because they had something in common with them and yielded themselves to their teacher's purpose for living. The necessity of the new birth experience is fundamental for a man to take upon the common nature of the Son of God. Natural man is opposed and hostile to God's ways. To be a follower of Jesus, a man must be born again in order to have a common nature with Jesus.

Principal Law #4 - There must be a personal relationship. Without a personal relationship, there is no possibility of authentic discipleship. Through the new birth and being reconciled with God through the Lord Jesus Christ, we enter into a personal relationship with God and His Son and experience what Christ has come to do. We are connected to Christ and now can relate to Him physically, mentally, emotionally, and spiritually.

Principal Law #5 - There must be clear communication. Without being in intimate fellowship, there is no discipleship. To know what one believes, there must be clear communication. A teacher finds out where his followers are through quality time spent communicating with one another. A follower knows what his master thinks about things because they talk about it together. Clear communication sets the stage for authentic discipleship.

Principal Law #6 - There must be life-altering instruction. A life of discipleship is built on this foundational principle. The student wants to be like his teacher, and for this to happen, life-altering instruction must be given and received. All followers want to be led by their master. Instruction from a master is the lifeline of the disciple.

Principal Law #7 - There must be lifestyle affirmation and allegiance. The student wants to be like his teacher. Both teacher and student will affirm the progress of each other. The student will affirm and authenticate the effectiveness of His teacher in everyday life. The teacher is sensitive to the needs of his follower and discerns when it is the right time to affirm and authenticate the diligence and determination of his student's effort to follow his instruction. They also are pleased to affirm their allegiance to each other. The teacher affirms his commitment to the student by allowing him to do things that would identify him as his disciple. The student makes every effort to honor his master and points everyone to his master's influence over his life. It will always be known verbally and visually who is the master and who is the disciple. Both the teacher and the disciple see it as an honor to be identified with one another because they are not ashamed of each other.

WHY THEY WERE CALLED

In our modern world, the title "Christian" is often used to describe someone affiliated with the church. This title was used in the New Testament only three times, and it was always in association with individuals or a group of people who were disciples of the Lord Jesus Christ. Why did they call them Christians? They were followers of Christ. They did not call them Christians because they belonged to the group that followed Christ. They did not call them Christians because they went to someone who followed Christ. They called them Christians because they were diligent learners and dedicated followers of God's Anointed One, Jesus Christ.

HIS NAME

The name *Christ* means "Anointed One." When God used a prophet, priest, or king to do His work, He always had them anointed. The anointing symbolized the effusion of God's presence and the authority of His commission, which approved them for a unique task. Why did He anoint them? God anointed His people in order to approve them for His work so He could accept what they offered to Him. If God does not approve us in a work, He will not accept what we offer to Him. God promised to send a Person with an anointing upon His life for the purpose of accomplishing a specific assignment. Christ the Lord is the Person whom God promised to send.

ANOINTED FOLLOWER

Jesus was anointed to accomplish a God-sized task, but more than that, He is the Anointed One. God chose to use Jesus to disciple His people for His own glory (a God-ordained assignment). The thought that a person can be a Christian without any evidence that this same person has also been approved by God to learn and follow Christ is ludicrous. All authentic believers are disciples, and as disciples they have been anointed by the Holy Spirit to follow the teachings of Christ: "But ye have an unction from the Holy One, and ye know all things. But the anointing which ye have received of Him abideth in you, and ye need not that any man teach you: but as the same anointing teacheth you of all things, and is truth, and is no lie, and even as it hath taught you, ye shall abide in Him" (1 John 2:20, 27). All disciples of Jesus Christ have the Holy Spirit living within them to guide and teach them truth so they can have the understanding and discernment needed to stay connected to Jesus.

CAN'T POSSIBLY BE HIS

The error being taught in our day is that there is a difference between being a "Christian" and a "disciple." It is actually being promoted and advocated by the majority that we can be a "Christian" without ever becoming a "disciple." Jesus came to this world to make sinners into disciples. Jesus deals with this blasphemy in Luke 14 when He says, "If any man come to Me, and hate not his father, and mother, and wife, and children, and brethren, and sisters, yea, and his own life also, he cannot be My disciple. And whosoever doth not bear his cross, and come after Me, cannot be My disciple" (Luke 14:26-27). In this passage, Jesus is merely stating a fact. If anyone came to Him and preferred others over Him, there is no possible way this person could belong to Him. He is not giving us a command to discipleship in this passage, but facts that would be true about His disciples. Continuing in the teachings of Jesus does not make you a disciple it is only a validation that you are a disciple. "Then said Jesus to those Jews which believed on him, If ye continue in My word, then are ye My disciples indeed" (John 8:31). He did not say you'll be His disciples, but you are His disciples because you are the workmanship of the Father.

In Luke 14:33-35, Jesus uses an analogy with salt to show how it compares to our perception of relationships. He says salt is good as long as it's useable. But once it loses its flavor, we have no problem disposing of it. The same applies with a new creature in Christ, the workmanship of God. Family, friends, and our own agendas are very valuable and useful to us before we meet Jesus. But when Jesus interrupts our lives, they lose their "flavor" in comparison to Him, and we now have no problem properly prioritizing/disposing of any relationship that will hinder our devotion to Him.[139] We are willing to dispose all we have or have gained so we can gain Him. Everything in life loses its appeal next to Jesus. Paul says he counts everything as dung when he views it in comparison to the surpassing value of knowing Christ Jesus.[140] Hunting, fishing, racing, shopping, money, cars, homes, our education, and job training lose their ability to consume our hearts and thoughts.

ALL ARE DISCIPLINED

How did we go from being obsessed with earthly things to being consumed with Jesus? Our loving heavenly Father began to scourge and discipline our lives for His service. All disciples of Jesus are disciplined by God. Why does He do this? The idea of chastening is never pleasant because of the pain and personal conflict it causes within and without. God disciplines His people as He disciples them because He loves them. What is His primary means of chastening? He uses the ministry of teaching to deal with our individual issues that are contrary to His ways. The essence of discipleship is teaching. God uses everything in our lives to teach us His ways.[141] Why everything? Because everything in life is a teachable moment. In doing so, He uses His growing disciples who have already been disciplined by Him to teach His new disciples in the way they should go. His more mature disciples use His Word in teaching because it clarifies, convicts, corrects, confirms, and completes the disciple through a God-ordained process of disciplined instruction.

The Word of God is profitable for doctrine (clarity), reproof (conviction), correction, and instruction in righteousness (confirmation) so the man of God can be complete: "All scripture is given by inspiration of God, and is profitable for doctrine, for reproof, for correction, for instruction in righteousness: That the man of God may be perfect, thoroughly furnished unto all good works" (2 Timothy 3:16-17). True discipleship will always follow this matchless pattern as God uses His Word in our lives for disciplined instruction. Why is God's Word so important to His disciples? God's doctrine is truth that clarifies God's ways. A disciple longs to follow the way of his Master. God's Word also clarifies where we are in the process of growing in grace. God uses His truth to clarify to His disciples where He stands on everything in life. God's Word becomes the tool used by Him to rebuke us when we are in opposition to Him. This intentional rebuke is designed to bring us to a place of conviction over our sins. Why does He do this? He will use the same Word as a means of correction. His Word is a healing balm used by God's disciples to correct each others' lives. Why would we want to get into other people's business? All disciples are in the same business together. Disciples make disciples. Sin is the only thing that hinders this eternal work of disciple-making. When we are corrected and in agreement with God and the business of disciple-making, God will use His Word to confirm His instructions in righteousness. The heart of this process is so we can be used by God to help other disciples live their lives the way God intended. The word *perfect* is the idea of something that is mature or complete. Fruit that is ripe and ready to be picked for consumption is called perfect. The disciple of God follows the Lord Jesus Christ so he can be disciplined by Him to be an individual who has a fresh word of life to give away. This is the type of lifestyle that best identifies with Jesus according to Isaiah 50:4: "The Lord God hath given Me the tongue of the learned, that I should know how to speak a word in season to him that is weary: He wakeneth morning by morning, He wakeneth Mine ear to hear as the learned."

ALL ARE DELIVERED TO DEATH

All disciples of Jesus will be disciplined, but they will also be delivered to death for His sake. This thought process is so clearly taught in the Word of God that it is hard to miss. When we regard the facts that are revealed about Christ, we can't help but see how God uses suffering to advance and affirm His purpose and pleasure. We often will make every attempt necessary to avoid suffering. Knowing we will avoid suffering, God has taken matters into His own hand; He delivers His disciples to death. He does this to release Christ Jesus from our lives. Hebrews reveals that Jesus Himself learned obedience through suffering: "Though He were a Son, yet learned He obedience by the things which He suffered" (Hebrews 5:8). Jesus had no sin and lived a perfect life of submission to His Father's will, yet He had to endure suffering to learn obedience. If Jesus, who had no sin, had to suffer to learn obedience, how much more do you think we will have to suffer to learn to be obedient to the faith? We will have to be brought into the daily fires of suffering so Jesus can be seen through our life. All disciples are always delivered to death in order for the life of Christ to be manifested in their bodies.[142]

How does this all fit within God's purpose? Paul shares with the church at Corinth that we suffer affliction for two primary purposes and one ultimate goal:

Blessed be God, even the Father of our Lord Jesus Christ, the Father of mercies, and the God of all comfort; Who comforteth us in all our tribulation, that we may be able to comfort them which are in any trouble, by the comfort wherewith we ourselves are comforted of God. For as the sufferings of Christ abound in us, so our consolation also aboundeth by Christ. And whether we be afflicted, it is for your consolation and salvation, which is effectual in the enduring of the same sufferings which we also suffer: or whether we be comforted, it is for your consolation and salvation.
2 Corinthians 1:3-6

God afflicts and comforts His disciples so He can use them to see others delivered through their affliction and comfort them while in affliction. What is the ultimate goal? He is always glorified. I like to call this the "Cycle of Life." God uses affliction in one of His disciples' life to produce life in another disciple. While one is being delivered to death to see Jesus manifested, God is using His servant to produce life in another servant whom He is delivering to death. This is what Paul says in 2 Corinthians 4:10-12:

> Always bearing about in the body the dying of the Lord Jesus, that the life also of Jesus might be made manifest in our body. For we which live are alway delivered unto death for Jesus' sake, that the life also of Jesus might be made manifest in our mortal flesh. So then death worketh in us, but life in you.

This is the "Cycle of Life" of all disciples. Paul even reverses the thought yet says the exact same thing when writing to the church at Thessalonica:

> Wherefore when we could no longer forbear, we thought it good to be left at Athens alone; And sent Timotheus, our brother, and minister of God, and our fellow labourer in the gospel of Christ, to establish you, and to comfort you concerning your faith: That no man should be moved by these afflictions: for yourselves know that we are appointed thereunto. For verily, when we were with you, we told you before that we should suffer tribulation; even as it came to pass, and ye know. For this cause, when I could no longer forbear, I sent to know your faith, lest by some means the tempter have tempted you, and our labour be in vain. But now when Timotheus came from you unto us, and brought us good tidings of your faith and charity, and that ye have good remembrance of us always, desiring greatly to see us, as we also to see you: Therefore, brethren, we were comforted over you in all our affliction and distress by your faith: For now we live, if ye stand fast in the Lord.
>
> 1 Thessalonians 3:1-8

Paul, the great apostle to the Gentiles, is telling this church the way they are handling this affliction has produced life in him. Seeing they were standing fast in the faith and being delivered to death was working life in Paul and all those who were with God.

This is how God works. It is a "Cycle of Life." We all are being delivered to death and we're all being encouraged by the life of Christ, which is being manifested in us. Think for a moment about this in your own life. You have watched other disciples go through great affliction and persevere through it with the joy of the Lord as their strength. What did it do to you? It encouraged you and made you press on in your affliction. On the other hand, have you ever seen someone go through a trial they did not handle well? What did it do to your spirit? You were more than likely grieved by their actions and attitude during their affliction. Why were you aggrieved? Because they grieved the Spirit of God, and that same Spirit lives in all God's disciples, who also become burdened and grieved when other believers misuse God's opportunities to turn death into life. Why is it so? God has a "Cycle of Life" designed to deliver us to death to produce life in another. It is how He works. Is He working this in you? He delivers all His disciples to death. Some have to be disciplined during the affliction because they missed what God was doing and handled the affliction in their own strength rather than in the power of God's might. How about you? Are you really a disciple of Jesus?

ALL DIFFUSE HIS AROMA

All disciples of Jesus are disciplined and delivered to death so God can use them to diffuse the aroma of Christ through their life. This is the aroma of life that blesses the Lord and His disciples:

Now thanks be unto God, which always causeth us to triumph in Christ, and maketh manifest the savour of His knowledge by us in every place. For we are unto God a sweet savour of Christ, in them that are saved, and in them that perish: To the one we are the savour of death unto death; and to the other the savour of life unto life. And who is sufficient for these things?

2 Corinthians 2:14-16

The fragrance of Christ being diffused through our life is a miracle. God has done a wonderful and powerful work in the lives of all His disciples through the cross at Calvary.

INTIMACY

As disciples of the Lord, we will diffuse the fragrance of Christ because of the principle laws of discipleship. Intimacy and suffering are the two ingredients used to make up such a smell of life. To smell like Jesus, we have to be around Jesus. We have to be in His presence and in His bosom to give off His glorious aroma of life. Have you ever hugged someone who just put on perfume? You can walk away from them and still smell them on your clothes and skin an hour later. Closeness creates a transfer of aroma. When a husband and wife are intimate, there is an aroma that clings to each. The same applies to the life of the disciple that lives at the feet of His Master. Jesus longs to be intimate with us. Yet sin often hinders that intimate encounter. Therefore, the Lord chastens us and uses affliction to humble us so we will cry out for Him to come to us.

DEFILED

God at times had to deal with Israel concerning their defiled ways. He referred to them as being defiled in their own ways. Living life our way is appalling to God. We know it is impossible to please the Lord in the flesh, yet when we do things on our own, that's exactly what we do: "Moreover the word of the Lord came unto me, saying, Son of man, when the house of Israel dwelt in their own land, they defiled it by their own way and by their doings: their way was before Me as the uncleanness of a removed woman" (Ezekiel 36:16-17). God wanted to be intimate with His people, yet their sin defiled them from such an occasion. God's description is that of a women who has been removed from temple worship because of impurity. Women were not permitted to worship in the temple while they were on their monthly cycle. Men were not allowed to have intercourse with their wives as long as they were involved in their monthly cycle because they, too, would become defiled. Thus, God is saying to the people of Israel that when they were in the flesh and doing things in their own strength, He could not and would not be intimate with them. They were defiled.

TO DIFFUSE

To release the life of Christ, we must spend intimate time with Him. In chapter four we referred to this place as the "nest." We should always be "nesting" with our heavenly Father so we can flourish with His identity. It is in this secret place, the place of eternal release, the aroma of Christ is transferred to us. It is through suffering this aroma is released from us to bless others. We release eternity through being crushed or delivered to death by God. Like a flower, we release the life of Christ out of us when we suffer for God's glory. "Be ye therefore followers of God, as dear children; And walk in love, as Christ also hath loved us, and hath given Himself for us an offering and a sacrifice to God for a sweet smelling savour" (Ephesians 5:1-2). As with Christ, so it is with His disciples. He didn't look for suffering, yet it was His Father's will to teach Him obedience through it. Christ knew He would suffer, but His eye was upon the Father. It is through the crushing of our earthly life the life of Christ's aroma is released.

HOW?

The two ingredients that God uses to diffuse His aroma are intimacy and suffering. These two special ingredients have been divinely chosen for the Lord's anointed followers. The question is not do all disciples diffuse the fragrance of Christ, but is there really a fragrance of Christ or is it a metaphor used by God to drive a serious point home?

I REMEMBER

I've tried to smell Jesus on people, but I don't know what He smells like. Through the Word of God, I know what He looks like and how He acts. Think with me for a moment. Have you ever walked in a room and smelled a candle burning that really grabbed your attention? Something about the smell took you back to another place in time and you could remember what you were doing the first time you embraced that particular fragrance. The smell of the scented candle affected every dynamic of your life. You thought about what you smelled and where you first smelled it. Your demeanor and attitude changed all because of that smell. It affected your thoughts and emotions. Then it effected your actions because you wanted to know what scent it was so you either found the burning candle or you asked the owner about the candle and where they got it. This all happened because of a smell the effected your senses, thoughts, emotions, and spirit. It may not have been a candle, but food that stirred your insides when you smelled it. The point is the fact that smells can make us transcend time and they can affect our life and even control our actions.

IT HAS AN EFFECT

This is true of Jesus! When His life is manifested through the life of one of His disciples, it affects every part of that disciple's life. The life of Christ, when released through His disciples' lives, affects His disciples in a very positive way. Remember, it's the life of a teacher that consumes the learner. Disciples of Jesus are consumed with learning the life of Christ.

CAN WE SEE JESUS?

If we can't smell, Jesus what should we be looking for? I'll suggest seven things we should be looking for that manifest the presence of Christ and produce a life-altering smell. There are seven distinctions that will be a reality in our life when we are diffusing the Aroma of Christ.

1. Our reliance upon His Person and Presence (John 4:34). Jesus Himself was totally reliant upon His Father and His purpose to be accomplished. When we see a disciple living life reliant upon the leadership of the Lord through the power of the Holy Spirit, we see Jesus being lived out.

2. Our rights have been surrendered to Him (John 5:19, 30). Jesus deferred all rights and results over to His Father. When we find a disciple on a mission surrendered to the Lordship of Jesus, we see Jesus.

3. Our resources are at His disposal (John 6:37, 40). Jesus gave up His life at the Father's pleasure. When a disciple gives up all he has to the Father, we see Jesus.

4. Our readiness to be used by God (John 10:15-18). Jesus was a ready and available Shepherd who gave His life for the sheep. When His disciples lay down their lives for the Lamb of God and His sheep, we see Jesus.

5. Our race is His joy and that which He loves (Hebrews12:1-5). Jesus was not moved off the course God had given and endured the cross. When disciples are looking to Jesus and pressing on the high calling of God, we see Jesus.

6. Our report is His gospel (John 18:37, Mark 1:38). Jesus preached the gospel of the kingdom and said it would be preached to all the nations before He returned. When disciples are not ashamed of the gospel but preach it with conviction, confidence, and compassion, we see Jesus.

7. Our refusal to be influenced by this world (John 14:30-31, John 18:36). Jesus came to this world to reveal truth and what truth is, and He was not be tripped up by this world. When disciples refuse to be spotted by this world through compromise, we see Jesus in their lives. When we see Jesus in the face of adversity and affliction, it has a lasting and life-altering

effect upon our senses, intellect, emotions, spirit, and our actions. As with certain smells, the life of Christ manifested in and through His people affects our very being. It is how God works. Is He working in you? Are you His disciple?

DUMB DOGS

In thinking about the report of all authentic disciples being part of the gospel, I thought of something that really bothers me. One of the most aggravating things in the world to me is when a dog gets in the trash and spreads it all over the yard and community. An old dog will go through layer after layer of nasty garbage to get one little morsel of leftover food. They'll dig through that garbage bag because they can smell something in the bottom they want. The problem with this is the dog never cleans up behind himself, yet he'll take my trash and play with it and bring a little here and there. My neighbors get a little of my trash, and I have to go clean it up because a dog won't do it.

THEY'RE WORSE

What bothers me more than an old dog getting in my trash is a gossiper who spreads everyone's trash throughout the community. They'll wade through the mire of someone's life to find that one little morsel of "news" they sniffed out while checking out their trash. They, just like a dog, will spread their neighbor's trash throughout the community, but they won't clean it up. They don't live to bring the good news to men, but frivolous and useless trash that will have no positive and eternal effect on the heart and mind of the hearer of their trash.

BEAUTIFUL FEET

Disciples of Jesus Christ are not known as gossipers. They are known to have beautiful feet because they live to bring good news of a Deliverer who came to set His people free from sin. Disciples are not trash cans either. We normally put our trash in a trash can.

If it seems like people are always bringing you trash about others, it is because you are more than likely a trash can and not a disciple. True anointed followers of Jesus do not have a problem with gossip or becoming a trash can for others' gossip. Why not?

FISHERS OF MEN

What will a disciple become? Jesus says, "Follow Me, and I will make you fishers of men" (Matthew 4:19). If you are a disciple of Jesus Christ, He is at work teaching you how to be a fisher of men. The clearest mark of an authentic disciple of Jesus is his passion and persistence to win men for God's glory. The individual who follows Christ will become a fisher of men. If you are not a fisher of men, you are not a disciple of Jesus Christ. If you're not fishing, you're not following. Whatever we do in life as we follow the leadership of Jesus will be used by Him to help us catch men. If what we're reading, studying, or being taught is not helping us become more effective as a fisher of men, something is wrong with us. Why do I say this? If we're following Christ, He's making us into fishermen. If we're not following Him, we're not being equipped to catch fish by what we're learning. If Christ has not led us into something, we need to get away from it. There are many wonderful truths that will be taught to us as we follow Jesus. All of the things He will teach us as His disciples will be used to make us a better fisher of men. If we're not passionate and persistent in the effort to win souls for God's glory, we're lost in sin or need to repent of sin. Why do I say this? Because Jesus said to come follow Him and He'll make you a fisher of men.

TIE A STRING AROUND IT

Take your right hand and count your fingers and thumb. Most of you counted five. Start with your thumb and use each finger to remember the primary reason you were made a new creature in Christ. The thumb stands for *fellowship*, the index finger stands for *follow*, the middle finger stands for *flourish*, the ring finger stands for *fish*, and the pinky finger stands for *free*. God delivered you from sin so you could fellowship with Him, follow His Son, flourish with His identity, fish for men, and help free them from the daily deception of the world. If you are going to follow, flourish, fish, and free, you must be approved for the work. That happens through intimate fellowship with the Father via His Son.

Life will always be thumbs up if you live in intimate fellowship with the Lord and His people each day. You, like Abraham and David, are His workmanship. Follow Him because He's greater than Solomon and He's even greater than life. Give up yours to Him. Magnify the Lord!

Who Is This New Man?
By Nick Holden
(2 Corinthians 5:9-21)

Delivered from the snare of pride and his own crime,
Freed from the guilt of his past sins for all time.
Now redeemed by the life blood of his New Master,
A New Man he is with no fear of a future disaster.

Changed by the sacrifice of the sinless Lamb of God,
Longing to live and walk where angels trod.
Living in harmony with God and His kingdom plan,
A New Ministry of life brought to sinful man.

Desiring no longer to promote himself to the lost,
He abandoned his pride, weighing the cost.
A New Message he's committed to love and live,
"Christ crucified" is a word he desires to give.

Overcome by the power of God to call on men,
To give their life to Jesus and come on in.
God's power is his New Means of grace,
Pleading for God and running His race.

Being compelled by an amazing work of love,
Seeing God's grace given from above.
Persuaded to abide by a New Motive and Mission,
Living a holy life so others would listen.

Who is this New Man with a true song to sing?
A disciple of Jesus, with his cross to cling.
Rescued he is, living free from willful sin and pride,
Walking with the faithful brethren by his side.

Chapter 8

Magnify the Lord
He's Come to Divide

WE MUST BE FREED

For some, the subject title has already created a needed tension. This tension is a natural thing even Jesus had to deal with while teaching His disciples why He came. It is important for me to note in our discovery of these ten reasons why Christ came that God is the Master of leading us into a crisis of conscience and convictions. In chapter seven, we learned how God continually disciplines His disciples through teaching them the truth. He uses His people and the truth that set them free to reveal to us the strongholds in our minds, emotions that are not being governed by truth, and lies about life that still have our hearts bound in a fortress of deception. These chains of deception must be unlocked and destroyed if we are going to be continually set free to follow the Lord in obedience. God uses His Word to bring us to a crisis of conviction in the process of freeing us from the lies we once believed. Truth is the means God uses to unveil His ways and the deceptions we have traditionally believed and fought to keep. When God confronts us with truth, we have to choose between following our past convictions or being transformed by the renewing of our minds to prove His perfect will. God is the best ever at confronting our core values with His truth, which creates in us a crisis. We can settle it in our hearts now because God uses His people and His truth to demand allegiance to His ways.

VANITY AND PRIDE

Growing up, I was taught to fight back. My dad trained my brothers and myself to know when and how to finish a fight that someone else started. He insisted we were never to start a war but if someone else provoked a battle we were commanded to strike and strike hard. Over time, I learned how to enjoy fighting. This way of thinking cost my dad, my brothers, and me in more ways than one. On the other hand, when I was delivered from the aimlessness I received from my earthly father to the will of my heavenly Father, I learned how to turn the other cheek:[143] "But I say unto you, That ye resist not evil: but whosoever shall smite thee on thy right cheek, turn to him the other also" (Matthew 5:39). God used His truth to confront the way in which I had been taught how to live and survive. This confrontation led to a crisis in my thought process. I had to either embrace God's way or defend mine. God, in His gracious and loving way, confronted me with His truth because I was His and He demanded my allegiance in knowing and supporting His Word. I must admit I have been tempted on a few occasions to smite someone, but I've learned how to take those thoughts captive to the obedience of Jesus Christ. Thank God temptation is not a sin! Amen! It's how we think or act upon a temptation that drags us into sin.

I STAND CORRECTED

The flip side of the coin is God had to teach me what He meant by turning the other cheek. I understood I was called on by God to not personally retaliate against someone who might smite me. But this new truth in my life created another crisis surrounding the military[144] and the concept of fighting a war. If we were called upon by Jesus to turn the other cheek, how could we as believers support the military? Then God used His Word to deal with this way of thinking and show me He uses the military and law enforcement agencies to deal with evil men or nations that exist to hurt others. He led me to see I was not personally authorized to fight back against someone, but others could get involved and deal with this problem. God is the one who has ordained the governing authorities for the purpose of punishing evildoers and rewarding the good:

> Let every soul be subject unto the higher powers. For there is no power but of God: the powers that be are ordained of God. Whosoever therefore resisteth the power, resisteth the ordinance of God: and they that resist shall receive to themselves damnation. For rulers are not a terror to good works, but to the evil. Wilt thou then not be afraid of the power? do that which is good, and thou shalt have praise of the same.
>
> Romans 13:1-3

HE HAS HIS WAY

God used His truth to teach me He has a system, a governing body, to handle individuals or nations that are evil. We as individuals are not authorized to fight back, but a God-empowered system can handle it on our behalf for His glory. The same applies to church order and discipline. Individuals in the body of Christ don't have the right to personally retaliate or punish those who persecuted them through gossip or slander. God has ordained the body of Christ has the right to intervene and confront an individual or group of individuals in the church who are slandering another person. The body of Christ can demand they repent of the sin of slander and be reconciled or be turned over to Satan for the destruction of their flesh.[145] What would be the motive of the governing group? They would do it because God said He hates the one who sows discord among brethren: "These six things doth the Lord hate: yea, seven are an abomination unto him: A proud look, a lying tongue, and hands that shed innocent blood, an heart that deviseth wicked imaginations, feet that be swift in running to mischief, a false witness that speaketh lies, and he that soweth discord among brethren" (Proverbs 6:16-19). They are to turn them over to Satan to cause shame and brokenness in the heart of the sinner so he will call out to God in repentance and be reconciled unto His offended brother and church.

Reconciliation should always be the motive of any action by the church or government.[146]

WE ARE STEWARDS

God had to also teach my wife and me the principles of biblical stewardship as parents of three daughters. We had no clue of God's design for a woman of virtue. Everything we knew about being a family was gleaned from watching our parents and the culture in which we lived. We had made so many mistakes in every area of our lives due to following the world's way of doing things. We initially recognized we had to be very careful with what type of instruction we gave our daughters. God revealed to us we couldn't raise three contentious women and then let another man inherit the problems we didn't deal with when they were under our authority: "It is better to dwell in the wilderness, than with a contentious and an angry woman" (Proverbs 21:19). The Bible teaches us that foolishness is bound up in the heart of a child: "Foolishness is bound in the heart of a child; but the rod of correction shall drive it far from him" (Proverbs 22:15). Every child is born with a rebellious and selfish spirit that must be dealt with as they're growing up. God showed us we can't let our daughters do as they please, have all they want when they want it, and be consumed with themselves and expect them to grow up to be godly women. While they are under our care and stewardship, we must deal with these issues in the Lord as He prepares them for the mate He has already chosen for them. It is our responsibility to deal with their foolishness so another man will not reap their folly.

SETTING THEM UP

God allowed us to see one of the biggest problems in our society is how dysfunctional we are as families. The truth of God's Word divided it straight down the middle. There is God's way or the world's way. We, as disciples of the Lord Jesus Christ and ambassadors of His kingdom, had to come under the orders of our new King. He demanded our allegiance in all areas of stewardship, but especially

in our responsibility as parents to teach our girls and the community of faith God's way and lead them by example. Did this cause a
crisis in our lives? Yes! Did His truth confront the lies this society
used to forge our opinions on marriage, parenting, and the role God
designed for daughters? You better believe it did. We had heard of
fathers teaching their daughters how important it was for them to be
independent and self-sufficient. They led them into believing this
was what God honored and it established a core value system that
was set and controlled by worldliness and not godliness. Everything
God spoke to our hearts about this issue revealed that our way of
thinking was opposite to why Christ came to this earth to put to
death the fleshly pursuit of worldly things. Our society functions to
have more and more. Holidays are not set aside to honor the birth
or resurrection of our Lord Jesus Christ, but for economic reasons.
The only reason our land hasn't stopped observing Christmas or any
other religious holiday is because our economy would suffer. Our
foundational economic structure in America is built on two-income
families. Money and the drive to gain more material possessions is
often the motivation that pushes Americans out the door each day.
Billions of dollars are spent on daycare so we can have more stuff
and a more comfortable life. We all need to look at what motivates
us to do what we do. If God has led you to do what you're doing,
follow His leadership. If other things are leading you, ask God to
help you out of the trap.

TRUTH IS NOT POPULAR

As stewards of God[147] we can and will not advocate a system
that is being used by the enemy to destroy the foundational unit
of society, the family. Is this popular or politically correct? No!
Was there anything Jesus did that was politically correct? He said
He did not come to bring peace, but a sword: "Think not that I am
come to send peace on earth: I came not to send peace, but a sword"
(Matthew 10:34).

We haven't come to this place in our lives overnight. There were
struggles, conflicts of thought, and we wrestled with these truths,
but God in His gracious and tender way always demanded our alle-

giance to Him. We had to come to that place where we deferred all our rights to Him.

God showed me a particular passage of scripture in the book of Proverbs: "The desire accomplished is sweet to the soul: but it is abomination to fools to depart from evil" (Proverbs 13:19). As I looked at God's ways and the world's ways in view of this passage, I realized how wrong and foolish I was to even consider the lure of secular culture. God says fools find it as detestable and appalling to leave something that is evil. When something is evil, it is good for nothing eternally. It is something that has no eternal value because it is actually opposed to promoting God's perfect design. Only fools will find it absolutely terrible to voluntarily leave something in opposition to promoting and advancing God's kingdom agenda. I agree with King David, who says, "Concerning the words of men, by the word of Thy lips I have kept me from the paths of the destroyer" (Psalm 17:4). He also says, "The proud have had me greatly in derision: yet have I not declined from thy law" (Psalm 119:51). The words of men are the thoughts of men. The thoughts of men are turned into the works of men. David magnified the Lord and thanked Him for His Word, which kept him from following works of men. Why was David thankful? God had kept Him from the path of the destroyer. The world's way is in the path of a destroyer. I agree with David; this way does have me in great derision, but God's Word can be trusted and followed.

IT CUTS

We can see how Jesus, the Word of God who took upon flesh to dwell among us, came to divide. God's people are given a Word that cuts like a two-edged sword. The fool can't see any way other than the world's way: "A prudent man foreseeth the evil, and hideth himself: but the simple pass on, and are punished" (Proverbs 22:3). The fool passes on into evil because their view of what is valued in heaven is different than the view of the prudent. God had to deal with our hearts about these things before we began to see the division the truth causes. God taught us we didn't have to like His truth to obey it. We have come to learn through our personal experiences that when we obey the truth, whether we like it or not, we will grow to enjoy the truth. The blessings of God are in being a doer of the Word.

HE HAS A DESIGN

God does not want any of us, man or woman, to be dependent upon themselves: "Trust in the Lord with all thine heart; and lean not unto thine own understanding. In all thy ways acknowledge Him, and He shall direct thy paths. Be not wise in thine own eyes: fear the Lord, and depart from evil" (Proverbs 3:5-7).

The more I have grown in the grace and knowledge of the Lord, the more I have come to learn God has designed women to always be under the protection and provision of a man. This very thought has created a crisis of conviction for some of you already. It did for me when I was first introduced to God's design. I searched the Scriptures to see if it was so. I found a flood of biblical evidence that revealed God had designed all women to be protected by a man. Daughters are to always be under the authority of their fathers, and they, in turn, are responsible for their daughters' protection and accountable to provide for them the care they need. A wife is to be protected by her husband, and she is accountable to him. A wife is a beautiful and precious blessing from the Lord. The Bible says a man finds two things when God brings his wife into his life: favor from the Lord and a good thing: "Whoso findeth a wife findeth a good thing, and obtaineth favour of the Lord" (Proverbs 18:22). The relationship between a husband and wife has been designed by God to represent the relationship Jesus has with His Bride, the church. Characteristically speaking, the church is subject to her Redeemer and Sanctifier. Even the widows are encouraged to either remarry or come under the protective authority of the church.[148]

RAISING CHAMPIONS FOR TRUTH

Life is not about accumulating things. It's not about larger houses and fancier cars and toys; it's about bringing glory and honor to the name of our great God and King. How do we do this? We start by giving the Lord our lives so we can follow His ways and desire not to be spotted by this world. Where do we start? We must start in our own homes and reform our own families. We, as parents, must act on our duty to raise up our sons and daughters as disciples who live to advance God's kingdom agenda. We are responsible to raise disciples who are dangerously strong for the truth on the earth. It is our duty then to be a champion for the truth ourselves. We have to lead by example and teach our sons how to be men who love, cherish, nurture, and protect the women in their lives for God's glory. We have to nurture our daughters to be godly women who will not be ashamed of such a precious and fundamental role as being the hearts of their home. A reformation of thought and a revival of God's glory being manifested through our families should be a desperate cry from the heart of the church during these dark days.

WITH TRUTH

How did this crisis of conviction in my life start in regard to my family? Jesus used the Sword of the Spirit, the Word of God, to divide truth from error in my life. We are told it is considered adultery to even look on a woman with lust in your heart. We are also taught it is considered trespassing and stealing when we look on a woman who belongs to another man:

For this is the will of God, even your sanctification, that ye should abstain from fornication: That every one of you should know how to possess his vessel in sanctification and honour; Not in the lust of concupiscence, even as the Gentiles which know not God: That no man go beyond and defraud his brother in any matter: because that the Lord is the avenger of all such, as we also have forewarned you and testified. For God hath not called us unto uncleanness, but unto holiness. He therefore that despiseth, despiseth not man, but God, who hath also given unto us His Holy Spirit.

1 Thessalonians 4:3-8

The idea of committing *spiritual* (sin of the spirit) or *physical* (sin of the flesh) **adultery** with someone is similar to the concept of walking over a clearly marked boundary to take advantage of someone else's belongings. It is like watching someone cross a fence with the intent to go on another individual's property and steal what they coveted when they saw it from the other side of the fence. Why such a vivid picture? Because this is actually what a man does when he looks at another man's wife or daughter. He has no right to look at what rightfully belongs to another man in an ungodly way. God created the woman to be seen in that way only by one person. God has given her father the responsibility to protect her for her future husband. It will be the honor and duty of her future husband to provide and protect her in the future. Keep in mind that when you reject this truth, you're not rejecting my thoughts but God Himself. God's design is right! God's Word will cut it straight and divide. May we all line up with it.

INTERRUPTED

For twenty-six years of my life, I lived and thought in perfect harmony with a secular culture. Then after being indoctrinated by my environment for these twenty-six years, I was interrupted and invaded by Jesus Christ. He used His Word and His servants to speak truth to me, and my life was in a crisis of conviction daily. My entire life was constantly being confronted and challenged with truths that exposed the strongholds in my life I once believed to be true. The things I learned from watching my parents, peers, teachers, and trusted mentors were now being tested by the truth. This created a conflict in my soul, and I was challenged to either defend my pride or the promises of God. I had to make a choice to either hold on to the lie or let God free me from its burden.

WHAT ARE WE DEFENDING?

This is a scenario that happens at times in our home with our three daughters. When it does, we have a saying we share with the girls. They will get in a heated debate over who has done what in the house. One will say, "I washed the dishes earlier," another one will say, "I washed them twice yesterday," and the third one will say, "I just walked the dog." Then this will lead into more of the "Cain Syndrome"[149] discussions of what each one has recently done. I was listening in on one of their deliberations and thought to ask each one of them, "Are you defending the promises of God right now or your pride?" It was like a punch in the gut to each of them. It took the air out of the room.

WE MUST CHOOSE

Can you see that each time God reveals truth to us we have to choose what we are going to defend? Disciples can choose either way. Characteristically, they will choose to defend God's promises. Yes, they will act out of character and defend their pride at times, but this won't be what characterizes their life. "Therefore as the church is subject unto Christ, so let the wives be to their own husbands in everything" (Ephesians 5:24). Disciples of the Lord Jesus Christ will live a habitual life of defending the promises of God, not their pride. What does the Lord do when His bride defends her pride? He loves her enough to take the water of the Word and wash her. He is also the One held accountable to the Father to sanctify His Bride and responsible to cherish and nurture her forever. What is Christ doing with His bride today? He's lovingly providing for and protecting her because she belongs to Him.

BATTLE IN THE MIND

This conflict of crisis is a reality for all disciples. Paul teaches us we are in a truth war. We are instructed to take every thought captive unto the obedience of Christ Jesus. We can't fight this battle of pride and the promises of God with natural means, but rather with a supernatural work of God.

For the weapons of our warfare are not carnal, but mighty through God to the pulling down of strong holds; Casting down imaginations, and every high thing that exalteth itself

212

against the knowledge of God, and bringing into captivity every thought to the obedience of Christ; And having in a readiness to revenge all disobedience, when your obedience is fulfilled.

2 Corinthians 10:4-6

Listen to this conflict of the mind that all disciples will have to face. It's not just our thoughts we must take captive and bring in line with Christ, but the thoughts of everything we hear and see.

PREPARING FOR IT

This is why Paul instructed Timothy to be prepared to endure hardship as a good soldier of Christ Jesus. Just before he told him this, he instructed him to be strong in grace and to commit the things he had heard and been taught to faithful men who would be able teach others: "Thou therefore, my son, be strong in the grace that is in Christ Jesus. And the things that thou hast heard of me among many witnesses, the same commit thou to faithful men, who shall be able to teach others also. Thou therefore endure hardness, as a good soldier of Jesus Christ" (2 Timothy 2:1-3). Paul knew how difficult it would be to deal with this crisis of conviction, and he also knew every disciple of the Lord would have to face this regularly. He let Timothy know the men he was to commit these things to would oppose the truth at times. They would also have strongholds that would not have been dealt with by the Lord. Timothy would be the man God used to tear down, root out, and destroy before he would be used to plant and build up.

Jeremiah was another young man challenged and commanded by God to do the same thing:

Then the word of the Lord came unto me, saying, Before I formed thee in the belly I knew thee; and before thou camest forth out of the womb I sanctified thee, and I ordained thee a prophet unto the nations. Then said I, Ah, Lord God! behold, I cannot speak: for I am a child. But the Lord said unto me, Say not, I am a child: for thou shalt go to all that I shall send thee, and whatsoever I command thee thou shalt speak. Be not afraid of their faces: for I am with thee to deliver thee, saith the Lord. Then the Lord put forth His hand, and touched my mouth. And the Lord said unto me, Behold, I have put My words in thy mouth. See, I have this day set thee over the nations and over the kingdoms, to root out, and to pull down, and to destroy, and to throw down, to build, and to plant.

Jeremiah 1:4-10

This passage is in the same vein as the thought we're dealing with—with Paul and his young protégé. Jeremiah was at a crisis and was sent to bring others to a crisis of soul and mind.

IT'S HARD WORK

This would be hard work, and Timothy had to be prepared to face conflict and opposition as a good soldier. This vitally important task had to be accomplished if the mission was to be a significant success. Therefore, Paul didn't leave anything out. God wanted Timothy prepared for the battle that was ahead of Him. Why did he do this? False expectations only led to depression: "Hope deferred maketh the heart sick: but when the desire cometh, it is a tree of life" (Proverbs 13:12). If anyone has an expectation that is deferred or prolonged, their heart will become sick. There is nothing more precious than a burning burden upon the heart of an anointed follower of Jesus, yet there is nothing more pitiful than a discouraged disciple. When someone gets discouraged, they get moved off course. Setting a false expectation is a sure way to set yourself up for failure.

STICK WITH IT

Paul is helping Timothy grow in the grace and knowledge of the Lord Jesus Christ so he can help others grow without being distracted, discouraged, and defeated. This is my objective in this chapter. Knowing the fact the heart is made sick when hope is deferred, I must warn you in advance you will have to deal with your own personal crisis and also the crises of others. It is equally important to let you know disciples have a choice in defending their pride or God's promises, but a lost person doesn't. This is why Jesus said He came to bring a sword.

TO BUILD

The objective we should have in the body of Christ is to always build up. Yes, there will be things that have to be torn down, but our objective is to edify the body so we can fulfill God's mission.

And He gave some, apostles; and some, prophets; and some, evangelists; and some, pastors and teachers; For the perfecting of the saints, for the work of the ministry, for the edifying of the body of Christ: Till we all come in the unity of the faith, and of the knowledge of the Son of God, unto a perfect man, unto the measure of the stature of the fulness of Christ: That we henceforth be no more children, tossed to and fro, and carried about with every wind of doctrine, by the sleight of men, and cunning craftiness, whereby they lie in wait to deceive; But speaking the truth in love, may grow up into Him in all things, which is the head, even Christ: From whom the whole body fitly joined together and compacted by that which every joint supplieth, according to the effectual working in the measure of every part, maketh increase of the body unto the edifying of itself in love.
Ephesians 4:11-16

This must be our aim when we set out to help others see God's ways.

GOD DIVIDES

It is fundamentally important to know when God makes a new creature in Christ and anoints them to follow Him through the Holy Spirit's regenerating and renewing work, He separates His sheep from the goats. This dividing of the godly and the ungodly is precisely what Christ Jesus came to do. Before sending out His disciples, Jesus warned them He was sending them out as sheep in the midst of wolves: "Behold, I send you forth as sheep in the midst of wolves: be ye therefore wise as serpents, and harmless as doves" (Matthew 10:16). Herein lays the challenge the disciples of the Lord must face. God is sending us out with only one means of protection against a ravenous beast. They're beasts and they live to consume. They live in order to eat. They live to consume and not transform. They hate good and love evil. They deal unjustly and pervert with equity.[150] The sheep, on the other hand, live to follow their Shepherd. They literally follow their shepherd to live. Their only means of protection is the voice and vitality of their Shepherd. The reward of following their Shepherd is life. The reward of the Shepherd is protection for sheep and the provision their wool (fruit) will bring Him.

TOTALLY DIFFERENT

Jesus spoke truth to His disciples about the difference He would make in their lives:

> But beware of men: for they will deliver you up to the councils, and they will scourge you in their synagogues; and ye shall be brought before governors and kings for My sake, for a testimony against them and the Gentiles. But when they deliver you up, take no thought how or what ye shall speak: for it shall be given you in that same hour what ye shall speak. For it is not ye that speak, but the Spirit of your Father which speaketh in you. And the brother shall deliver up the brother to death, and the father the child: and the children shall rise up against their parents, and cause them to be put to death. And ye shall be hated of all men for My name's sake: but he that endureth to the end shall be saved. But when they persecute you in this city, flee ye into another: for verily I say unto you, Ye shall not have gone over the cities of Israel, till the Son of Man be come. The disciple is not above his master, nor the servant above his lord. It is enough for the

disciple that he be as his master, and the servant as his lord. If they have called the master of the house Beelzebub, how much more shall they call them of His household? Fear them not therefore: for there is nothing covered, that shall not be revealed; and hid, that shall not be known.

Matthew 10:17-26

It would be such a distinct difference that the division would cause many to be killed over their stand for Him. He hits the nail on the head when He says,

Think not that I am come to send peace on earth: I came not to send peace, but a sword. For I am come to set a man at variance against his father, and the daughter against her mother, and the daughter in law against her mother in law. And a man's foes shall be they of his own household. He that loveth father or mother more than Me is not worthy of Me: and he that loveth son or daughter more than Me is not worthy of Me. And he that taketh not his cross, and followeth after Me, is not worthy of Me. He that findeth his life shall lose it: and he that loseth his life for My sake shall find it.

Matthew 10:34-39

CAN'T BE MISTAKEN

Jesus said He came to completely separate a man from others in such a radical way that He described it in terms of war. He referred to a sword, painting a very descriptive picture for His disciples of the effects they would have on homes and communities, which would not be hidden. Homes that used to be at peace and harmony would be disrupted and radically transformed because one individual in the home would be delivered from sin to follow the Anointed One, Jesus Christ.

Jesus came to change a man so his natural affection for his parents would pale in comparison to his appeal for Jesus. Jesus believes so much in the power of His work to change a life that He says, "If a man likes his father more than Me He is not been made fit for My presence in his life." (paraphrase of Mat 10:37) The idea is one that is not suitable to Him. What does He mean by this? He is emphasizing the power of God in the new birth to radically change the nature of a sinner into a person who supernaturally likes Jesus.

THEY WILL LIKE HIM

I've referred to this verse already, but it will be beneficial if we look at it again: "If any man love not the Lord Jesus Christ, let him be Anathema Maranatha" (1 Corinthians 16:22). This is exactly what Jesus was saying in Matthew 10. The word *love* in both I Corinthians and Matthew 10 is the kind of love that refers to a natural affection toward someone. It literally means liking someone without really knowing anything about them. It is the kind of love that draws you to learn and know more about someone. How can we who live a life opposed and hostile to the Lord and His ways be drawn to like Him? It happens through the work of God the Spirit, who is regenerating and renewing our life to be fit, suitable, and comparable in nature to Jesus. This is the result of being made a disciple, part of His workmanship created in Christ Jesus for God's holy service.

WHO?

In Matthew 24 and 25, we see Jesus dividing the faithful and wise servant from those who just claimed service. He warned the church of a future day that the enemy would make every effort to deceive God's elect.[151] He shares that the deception will be so strong that if it were possible, even His people would be deceived. Then He asks the question, "Who then is a faithful and wise servant?"[152] He used three parables to illustrate who would be the ones we could honestly trust. By doing this, He once again divided His people from the rest of the world. He was teaching us how to be ready for His return and how to recognize those who were involved, invested, and interested in affirming, applauding, and advancing God's kingdom purpose.

WHAT WILL THEY THINK?

Now we have been made a new creature and have a nature comparable to Jesus' nature, we are different from those in our home and community who have not been born again. God illuminates and opens the eyes of our understanding, and we can see that which we once couldn't see. We can see our family members and friends are lost and perishing in their sin. We now have a nature like Jesus, who came to save that which is lost, and we also want to see them saved. So we are burdened for their souls and tell them they are lost and dying in their sin. They then think we have gone crazy and flipped out with this Jesus thing, and they mock us and scorn our convictions. Why is this so? Jesus came to reveal us to the truth and make us a fisher of men. Our biological family can't see what we are seeing. But your new family, the church of the living God, knows exactly what you are going through.

A NEW FAMILY

We inherit a new family when we're made disciples of Jesus. The church is made up of sinners who have been forgiven and reconciled to God and who love and long to fellowship with other believers. Why do they love each other? They've been made new creatures in Christ and they love what their Shepherd loves. Jesus loves His Bride!

A DISRUPTION

When Jesus delivers a man from himself and his sins, He always delivers him to His service. It goes without question that this deliverance into discipleship will divide people. The sheep will be divided from the goats—or we could say the godly from the ungodly. This distinction is noted and validated throughout the Scriptures, but seen mainly in the book of Acts. The disciples—or followers of the Anointed One—disturbed, disrupted, and divided every city to which they went. They were involved with uproar after uproar. They went from one prison to another prison. The disciples of Jesus turned the world right side up and caused people to be divided in every community. These disciples didn't go looking for trouble. They were only fishermen who were fishing for souls on the ship of Zion. They preached the offensive message of the resurrected Christ. The gospel condemned sin and the darkness that men lived in and loved. It condemned humanistic thinking and revealed the consequences of self-centered living. The gospel revealed the righteousness of God and demanded the life of its recipients. Man then and now does not want the gospel. The gospel is not what mankind really wants in any age.

EVEN TODAY

This is why the gospel still divides today. If you are a true follower of the Anointed One, you will be a person who is known as one who believes Jesus Christ is the only way anyone will ever have a relationship with God the Father.[153] You will be known to be narrow-minded and a bigot who believes in the exclusivity of Christ and the supreme authority He exercises over your life. You will be known as a Bible thumper because you rest your life upon Jesus and His Word. You will be seen as a troublemaker and disrupter who can't be a follower of Christ because "He came to bring unity and peace."

DON'T LET THEM

Jesus said to not entertain the thought He came to bring peace for even one second: "Think not that I am come to send peace on earth: I came not to send peace, but a sword" (Matthew 10:34). Jesus told His disciples to not let anyone put it in their mind that He came to bring peace. Do not think like that and do not let the culture around you shape what think about Jesus and the reasons He came. When He saves, it is truly forever. If anyone is ever saved, they are forever saved. His deliverance is so uncontainable that He warns us from the beginning everything about our life will be altered. And these altered lives will see to it that other lives will be altered, too.

Jesus' family didn't believe Him at first either. He even said a prophet is not without honor except in his own home and country. He doesn't want us to have a false expectation. He wants us to wait on Him while we work His field. He doesn't want us to procrastinate either because the fields are white for harvest. He knows hope deferred makes the heart sick. I want you to know in advance these things are going to happen. It's not the enemy as much as it is the power of God who has changed your life:[154] "He ruleth by His power forever; His eyes behold the nations: let not the rebellious exalt themselves. Selah" (Psalm 66:7). Notice what He just said in that passage. "Let not the rebellious exalt themselves" is what He said. What does He mean by this? Can we make the rebellious stop exalting themselves? Not really! He must mean we must not let them exalt themselves in their own mind's eye. In your mind, don't let the enemy take credit for the world's response. Don't think for one second this is the product of the enemy. Notice what the rest of the verse says:

O bless our God, ye people, and make the voice of His praise to be heard: Which holdeth our soul in life, and suffereth not our feet to be moved. For Thou, O God, hast proved us: Thou hast tried us, as silver is tried. Thou broughtest us into the net; thou laidst affliction upon our loins. Thou hast caused men to ride over our heads; we went through fire and through water: but Thou broughtest us out into a wealthy place.

Psalm 66:8-12

God has done this work to prove His grace in our life and to provide our lives with His richest blessing. Don't let the enemy exalt himself in your mind, my friend. This is the work of God in your life. So I'll tell you again that Jesus has come to divide. Magnify the Lord! Amen!

TAKING IT SERIOUSLY

Has God separated you from the world unto Himself?

Is He creating a crisis of conviction in your life?

Has He anointed you to have an impact on the world for His own glory?

Are you glad He is correcting your life to be a usable vessel?

Is He using you to help correct others?

Is your objective to edify or be exalted yourself?

What does God do to the proud?

What does He do for the humble?

Chapter 9

Magnify the Lord
He's Come to Defend

OUR PORTION

The previous chapter created a natural tension for most of us. As we continually seek God's face and grow in His grace, we come to see how He uses conflict to advance His kingdom and mature us in the faith. The subject we'll look at in this chapter should create a great sense of trust. The Lord wants us to know He is our Portion in this life. What a blessing it is to know God is our Portion. He is also our Provider and Protector. We are His sheep and He is our Shepherd. He is accountable for our lives. The Father has entrusted the sheep of His pasture to the loving and tender care of His Son.

MAGNIFY THE LORD

The Father cares about the cause and well-being of His Son and the lives He's changed through His grace. We can rest assured that God will protect the subjects of His kingdom: "Let them shout for joy, and be glad, that favour my righteous cause: yea, let them say continually, Let the Lord be magnified, which hath pleasure in the prosperity of His servant" (Psalm 35:27). The Psalmist called on the saints of God to manifest their joy with a shout. He invited those who favored His righteous cause to be glad and rejoice in the blessings of God. He described His audience as those who took pleasure and delighted in God's ordained and eternal purpose that was being expressed through His personal testimony. He said be glad and magnify the Lord because He was the One who deserved the glory. Why does He deserve the glory? He has given both the cause and the well-being of His servant to fulfill His purpose. He is the One who takes pleasure in the well-being or significant success of His servant. The Father is well pleased with His Son and takes pleasure in the prosperity of His Son's work. We are His Son's work. Therefore, we can rejoice and be glad He is not out to punish or push aside the work of His Son, but He will preserve and prosper it.

PROTECTION OF A FATHER

How can we see the hand of God preserving and protecting the work of His Son? We see it in the lives of His people: "The blood-thirsty hate the upright: but the just seek his soul" (Proverbs 29:10). God, working in the hearts of His people, seeks the well-being of His own. The righteous are not and should not ever be threatened by the eternal purpose of his brethren. God's people love each other. The blameless are a blessing to God. The wicked always have their eye on the righteous, seeking to trap and slay them: "The wicked watcheth the righteous, and seeketh to slay him" (Psalm 37:32). The righteous may slip, but the Lord honestly delights in the way of the righteous; therefore, He upholds him with His hand: "The steps of a good man are ordered by the Lord: and He delighteth in his way. Though he fall, he shall not be utterly cast down: for the Lord upholdeth him with His hand" (Psalm 37:23-24). Why do the wicked attempt to take down the life of the righteous and destroy their livelihood? Because the wicked hate the righteous and the righteous utterly despise the wicked: "An unjust man is an abomination to the just: and he that is upright in the way is abomination to the wicked" (Proverbs 29:27). Thank God for His defense. If it wasn't for His protection and purpose, we would be overtaken and consumed by the wicked.

DECEITFUL

The unjust may not always show their hatred for the righteous. They use flattery and other means to cover up the poison that's in their heart:[155] "He that hateth dissembleth with his lips, and layeth up deceit within him; When he speaketh fair, believe him not: for there are seven abominations in his heart. Whose hatred is covered by deceit, his wickedness shall be shewed before the whole congregation" (Proverbs 26:24-26). God warns the wicked man and brings comfort to His servant: "Lay not wait, O wicked man, against the dwelling of the righteous; spoil not his resting place: For a just man falleth seven times, and riseth up again: but the wicked shall fall into mischief" (Proverbs 24:15-16). God will protect His servants from their deceit and punish those who attempt to overthrow His disciples.

THEY'RE HIS

Why does God protect the righteous? They belong to Him, and He has made them the apple of His eye.[156] He will protect them like an eagle protects its young in the nest: "The eyes of the Lord are upon the righteous, and his ears are open unto their cry" (Psalm 34:15). God's eye is on the righteous because they hope in His mercy and fear Him: "Behold, the eye of the Lord is upon them that fear him, upon them that hope in His mercy" (Psalm 33:18).

God promises to surround those who fear Him with four things. First, He will surround them with the angel of the Lord: "The angel of the Lord encampeth round about them that fear him, and delivereth them" (Psalm 34:7). Second, He promises to surround them with His mercy: "Many sorrows shall be to the wicked: but he that trusteth in the Lord, mercy shall compass him about" (Psalm 32:10). Third, He will use His other disciples, the righteous, to surround and comfort His people with their presence: "...the righteous shall compass me about; for thou shalt deal bountifully with me" (Psalm 142:7). Fourth, as the righteous surround His people, they encourage them with songs of deliverance: "Thou art my hiding place; Thou shalt preserve me from trouble; thou shalt compass me about with songs of deliverance. Selah" (Psalm 32:7). In His mercy, He surrounds His servants with His people as they sing songs of God's faithfulness to forever preserve and protect them. Why does He do this for those who trust Him enough to hope in His covenant faithfulness? He is their Portion!

HE'S READY TO GIVE

He also promised to store up two things for those who fear Him. First, He promised to store up His goodness so they might trust Him in the midst of a wicked and perverse generation: "Oh how great is Thy goodness, which Thou hast laid up for them that fear Thee; which Thou hast wrought for them that trust in Thee before the sons of men!" (Psalm 31:19). Second, the Father has sound wisdom stored up for those who understand the fear of the Lord, and as a result of this understanding, walk uprightly with Him:

My son, if thou wilt receive my words, and hide my commandments with thee; So that thou incline thine ear unto wisdom, and apply thine heart to understanding; Yea, if thou criest after knowledge, and liftest up thy voice for understanding; If thou seekest her as silver, and searchest for her as for hid treasures; Then shalt thou understand the fear of the Lord, and find the knowledge of God. For the Lord giveth wisdom: out of His mouth cometh knowledge and understanding. He layeth up sound wisdom for the righteous: He is a buckler to them that walk uprightly.

Proverbs 2:1-7

He stores up His goodness and sound wisdom to feed His servants with truth, and He surrounds them with His presence to deliver and defend them from the lies and lust of the enemy. We have an awesome Defender in our heavenly Father.

NO GRAY

Have you ever considered the paradox of God's defense? One of His greatest measures of defense is actually the reason why we need a Defender. The lifestyles of the righteous and the wicked are completely opposite. Like the truth and a lie are opposite to one another, so are the righteous and the wicked. The word *wicked* is a word that is usually given to indicate someone is wrong. The word *wicked* means "wrong." Wrong is the opposite of right. God deals with men on the basis of what is either declared by Him as being right or wrong. We do not have the authority to say what is right or wrong. The power belongs solely to God. Therefore, to know what is right and wrong, we must know the Lord and what He has declared to be right or wrong. When God declares someone or something as right, they or it are in right standing before God and approved to promote righteousness. When someone or something is wrong, they or it are not in right standing with the Lord and not approved to be or do anything righteously before the eyes of the Lord. When someone is declared wrong by God, everything they do, good or bad, is wrong. Cain was a man declared by God to be wrong/wicked; therefore, nothing he offered God was acceptable because he was not right with God. When anyone is known by God to be wrong, everything he does before God is seen as wrong and also hated:

> The sacrifice of the wicked is an abomination to the Lord: but the prayer of the upright is His delight. The way of the wicked is an abomination unto the Lord: but He loveth him that followeth after righteousness.
>
> Proverbs 15:8-9

> The thoughts of the wicked are an abomination to the Lord: but the words of the pure are pleasant words.
>
> Proverbs 15:26

> The sacrifice of the wicked is abomination: how much more, when he bringeth it with a wicked mind?
>
> Proverbs 21:27

He that turneth away his ear from hearing the law, even his prayer shall be abomination.

Proverbs 28:9

God said the thoughts, prayers, ways, and sacrifices of those who are wrong are detestable and utterly despised before His eyes. Why does He hate their actions? He does not accept them; therefore, He will not accept anything they do, good or bad, because everything they do is wrong/wicked in God's eyes. Their heart is not right with God, so nothing in their life is right.

IT'S A FACT

The opposite can be said about those who are declared righteous before God. They are not righteous in and of themselves, but God declares them right because of the righteousness of Christ that has been imparted on them. Because of this imparted righteousness, they are accepted and the things they do through the help of the Lord are acceptable in His sight. The results of this imparted righteousness go beyond the fact the righteous are declared right; they are now enabled by God to live right. Those who are wrong are not enabled to live life God's way. On the other hand, those who are right can and do.

FIRST LINE OF DEFENSE

The fact the righteous are empowered to live right is one of the most essential dynamics of God defending His people. They are capable of and walk in the wisdom that God has stored up for them. God is the One who preserves their way and guards their paths: "He layeth up sound wisdom for the righteous: He is a buckler to them that walk uprightly. He keepeth the paths of judgment, and preserveth the way of His saints. Then shalt thou understand righteousness, and judgment, and equity; yea, every good path" (Proverbs 2:7-9). God is a proactive Defender.[157] In Proverbs 2, we see how God defends us by releasing into our lives the wisdom, knowledge, understanding, and discernment necessary to deliver us from the

228

way of evil, from the lies of men, and from the following people who walk in darkness: those who rejoice in evil, those who delight in the perversity of those who are wrong, and those whose ways are crooked and devious. We also see how He delivers us from immoral women who seduce men with flattery, who do what they want, and who do not live for the glory of God. Additionally, we see how He delivers us to God's purposes, to walk in His goodness, and to walk in His righteousness.

PLACED IN THE CROSSFIRE

It is this defense dynamic of God which puts us in a position that needs defending. We become a target for the enemy when God delivers us from the path of the destroyer to His path: "Yea, truth faileth; and he that departeth from evil maketh himself a prey: and the Lord saw it, and it displeased Him that there was no judgment" (Isaiah 59:15). When the righteous departs from that which has no eternal value (evil), the wicked (those who are wrong) target their lives. The righteous are marked men and women: "Yea, and all that will live godly in Christ Jesus shall suffer persecution" (2 Timothy 3:12). They are so different from the world that they could walk around with a sign that says, "God is right; man is wrong," and be persecuted for it because this is the message they live.

THE JOY OF THE LORD

Paul the apostle encouraged and strengthened the souls of the disciples in Lystra, Iconium, and Antioch by "...exhorting them to continue in the faith, and that we must through much tribulation enter into the kingdom of God" (Acts 14:22). It was in this area Paul had been stoned and left for dead simply because He preached God was right and man was wrong. These disciples knew what he meant when he said they would have to go through much affliction while on their journey of discipleship. Keep in mind what he did. He strengthened their souls. What are we told about the source of the disciple's strength? We are told the source of a disciple's strength is in the Lord. Their strength is in the way, joy, or pleasure of the

Lord: "The way of the Lord is strength to the upright" (Proverbs 10:29a). God's joy is centered in His will: "…Go your way, eat the fat, and drink the sweet, and send portions unto them for whom nothing is prepared: for this day is holy unto our Lord: neither be ye sorry; for the joy of the Lord is your strength" (Nehemiah 8:10). A disciple's strength is the will of God. God's will, His way and joy, is our strength. Paul encouraged the disciples to continue to grow in the faith and to understand that suffering for Jesus' sake was God's will and they would be strengthened the more they suffered: "A wise man is strong; yea, a man of knowledge increaseth strength. If thou faint in the day of adversity, thy strength is small" (Proverbs 24:5, 10). Suffering for the glory of the kingdom is strength for growing disciples.

THEY CAN'T SEE IT!

The reason why the righteous are persecuted is because man likes being wrong. Why does he like being wrong? He sees no wrong with what he's doing: "He that justifieth the wicked, and he that condemneth the just, even they both are abomination to the Lord" (Proverbs 17:15). His wrong is right to him. Dare anyone to tell him he's wrong! How could he be wrong when it feels so right? How could he be wrong when the majority feels the same way he feels? How could he be wrong when it works so well? How could he be wrong for investing all of his life and resources into his children? How could he be wrong to leave a successful name as a legacy? How could he be wrong to be good to his neighbor and community? How could he be wrong to fight for the personal rights of a woman to make her own choice? How could he be wrong to teach his children how to be the best students, athletes, businessmen, and businesswomen? How could he be wrong to think people can believe in whatever they want? How could he be wrong to live life how he chooses? How could he be wrong to think and know he's right? How could he be wrong to think there is no absolute truth? Why do men persecute the righteous? Because the man who sees his wrong as being right also thinks the righteous are wrong for seeing as wrong what he thinks is right. What is the point of this madness? Those who are right and those who are wrong see life and eternity differently! They see evil and good differently! They see right and wrong differently! They see each other differently! They see God and man differently! They see everything differently! Why? They are totally different![158] Who made them different? The One who defends the righteous!

HIS WORK OF ART

The righteous are the workmanship of God, the vessels of His eternal mercy, prepared for every good work in Christ:

> For the grace of God that bringeth salvation hath appeared to all men, teaching us that, denying ungodliness and worldly lusts, we should live soberly, righteously, and godly, in this present world; Looking for that blessed hope, and the glorious appearing of the great God and our Saviour Jesus Christ; Who gave himself for us, that he might redeem us from all iniquity, and purify unto himself a peculiar people, zealous of good works.
>
> Titus 2:11-14

God and His amazing grace have made His people into the vessels of His mercy.

OUR SHEPHERD

The New Testament provides us with even better promises in Christ. In John 6, Jesus says He is accountable to rescue and retain all the sheep that have belonged to His Father since before the foundation of the world:

> All that the Father giveth Me shall come to Me; and him that cometh to Me I will in no wise cast out. For I came down from heaven, not to do Mine own will, but the will of Him that sent Me. And this is the Father's will which hath sent Me, that of all which He hath given Me I should lose nothing, but should raise it up again at the last day. And this

is the will of Him that sent Me, that every one which seeth the Son, and believeth on Him, may have everlasting life: and I will raise him up at the last day." (John 6:37-40) Jesus reassured His disciples of His objective to accomplish His Fathers will in John chapter ten. "I am the good shepherd, and know My sheep, and am known of Mine. As the Father knoweth Me, even so know I the Father: and I lay down My life for the sheep. And other sheep I have, which are not of this fold: them also I must bring, and they shall hear My voice; and there shall be one fold, and one shepherd.

John 10:14-16

CALLED TO FOLLOW

What a defending Shepherd! He has and will go to great extremes to protect and provide for His sheep. He has made an eternal covenant with His Father; therefore, He is eternally responsible for His sheep. As sheep, our only defense is the voice and vitality of our Shepherd. Hearing the voice of our Shepherd, the Lord Jesus Christ, is the strength of our confidence and gives us the courage to keep walking toward our heavenly Father and His eternal dwelling place. Notice how Jesus describes this principle:

My sheep hear My voice, and I know them, and they follow Me: And I give unto them eternal life; and they shall never perish, neither shall any man pluck them out of My hand. My Father, which gave them Me, is greater than all; and no man is able to pluck them out of My Father's hand. I and my Father are one.

John 10:27-30

IN CHRIST

Jesus is responsible for the life of the sheep. He is also accountable to present every one of them to His Father. God the Father has granted all authority in heaven and on earth to His Son, our Shepherd, the Lord Jesus Christ: And Jesus came and spake unto them, saying, "All power is given unto Me in heaven and in earth" (Matthew 28:18). We are more than conquerors because of Jesus.

SEE IT

Can you see why Paul and Jesus preached the gospel of the kingdom with an eager anticipation and excitement? Can you sense the joy of their expectation in a God who cannot lie? We can trust and expect Jesus to defend us and His purpose for our lives. Jesus, with all authority, has sent out His disciples into the world to call on men everywhere to come to Him for eternal life. He is at work today calling the Father's sheep to their eternal glory. We know that not one sheep will escape the call of His voice. They all will hear and they all will come to their eternal Shepherd. Those who hear and come will be given everlasting life through the provided promise, Jesus Christ. Whosoever will do this, let him come to Jesus; take from the water of life freely; embrace and enjoy the good news of his salvation in Christ Jesus, his Master; and prepare his heart for the kingdom. How can I know such wonderful news? "Then shall the King say unto them on His right hand, Come, ye blessed of My Father, inherit the kingdom prepared for you from the foundation of the world" (Matthew 25:34). This will not happen accidentally. Jesus is responsible and accountable for all His Father's sheep. The sheep have always belonged to the Father since eternity past. He sent His Son, in time, to bring His sheep home. Through the gospel, we who are God's sheep are made aware we have always belonged to the Father. Jesus said even we Gentiles (the sheep of another fold) must be brought by Him to the Father so we can all be one.[159]

TOUCHED BY GOD

They are His sheep, and He is their Shepherd. They know and hear His voice and follow Him. Hearing and following Jesus is their defense! How can they know Him and hear His voice in order to live and follow? They have been created in Christ (God's workmanship) to be subject to Christ. They are disciplined followers of the Anointed One. They are disciples who have given themselves over to the Lordship of their Master and Teacher. They are anointed by the Holy Spirit to know how to discern the voice of Jesus. Disciples are supernaturally endowed with the power to walk with Jesus, and as a result, be His witness. He is their Shepherd and He is responsible and accountable for their life and livelihood.

HE'S ACCOUNTABLE

The prophet Amos reveals the duty of the shepherd and just how accountable he is to give an account of all the sheep entrusted to his care: "Thus saith the Lord; As the shepherd taketh out of the mouth of the lion two legs, or a piece of an ear; so shall the children of Israel be taken out that dwell in Samaria in the corner of a bed, and in Damascus in a couch" (Amos 3:12). The shepherd was accountable for every sheep. He had to make every effort to defend and protect the sheep that belonged to his master; therefore, he would fight the lion who attacked his sheep. There were times when all he had to bring to the sheerer were parts of a sheep. Why would he bring body parts? Integrity! He was accountable to protect but also to prove what happened to the sheep. If a sheep was lost to a lion, he would make every effort to take whatever remained to validate he did not sell the sheep for his own profit. The shepherds were held to a high calling of accountability.

WORTHY TO TRUST

God will hold His Son to an even greater sense of accountability for the lives of His precious sheep. We can count on our Shepherd. He is forever faithful and true. He will preserve the wholeness of His own sheep for His eternal glory: "And the very God of peace sanctify you wholly; and I pray God your whole spirit and soul and body be preserved blameless unto the coming of our Lord Jesus Christ. Faithful is He that calleth you, who also will do it" (1 Thessalonians 5:23-24). What an awesome God we serve. Does this mean we will be free of trouble? Not at all! We live in the valley of the shadow of death.[160] We are continually delivered to death for His glory, as we have already learned. Suffering for God's glory is a given for every sheep. If there's not a battle going on within us and outside us because of Jesus, we're not His sheep. Pride always goes before a fall. In like manner, suffering in this life for Jesus' sake will precede glorification.

> For as many as are led by the Spirit of God, they are the sons of God. For ye have not received the spirit of bondage again to fear; but ye have received the Spirit of adoption, whereby we cry, Abba, Father. The Spirit itself beareth witness with our spirit, that we are the children of God: And if children, then heirs; heirs of God, and joint-heirs with Christ; if so be that we suffer with Him, that we may be also glorified together.
>
> Romans 8:14-17

The sheep suffer with the Shepherd. The lion is after the Shepherd's sheep, and the Shepherd will always defend and deliver His sheep. Read and meditate upon this comforting word that brings hope to God's sheep:

> Now the God of peace, that brought again from the dead our Lord Jesus, that great Shepherd of the sheep, through the blood of the everlasting covenant, make you perfect in every good work to do His will, working in you that which is well pleasing in His sight, through Jesus Christ; to whom be glory for ever and ever. Amen.
>
> Hebrews 13:20-21

ON DUTY

Jesus has been given an all-important assignment by His Father to make all things subject to Himself. Why is this important? Jesus will one day take everything that is subject to Him and hand it over to the Father. What is Jesus doing right now? He's making sinners subject to Himself. This is very important to note. If you're not subject to what you know about Jesus and His lordship, you're still lost. The church (God's sheep) is subject to Christ.

YES HE IS!

Jesus is the only One able to make all things subject to Himself: "Who shall change our vile body, that it may be fashioned like unto His glorious body, according to the working whereby He is able even to subdue all things unto Himself" (Philippians 3:21). Can we say we know what Christ Jesus is doing until the end of time? Yes! He is doing two things in particular: He's making subjects and interceding for His subjects.

Then cometh the end, when He shall have delivered up the kingdom to God, even the Father; when He shall have put down all rule and all authority and power. For He must reign, till He hath put all enemies under His feet. The last enemy that shall be destroyed is death. For He hath put all things under His feet. But when He saith, all things are put under Him, it is manifest that he is excepted, which did put all things under Him. And when all things shall be subdued unto Him, then shall the Son also Himself be subject unto Him that put all things under Him, that God may be all in all.

1 Corinthians 15:24-28

HE LIVES

Christ Jesus lives to make intercession for His disciples. Why would He have to make intercession for us? We are His sanctified servants He sent into the world to do His work. For it to be His work and to accomplish His agenda, we have to be put to death so the life of Christ can be manifested through our life. Have you ever considered the fact God doesn't resurrect anything that has not died first? There must be a death before there can be a resurrection. If we are going to live in the resurrection power of Jesus, we must be delivered to death daily.[161]

TO GAIN

When we were born again, there was a death that took place. Old things have passed away; behold, all things become new.[162] From that point, we were set on a continual path of being conformed to the image of the Son of God. The life of Jesus is the pattern which the disciple of Jesus is predestined to follow. Jesus lived; suffered many things; was rejected by the elders, chief priest, and scribes; and was murdered, only to be raised on the third day for God's glory: "Saying, The Son of Man must suffer many things, and be rejected of the elders and chief priests and scribes, and be slain, and be raised the third day" (Luke 9:22). This lifestyle is how the follower of Christ will live his life as He follows the Lord. In Christ, he is given over to suffer, be rejected, die to self, and be raised with power and victory. Paul speaks about this lifestyle in Philippians 3:7-11:

> But what things were gain to me, those I counted loss for Christ. Yea doubtless, and I count all things but loss for the excellency of the knowledge of Christ Jesus my Lord: for whom I have suffered the loss of all things, and do count them but dung, that I may win Christ, and be found in Him, not having mine own righteousness, which is of the law, but that which is through the faith of Christ, the righteousness which is of God by faith: That I may know Him, and the power of His resurrection, and the fellowship of His sufferings, being made conformable unto His death; If by any means I might attain unto the resurrection of the dead.

When we place faith in the truth that we died with Christ and have been resurrected to newness of life, we can present our bodies unto the Lord for His service. We know our lives are not our own, so we need resurrection power to know the fellowship of His suffering has been conformed to His death. A great picture of this is found in 2 Corinthians 1:8-10:

> For we would not, brethren, have you ignorant of our trouble which came to us in Asia, that we were pressed out of

measure, above strength, insomuch that we despaired even of life: But we had the sentence of death in ourselves, that we should not trust in ourselves, but in God which raiseth the dead: Who delivered us from so great a death, and doth deliver: in whom we trust that He will yet deliver us.

HE'S ACQUAINTED

Whom do we really trust? We started off this chapter with this in mind. The fact that Christ came to defend His people brings great trust and confidence to His disciples. I mention this idea of suffering again because it connects us to the reality of Christ's intercession. He, as our Mediator and Advocate, not only defends us, but He also understands what it's like to be tempted in the world. Christ's intercession is not without His tender mercies. He knows what it is like to live among the wicked. He experienced the temptation of Satan in the wilderness. He is acquainted with our grief and our sorrow:[163] "For it became Him, for whom are all things, and by whom are all things, in bringing many sons unto glory, to make the captain of their salvation perfect through sufferings. For both He that sanctifieth and they who are sanctified are all of one: for which cause He is not ashamed to call them brethren" (Hebrews 2:10-11). He is able to render eternal aid and comfort through His everlasting mercy to His own people with tenderness and compassion. Praise God! Halleluiah! Amen! He is better than we could ever imagine. He is more excellent than what truth can reveal. He is our indescribable and matchless gift of grace. He is the perfect Defender of our life.

But this Man, because He continueth ever, hath an unchangeable priesthood. Wherefore He is able also to save them to the uttermost that come unto God by Him, seeing He ever liveth to make intercession for them. For such an high priest became us, who is holy, harmless, undefiled, separate from sinners, and made higher than the heavens; Who needeth not daily, as those high priests, to offer up sacrifice, first for his own sins, and then for the people's: for this He did once, when He offered up Himself. For the law maketh men high priests which have infirmity; but the word of the oath, which was since the law, maketh the Son, who is consecrated for evermore.

Hebrews 7:24-28

A HIGH STANDARD

The standard that God demands is no sin, not even one. We are commanded not to sin: "My little children, these things write I unto you, that ye sin not. And if any man sin, we have an Advocate with the Father, Jesus Christ the righteous" (1 John 2:1). We are told to be perfect and holy, as our Father is perfect and holy. The problem we face is that we are going to sin. For the child of God, it ought to be their heart's aim to lead a sinless life. Yet the reality is that's not going to happen until we are glorified with Jesus in heaven. This is why John also says, "And if any man sin, we have an Advocate with the Father, Jesus Christ the righteous." Jesus is always pleading His cause as our Advocate. He's not going to attempt to get us off on a technicality. No! We belong to Him. We are His property. We are His body! He is pleading His cause over our life. He is the only One who can satisfy the wrath of a Holy God and supply His favor on our condition. If we want to stay in fellowship with Him, we must confess our sin as it is revealed: "If we confess our sins, he is faithful and just to forgive us our sins, and to cleanse us from all unrighteousness" (1 John 1:9).

HE KNOWS

Jesus knows there is a battle going on in the heavenly realm.[164] He also knows there is a war going on in the lives of His people. "For the flesh lusteth against the Spirit, and the Spirit against the flesh: and these are contrary the one to the other: so that ye cannot do the things that ye would" (Galatians 5:17). He is aware Satan walks about like a roaring lion seeking those whom he may devour.[165] Jesus knows how long and just how much pressure to put on you so you can be crushed and He released.[166] He knows you better than you know yourself, and He is still willing to defend you.

BY HIS BLOOD

We have an accuser who regularly presents himself before the throne of God to bring accusations against us and our brethren: And I heard a loud voice saying in heaven, "Now is come salvation, and strength, and the kingdom of our God, and the power of His Christ: for the accuser of our brethren is cast down, which accused them before our God day and night. And they overcame him by the blood of the Lamb, and by the word of their testimony; and they loved not their lives unto the death" (Revelation 12:10-11). What a great defense we have in Jesus. His blood has worked a mighty miracle in our life. His life has become our life. He is our testimony we want to share. We love to tell when and how Jesus interrupted and invaded our lives by His marvelous grace.

By the Blood
By Nick Holden
(Revelation 12:11)

By the Blood of Jesus
They stood so strong.

By the Blood of Jesus
They sang His song.

By the Blood of Jesus
They Praised all day long.
By the Blood, By the Blood Victory is WON!

By the Word of Truth
They shared the Way.

By the Word of Truth
They saved the Day.

By the Word of Truth
They plan to Stay.

By the Blood, By the Blood Victory is WON!

By the Life of One
They gave their All.

By the Life of One
They stand so Tall.

By the Life of One
They never will Fall.
By the Blood, By the Blood Victory is WON!

HOLY SPIRIT

We can take it another step and consider the reality of the Holy Spirit, who knows the heart and mind of God also intercedes for us. He prays for things in our life we can't even utter. We are weak and need such a defense.

Likewise the Spirit also helpeth our infirmities: for we know not what we should pray for as we ought: but the Spirit itself maketh intercession for us with groanings which cannot be uttered. And He that searcheth the hearts knoweth what is the mind of the Spirit, because he maketh intercession for the saints according to the will of God. And we know that all things work together for good to them that love God, to them who are the called according to His purpose.

Romans 8:26-28

RESIST THE DEVIL

The Spirit also teaches us how to fight the enemies we face. Through praying in the Spirit and adorning our life with the full armor of God, we can face the enemy in the strength of the Lord.[167] We are instructed by the Word of God to resist the devil in the faith and he'll flee from us.[168] The word *resist* means "to stand in battle against a foe." It means to be completely and utterly opposed to the purpose and pleasure of the enemy. We must humble ourselves under the mighty hand of God if we're opposed to the devil and his agenda. Therefore, the answer to dealing with the devil is making sure we are in full agreement with the Lord. We should test every spirit by the Word of God to see who or what agenda is driving this spirit.

MORTIFY THE FLESH

We are taught by the Lord in His Word to mortify the flesh. We are commanded by the Lord to cut off the flesh. I can't help but think about Moses and the children of Israel as they went into the Promised Land. God commanded them to utterly kill everything that breathed.[169] Why did they have to kill everything? If they didn't kill everything, it would eventually kill them. This is a picture of the flesh. We are commanded to make no provision whatsoever for the flesh. We must deny its influence by submitting to the truth.

HATE THE WORLD

We are also instructed to hate the world system so much that we long to be separated from it. We should even hate the garments defiled by the world system, which are opposed to the things of Christ. We're even told that if a man makes a willful choice to love this world based on the information and facts he has about it, the love of God can't be in him. The world system we live in thrives on its lust. The lust for things, pleasure, and success is what drives and draws this world we live in to do what it does.

> Love not the world, neither the things that are in the world. If any man love the world, the love of the Father is not in him. For all that is in the world, the lust of the flesh, and the lust of the eyes, and the pride of life, is not of the Father, but is of the world. And the world passeth away, and the lust thereof: but he that doeth the will of God abideth for ever.
>
> 1 John 2:15-17

LUST

The world makes **instant gratification** its aim in life in order to fulfill the lust of the flesh. The lust of the flesh survives by being *amused* and *entertained*. Its chief aim is to enjoy physical pleasure, and it will pay whatever price to be fulfilled. Why do you think the entertainment industry and sports venues are the single most popular categories in most every culture worldwide? The lust of the flesh is what provides these industries with their platform and agenda. And anyone that has breath can be taken by it!

HOW IT WORKS

The world makes its living to gain more and more. The world wants what it sees. Have you ever considered how messed up our society is? The Bible teaches us pride and self-promotion always come before the fall. The next commercial you see or advertisement you read, notice how each company is promoting its product as the very best. We're not talking about others promoting their product or company, but the company promoting itself to the public. The company pays money to boast about itself. Why does a business get away with doing this? Natural man is led by the lust of his eyes. The world wants what it sees. When an individual stands up and promotes himself above every other competitor, we are bothered by this. We know it shouldn't be this way. On the other hand, because of the lust of the eyes, we allow someone who has what we want say whatever they want about it, as long as there is a chance we can get what we want. We don't care how they do it; we just want what we want. It's called the lust of the eyes.

> Thus saith the Lord, Let not the wise man glory in his wisdom, neither let the mighty man glory in his might, let not the rich man glory in his riches: But let him that glorieth glory in this, that he understandeth and knoweth Me, that I am the Lord which exercise lovingkindness, judgment, and righteousness, in the earth: for in these things I delight, saith the Lord.
> Jeremiah 9:23-24

THEY GET AWAY WITH IT

A company paying to tell the world or a targeted audience their product is the best is completely and totally opposed to the pleasure of God. It is one thing to inform people about your product's availability, and it's another thing to say you're the best. Why will they do this and not let the people who use their product be their source of promotion? Carnal men are driven by the pride of life. They have a compelling desire to be noticed, respected, and overrated. It is that spirit that drives them, and it demands respect and honor. The spirit of this world will insist and ultimately fight for our admiration and for us to pay tribute to its success. People and companies want to be praised with either your adoration or your money.

FEEDS THE FLESH

This way of thinking and living is a natural inclination we're all born with. We can't forget we were all born with an inclination that is bent on evil.

And God saw that the wickedness of man was great in the earth, and that every imagination of the thoughts of his heart was only evil continually.

Genesis 6:5

And the Lord smelled a sweet savour; and the Lord said in His heart, I will not again curse the ground any more for man's sake; for the imagination of man's heart is evil from his youth; neither will I again smite any more every thing living, as I have done.

Genesis 8:21

The only option we have is to submit to God's way of dealing with the world. Our weapons are not natural but supernatural, and they are mighty for the pulling down of these strongholds.[170]

PROMOTE JESUS

The church must be cautious about the subtle deceptions of the enemy. We have become so influenced by a secular culture that we promote our church more than the Lord Himself. Very few soul-winners go out day after day, calling on sinners to repent. What are the people doing today? They are inviting people to "the best church in town." We're not edifying the body of Christ and seeking to save those who are lost, but promoting ourselves. If your church is the best, let someone else tell them about your church. You go tell them about Jesus. We have churches that advertise and promote their church in the paper and on TV these days. There is nothing wrong with letting people know where we are located. Keep in mind that our location is the place where the church, that is blood bought, redeemed and sanctified believers, gather to collectively equip, edify, worship, and sharpen one another on to good works of missions and ministry. The redeemed are precious in the eyes of the Lord because its through them that He glorifies His Father. (Eph. 3:20-21)

LOOKING LIKE THE WORLD

I believe the Lord is disgusted with our way of doing things today. We are all guilty of promoting our churches over the Lord. We must repent of this travesty. We should love and like our church. We should love and lift up our pastor. We should never be ashamed of our blood bought brethren. We ought to want people to come and fellowship with us, but not so we can say we had many people in the church on Sunday. That's the pride of life at work, and not the grace of God working through us. Numbers are people, I will agree with you. But numbers can never be what motivates us. The love of Christ and His life sacrifice should be what compels us, not our church. Jesus is who we should promote with **great intensity**, and not our church.

WE NEED HELP

I love my church and my pastor, and I believe in the vision and mission our church is accomplishing. I believe it is what Jesus would have us to do. What has He called us to do? To heavily promote the purpose and pleasure of our heavenly Father and what He accomplished through the life's work of His Son. Can we do this on our own? No! He has given the Holy Spirit to defend us in this effort to support our Father's will on earth.

GOD WILL BUILD IT

When we yield ourselves to the Lord, He'll work in and through us.

For unto us a Child is born, unto us a Son is given: and the government shall be upon His shoulder: and His name shall be called Wonderful, Counsellor, The Mighty God, The Everlasting Father, The Prince of Peace. Of the increase of His government and peace there shall be no end, upon the throne of David, and upon His kingdom, to order it, and to establish it with judgment and with justice from henceforth even for ever. The zeal of the Lord of Hosts will perform this.

Isaiah 9:6-11

Who will perform this? The Lord of Hosts will see to it everything mentioned in this verse is accomplished. Jesus will be brought into the world miraculously, magnified, and exalted upon His throne. He will increase His reign and rule forever. He has promised to order and establish His kingdom; therefore, we can know for sure He will also defend His kingdom. This means He'll be at work in and through the lives of His servants protecting His assets. This would include His people and the work He is performing in their lives. Knowing God has an order helps me understand how we're to defend the faith.

FOLLOW HIS WAY

God uses His Word and His people to help guide us through the battles we will fight. It is important to remember we can't **cut off** the devil. We can **hate** our flesh all day long and be defeated by it. We can also try to **resist** the world and be totally overcome by it. Why? Jesus came to defend us through also teaching us how to fight the enemy. We're not taught to hate the flesh, but to crucify the flesh by making no provision for it. How do we mortify the flesh? We **mortify** the flesh when we put faith in the fact we died with Christ upon the cross and our life is not our own. We are His slaves; therefore, we must give ourselves to Him to prove His perfect will. We must **resist** the devil and not try to kill him. How do we resist the devil? We resist him by humbling ourselves before God and placing our life at His mercy while being submissive to God's ways. We have to **hate** the world (the system that does not factor God in and is governed by Satan and his demonic forces), not resist it. How do we do this? By knowing Jesus has overcome the world and in Him we have the victory already. How can this be a reality in our life? It becomes a reality when we do not allow the world to shape us into its mold. How can we prevent this from happening? When we trust the Lord enough to present ourselves to Him daily in order to be transformed by the renewing of our mind with a motivation to promote God's will on earth. Jesus, our great Defender, will help us because He lives to defend us, His sheep.

HE'S THE GREATEST

What a confidence booster! We have a great defender in Jesus. He's come to defend His own. Knowing all things work together for the good of those who love the Lord and for those who are called according to His purpose makes me want to shout and tackle the world for Christ. I often ask people a series of questions that goes like this: In your opinion, who is the greatest football player who ever lived? Who is the greatest boxer who ever lived? Who is the greatest race car driver ever? Who is the greatest baseball player ever? Then I'll ask them this: Who is the greatest Interrupter who ever lived? I want to tell His name. His name is Jesus! Jesus is the greatest Interrupter ever. Has He interrupted your life? If He has, you'll come to learn He's also the greatest Defender who ever lived. If He's interrupted your life, it was a permanent interruption; therefore, you also have a permanent Defender. You need Him today. Make sure He's your defense. Magnify the Lord! He came to defend!

TIPS FOR DEFENSE

- **Prayer:** Talking.[171]
- **Devotion:** Devote your works unto the Lord and make yourself available to Him each morning; He has promised to establish your thoughts (Proverbs 16:3).I recommend you let the Lord lead you to a Bible and start reading one chapter a day for your devotion material. Don't let someone else's devotional material replace God's Word. Seek the face of God with singleness of heart and He'll give you a word for the weary (Isaiah 50:4-5).
- **Spirit-Filled Living:** You must submit your life to the Lordship of Jesus and the authority of His Word through the leadership of the Holy Spirit in order to live in, walk in, and be led by the eternal influence of the Holy Spirit. You will grieve and quench the Spirit if your lifestyle is not in agreement with the pleasure of God (Ephesians 4:30, 5:18; Galatians 5).
- **Praise:** God is enthroned and abides in the praises of His acceptable servants (Psalm 22:3). Sing a new song unto the Lord because of the fresh work He is doing in your life (Psalm 42:8). Receive His Word with gladness and live to sing His praises (1 Peter 2:10).
- **Practice:** Be a doer of the Word. It's not enough to only hear the Word. Faith cometh by a report and the report must be from the Word (mouth) of God (Romans 10:17). You cannot accidentally obey God. Take the Word He gives you while praying and through your devotion and walk in it. Let everything in life be a teachable moment (Hebrews 11:6-7).
- **Persistent Passion:** Be diligent in whatever God gives you to do. He is the One who works in you to do according to His good pleasure (Philippians 2:12-14). It's not enough to desire some-

thing (disciple making); you must be diligent in making disciples (Proverbs 13:4).

- **Water:** Live life as an encourager. Take the Water of Life and water others with it and God will ensure you are watered as needed (Proverbs 11:25). Give and it will be given back to you. Whatever God gives to you and permits to be given away, go give it away and you'll always have more than enough to live a fruitful life. Do you want to remember Scripture? Go give it away and it will be yours to have. Give love, truth, supernatural gift, mercy, money, and time and they will be given back to you (Luke 6:38, 2 Corinthians 9:6-9).

- **Rescue the Perishing:** Go make disciples. Be a deliverer of souls. Go forth weeping and bearing precious seed for sowing and you will return with a glad heart during the harvest. Let God thrust you out into His harvest (Proverbs 24:11, 14:25, Psalm 125:5-6, Luke 10:2).

- **Have and Be a Disciple:** Invest your life into another disciple (Matthew 28:18-20).

- **Repent as Needed:** Learn to live a lifestyle of repentance (Proverbs 28:13).

- **Submit to Godly Preaching:** Get under the leadership of an anointed preacher. Love him and his family, listen to him, learn about his life, lift him up in prayer before others, and learn how to protect him from the vicious attacks of ungodly men and women (Ephesians 4:11-16, Hebrews 13:17, 2 Thessalonians 3:1-3, 1 Thessalonians 5:11-23, Revelation 12:11).

- **Invest in the Kingdom:** Serve the Lord by serving his people in a local church. Invest your life and livelihood in advancing the kingdom of God through a group of missionaries who are Christ-honoring, truth-based, and God-fearing. Be part of a church that follows the oversight of its pastor and has a prophetic voice of calling on men to repent as they prepare the way for the Second Coming of Christ (Titus 2:11-14, 1 Timothy 3:14-16).

- **Mortify the Flesh:** Make no provisions for the flesh. Stay away from teachers and teachings that appeal to the carnality of men. If they affirm and aid you in living a life to pursue things the world loves and treasures, get away from this kind of teaching (Jeremiah 23:21-22; Malachi 2:5:7; Is. 66:1-4; Acts. 20:17-38, 26:17-20).

- **Love the Brethren:** Cherish and nourish the saints of God. The truth that is in you and them will connect your hearts together (2 John 1:1-3, 2 Timothy 2:22, 1 John 4:7-11).
- **Use a Creed:** I recommend Psalm 34:1-3[172]. It will bless you, humble you, and keep you accountable. Share it with others. There will be times when you are not glad to hear the praises of God, and it will be a revelation that pride is in your heart and you need to repent. Why? When a humble man hears the praises of the upright, it makes His heart leap with gladness. If you're not glad about praising God, you're not humble and you're living in sin. Praise His name together (Psalm 33:1).

TAKING IT SERIOUSLY

Do you have the confidence you need in Christ to be His servant?

Do you live to make Him known?

Does knowing He has all authority in heaven and earth strengthen you?

Have you been made subject to Jesus?

Do you let the Spirit lead?

Who are you promoting?[173]

Who or what gets the most promotion in your life?

What is promoted the most in your home?

What is promoted the most in your church?

Chapter 10

He's Come to Deploy

IT'S TRUE

He's come! What a thought to ponder! What a life to consider! What a lifestyle to commit to! Jesus has come and He's coming again. We do not know the day or the hour of His coming. We can be sure He is coming physically very soon for His church. The angels comforted the disciples by affirming this eternal truth to them on the day of Christ's ascension into heaven:

> And while they looked steadfastly toward heaven as He went up, behold, two men stood by them in white apparel; Which also said, Ye men of Galilee, why stand ye gazing up into heaven? this same Jesus, which is taken up from you into heaven, shall so come in like manner as ye have seen Him go into heaven.
>
> Acts 1:10-11

HE'LL BE BACK

Jesus told His disciples He was going to prepare a place for them. This truth implied He would also come back to get them.

Let not your heart be troubled: ye believe in God, believe also in Me. In My Father's house are many mansions: if it were not so, I would have told you. I go to prepare a place for you. And if I go and prepare a place for you, I will come again, and receive you unto Myself; that where I am, there ye may be also. And whither I go ye know, and the way ye know. Thomas saith unto Him, Lord, we know not whither thou goest; and how can we know the way? Jesus saith unto Him, I am the way, the truth, and the life: no man cometh unto the Father, but by Me.

John 14:1-7

With this thought placed before us, we must consider the reality of this truth as being a fundamental element of the gospel. Why would I say it's a fundamental element of the gospel?

A LIVING HOPE

Peter, writing to a group of believers who were pressing on through heavy persecution, confirmed what they already knew regarding the hope by which they were saved. He made every effort to comfort the brethren with the truth about their current position in Christ and their assured future with Him: "Blessed be the God and Father of our Lord Jesus Christ, which according to His abundant mercy hath begotten us again unto a lively hope by the resurrection of Jesus Christ from the dead, to an inheritance incorruptible, and undefiled, and that fadeth not away, reserved in heaven for you, who are kept by the power of God through faith unto salvation ready to be revealed in the last time" (1 Peter 1:3-5). He goes on to affirm what they already know and the truth that is sustaining them in this trial:

Wherein ye greatly rejoice, though now for a season, if need be, ye are in heaviness through manifold temptations: That the trial of your faith, being much more precious than of gold that perisheth, though it be tried with fire, might be found unto praise and honour and glory at the appearing of Jesus Christ: Whom having not seen, ye love; in whom, though now ye see Him not, yet believing, ye rejoice with joy unspeakable and full of glory.

1 Peter 1:6-8

This is the lively hope we have in Christ that we embraced and experience through the gospel. What is the "wherein" that Peter said "they greatly rejoice over?" It is the truth about their deliverance from sin through the new birth, to an inheritance that is incorruptible, undefiled, everlasting, and reserved for them in heaven. It is ready to be revealed at any time. This is what they were rejoicing over. They were looking for Jesus. He's the One they trust and love. He promised He was coming back for them. Peter also encouraged them to look for more grace at the revelation of Jesus Christ. He even insisted they eagerly look for it without wavering, having already been persuaded about it through the gospel:

Unto whom (prophets) it was revealed, that not unto themselves, but unto us they did minister the things, which are now reported unto you by them that have preached the gospel unto you with the Holy Ghost sent down from heaven; which things the angels desire to look into. Wherefore gird up the loins of your mind, be sober, and hope to the end for the grace that is to be brought unto you at the revelation of Jesus Christ.

1 Peter 1:12-13

UNMOVED

Paul, in the same vein, affirms this identical principle when he writes to the church at Colossae: "We give thanks to God and the Father of our Lord Jesus Christ, praying always for you, since we heard of your faith in Christ Jesus, and of the love which ye have to all the saints, for the hope which is laid up for you in heaven, whereof ye heard before in the word of the truth of the gospel..." (Colossians 1:3-5). He goes on to say to the church at Colossae this is such a fundamental truth that if one is moved away from it, it is evident they have never been delivered to such a great expectation: "If ye continue in the faith grounded and settled, and be not moved away from the hope of the gospel, which ye have heard, and which was preached to every creature which is under heaven; whereof I Paul am made a minister" (Colossians 1:23). This passage helps us to see the power of the gospel in radically changing a life. We go from living with our eyes on the world to living in the light of the return of Jesus.

IN HOPE

The Scriptures validate we were saved in this hope. Even all creation, which was subjected to futility as a result of the fall, groans and eagerly waits for the revealing of Jesus and His people:[174]

> And not only they, but ourselves also, which have the first-fruits of the Spirit, even we ourselves groan within ourselves, waiting for the adoption, to wit, the redemption of our body. For we are saved by hope: but hope that is seen is not hope: for what a man seeth, why doth he yet hope for? But if we hope for that we see not, then do we with patience wait for it.
>
> Romans 8:23-25

This hope was established in the life of all believers through the gospel Jesus said would be preached until He returns. He promised to come for us. Yet He also promised the gospel would be preached to all the nations: "And this gospel of the kingdom shall be preached in all the world for a witness unto all nations; and then shall the end come" (Matthew 24:14).

GOD'S WAY

Why does the gospel of the kingdom have to be preached? God has chosen the method of preaching to save sinners. The emphasis is not on the preaching, but on the foolishness of the message that is preached. The gospel is a stumbling block to Jews and foolish to the Greeks. To the religious, it is too easy for them, so they stumble all around it. And to the intellectual it is foolish nonsense and disregarded as fables of no value. But God chose preaching and the gospel as the means to call His sheep to repentance and humble service through faith. God, in His wisdom, chose this way in particular so no man could come to know Him in any other way. Through the gospel, God has shown us just how foolish the wisdom of the world really is:

> Where is the wise? where is the scribe? where is the disputer of this world? hath not God made foolish the wisdom of this world? For after that in the wisdom of God the world by wisdom knew not God, it pleased God by the foolishness of preaching to save them that believe. For the Jews require a sign, and the Greeks seek after wisdom: But we preach Christ crucified, unto the Jews a stumbling block, and unto the Greeks foolishness; But unto them which are called, both Jews and Greeks, Christ the power of God, and the wisdom of God. Because the foolishness of God is wiser than men; and the weakness of God is stronger than men.
>
> 1 Corinthians 1:20-25

The gospel is the power of God to unveil to His sheep their eternal salvation through Christ Jesus: "For I am not ashamed of the gospel of Christ: for it is the power of God unto salvation to every one that believeth; to the Jew first, and also to the Greek. For therein is the righteousness of God revealed from faith to faith: as it is written, The just shall live by faith" (Romans 1:16-17).

HIS MESSAGE

God has chosen both the method of preaching and the message that is to be preached. Since He has chosen both the method and the message, we can see how important it is He should also choose the messengers. It is His message and method, and they are His messengers. It is true we must hear God's gospel to be saved, and it is also true someone has to be sent by God to preach His saving message.

God uses Paul to affirm His method of preaching and that He is still sending out His messengers in Romans:

> How then shall they call on Him in whom they have not believed? and how shall they believe in Him of whom they have not heard? and how shall they hear without a preacher? And how shall they preach, except they be sent? as it is written, How beautiful are the feet of them that preach the gospel of peace, and bring glad tidings of good things! But they have not all obeyed the gospel. For Esaias saith, Lord, who hath believed our report? So then faith cometh by hearing, and hearing by the word of God.
>
> Romans 10:14-17

Who are the preachers? I must say they are anyone who has been made a new creature in Christ Jesus. God has set apart for Himself certain men to preach and teach in order to equip the other missionary preachers (disciples) for the work of ministry. But He has commissioned all His servants to preach the gospel. Christ came to deploy all His delivered disciples into His harvest.

COMMISSIONED

Jesus closed out His earthly ministry with a commission:

> And Jesus came and spake unto them, saying, All power is given unto Me in heaven and in earth. Go ye therefore, and teach all nations, baptizing them in the name of the Father, and of the Son, and of the Holy Ghost: Teaching them to observe all things whatsoever I have commanded you: and, lo, I am with you always, even unto the end of the world. Amen.
>
> Matthew 28:18

Just as Jesus closed out His earthy ministry, I want to close out this book with an urgent command to go preach the gospel of the kingdom and teach those things which concern the Lord Jesus

Christ.[175] I believe Jesus Christ came to deploy His champions for truth without hesitation or reservation. He did come to defer, define, declare, demonstrate, destroy, deliver, disciple, divide, and defend so He could deploy His troops into the war over the souls of men and women, boy and girls. On more than one occasion we have been commanded and commissioned with authority and power to make disciples for God's glory.

AUTHORIZATION NEEDED

If we're not fishing, we're not following! If we're not following, we're in unauthorized territory. Jesus has been granted all authority, and He authorizes us to go make disciples. We are not authorized to live and do what we want. We have the delegated responsibility to rescue the perishing. We can neglect that responsibility, but we will never get away from being accountable to rescue the perishing.

BLESSED

During one of our recent revival meetings, we saw firsthand the reality of the consequences of going in an unauthorized area. The church we were serving was near a beautiful lake. There was a family in the church who owned a very spacious and pleasant lake house that was only three miles from the church. This family was very kind and generous to open up their house to us. They opened the doors to the lake house and invited us to stay there while we were in the meeting with them that week. It was absolutely beautiful and a blessing. The house sat on a small peninsula in the lake and had water on all three sides. They took us on a tour of the lake, fed us fish, and did many other things. They treated us just like kings.

WARNED

During our tour of the lake, they pointed out an unauthorized swimming area about two hundred yards from the house. Our tour guide mentioned a young man had drowned in the area within the last year. It was roped off and had signs posted in all the right places, but people would often ignore the warnings and go swimming. The reason it was unauthorized and roped off was because it was an area used as a reservoir for community water. In the center of the reservoir area there was a tower that was used to open and close valves to regulate water as needed. Within about fifty to seventy-five yards of this tower was a drop-off of about one hundred feet. This drop off had a natural current that pulled water toward it even though the water was barely making it over the side. They had this area roped off so boaters and swimmers would stay out.

TRAGEDY STRUCK

On that Tuesday night of the meeting while we were in the midst of seeking God's face for revival, there were some young men who decided they would go swimming in this unauthorized area. While we were learning how to follow Jesus so we could rescue the perishing, one of the young men drowned. A family would have to face the reality of death.

SAW THE LIGHTS

None of us at the time knew anything about it. We fellowshipped after the service and eventually made our way back to the lake house at around 9:30 p.m. We noticed lights all along the levy and near the unauthorized area when we made it home. We wondered what was going on. The thought crossed our minds they might be gigging for frogs or even fishing. The thought did cross our minds that someone might have drowned and they were searching for the body. We had no clue what was really happening. We couldn't see any cars or rescue personal, so we stayed in and went to bed at around 12:30 a.m.

BAD NEWS

The following morning we received the news that a young man had drowned and they were in the process of locating and recovering his body. People far and wide came in to help with the recovery. The intense involvement of several rescue and police units from other parishes became very noticeable. All we could do was pray for the family and everyone else involved.

OBLIVIOUS

What I didn't know was that the pastor of the church I was preaching in and many others were stationed on the other side of the levy all night. We couldn't see them because of the levy. We were oblivious to the reality there was a rescue effort in process. We slept while others spent all night looking for someone for whom they loved and cared. We were ignorant of what was happening.

WE NEEDED A WORD

The following day, I sought the face of the Lord to give me a word for the people of that community and for my family. I knew I would be standing before a community of believers who had been stunned by the death of one of their own and would need to hear from God in regards to this tragedy. The Lord laid Proverbs 24:11 upon my heart all day: "If thou forbear to deliver them that are drawn unto death, and those that are ready to be slain; If thou sayest, Behold, we knew it not; doth not He that pondereth the heart consider it? and He that keepeth thy soul, doth not He know it? and shall not He render to every man according to his works?" (Proverbs 24:11-12). This passage burned in my heart like a fire. I had to call on God's people to wake up to the reality that people are drowning all around us in the sea of self-centered living. The Chief Lifeguard has blown His whistle to **awaken** and **alert** His rescuers that sinners are sinking into the open waters, and the depths of eternal separation and damnation are impossible to overcome by a drowning sinner. I was convinced that God was going to clearly speak to His people.

A COVENANT RENEWAL

There was a cloud of suspense that hovered over the service that evening. I'm sure there was talk amongst the people about the reality of suddenly losing a loved one and how sympathetic they felt for the family that has to now bury a son, brother, and friend. But up until I stood in the pulpit there was not a word mentioned about the drowning in the service. I sensed the pastor was using discernment and discretion about how he would minister to his church and community. He knew something I didn't know about those in attendance that night. In the congregation was one of the young men who had been swimming with the young man when he drowned. I was informed after the service that this young man had made every effort to pull him from the destructive waters. I preached Proverbs 24:11-12 and it was a very quiet service. The people were taken by the reality of the parallel between what had taken place the evening before and how people all around us are living in unauthorized lifestyles of sin. They responded to God's call to renew their covenant commitments to the great commission. The majority stepped out and bound themselves together to live a life committed to rescuing the perishing. I can only assume that it was a night that many will use as a landmark to remember that they have been saved to be spent for God's glory. **"For the Son of man is come to seek and to save that which was lost." (Luke 19:10)**

RESCUED TO RESCUE

We have been rescued to become a follower of Jesus and to rescue the perishing. Many times we are oblivious to the fact there are countless amounts of people who are avoiding all the warning signs in life and swimming deep in the mire of sin and shame. We have been called on by God to rescue them. Yes, they are drawn toward death. Yes, they are stumbling to the slaughter. Yes, they are living in an authorized area. But we can't let them drown in it and gather the forces afterward to look for and investigate what happened. No! We must rescue the perishing before they die in their sins. We are responsible and accountable to God and man to do so. Can we neglect this responsibility? Yes! Will we be held accountable if we do? Yes! We must increase our intensity and involvement in this rescue effort.

Why Do You Watch?
By Nick Holden

I've often asked that question too,
I'm not ashamed, I must tell you.
Watching each night from my perfect view,
Weeks I worked without one rescue.

Wondering why I came this way,
Maybe to help someone someday.
Month after month, though here I stay,
Watching the waters, day by day.

Then I watched a ship draw near,
Moving closer to the shore I fear.
I signaled my light, "Port, port now steer!"
Praise God, I watched her sail clear.

Why watch each night from my perfect view,
I'm not ashamed, I must tell you.
Though I've only help save a few,
I'll never, never forget my first rescue.

Have you gone to sleep on Jesus and been utterly oblivious to the fact you work with, live around, and go to school and church with people who are drowning in sin? It's time to wake up. You have been saved to be a rescuer. Live like one! If you're not seeing lost people, you're not looking. Amen!

WE NOTICE

We recently bought a new car. After we purchased our new vehicle, we started to notice how many more of them were on the highways. Has this ever happened to you? When we get something new, we start noticing it everywhere. Before we bought it, we rarely ever noticed it. The same principle applies to lost souls. When God allows us to really see a sinner drowning in his sin, we'll start seeing sinners everywhere. The reason why we are not noticing sinners is because we have not taken on the personal ownership of being a rescuer. When we take possession of something, we start noticing it everywhere.

AN EYE TO SEE

When professional painters walk in a room they have a trained eye to immediately notice the level of expertise of the individual who painted that room. Skilled craftsmen have an eye for quality workmanship and they can pick up all the flaws in a newly built house. Musicians who have perfect pitch will hear every mistake an instrumentalist or vocalist makes. Trained lifeguards see the signs of a swimmer in distress before others ever notice their swimming buddy is in trouble. Soul-winners see sinners dying in their sins while others see them as lifelong friends, co-workers, neighbors, and strangers living life the best way they know how. We all have an eye trained to see something. What is our eye trained to see?

WHAT DO YOU THINK OF?

When you hear the name Ford, what do you automatically think of? What do you think about when you hear the name Toyota? What do you think about when you hear the name Peavey or Dell? What do you automatically think about when you hear the word *disciple*? Most people normally respond to this last question with the name or label of "Christian." Yet with the other questions, they probably thought of things the company does. For example, with Ford and Toyota, they would say the first thing they thought of was cars or trucks. With Peavey or Dell, they would think about amps, speakers, electronics, and computers. Why? In general, we associate people or companies with what they do and not who they are. Yet when I say the word *disciple*, most believers automatically think about who they are—Christians—and not what they do. Why is this? It is because they see very little disciple-making happening and they don't have an eye trained to look for it. The reason we think of cars and trucks with Ford is because we see Ford cars and trucks everywhere. Most professing believers see little to no disciple-making going on today. If Ford exists to make cars, what do disciples exist to do? If Ford doesn't make cars, they make no money. If disciples do not make disciples, they do not glorify God.

WHAT ARE THEY?

What is Ford Motor Company? It is an automobile manufacturing company, but it is more than that. It is the manifest vision of Henry Ford. Ford Motor Company is the reality of Henry Ford's vision. Walt Disney World is the manifest vision of Walt Disney. There is no doubt that each of these companies have taken the vision of their founder and possibly created something the original visionary did not intend to do. That happens with all visions when passed down from one generation to another. Wal-Mart is an expression of Sam Walton's visionary capabilities.

What is a disciple of the Lord Jesus Christ? It is a new creation! It is a Christian or an anointed follower of Christ, the Anointed One! A disciple is more than just a Christian. It is the manifest evidence of the vision of God. The Bible calls all disciples the workmanship of God created in Christ Jesus: "For we are His workmanship, created in Christ Jesus unto good works, which God hath before ordained that we should walk in them" (Ephesians 2:10). Disciples are the workmanship (manifest evidence or reality of God's vision) of God. Are you an authentic representation of God's vision for His new creation? Are you following the call of Jesus? Are you a fisher of men? Are you seeing sinners in need of rescuing? Are you rescuing the perishing?

GIVEN THE MEANS

When anyone is made a new creature in Christ Jesus, God commits to them the ministry and message of reconciliation.

Therefore if any man be in Christ, he is a new creature: old things are passed away; behold, all things are become new. And all things are of God, who hath reconciled us to Himself by Jesus Christ, and hath given to us the ministry of reconciliation; To wit, that God was in Christ, reconciling the world unto Himself, not imputing their trespasses unto them; and hath committed unto us the word of reconciliation. Now then we are ambassadors for Christ, as though God did beseech you by us: we pray you in Christ's stead, be ye reconciled to God. For He hath made Him to be sin for us, who knew no sin; that we might be made the righteousness of God in Him.

2 Corinthians 5:17-21

If God is at work in your life, this will be a distinct reality. He will use you to plead with the men and women of this world to be saved from this perverse generation in which we live. If you are not burdened by the eternal condition of a lost world, you need Jesus yourself. If you believe the preaching of the gospel is for others to do and not for you, you are still lost in your sins. If you are not a deliverer of souls, you are a false witness and are perishing in your iniquity and unbelief: "A true witness delivereth souls: but a deceitful witness speaketh lies" (Proverbs 14:25). I'm not going to tell you a lie. If you have never been purposeful and intentional in making disciples, you are perishing in your sins. If you had been a disciple-maker in the past and you're not at work making disciples for God's glory at this time in your life, you are acting like a fool. No matter how you look at it, you need to repent and get right with God.

HE WON'T GIVE IT

God gives us a wise warning in the book of Proverbs about giving a message to a fool: "He that sendeth a message by the hand of a fool cutteth off the feet, and drinketh damage" (Proverbs 26:6). God does not tell us to do something He Himself does not practice. No! He's teaching us how He works, and He desires us to do the same. Giving a message to a fool is a foolish idea. It will only hurt you in the end. Paul says God gives His servants a message. The gospel is the message He gives to His servants. If you know you belong to the

Lord and you're not preaching the gospel, you must be acting like a fool. You have room for repentance. If God will perhaps grant you repentance, He will also give you a responsibility to preach Jesus. Examine yourself and see if you have ever been commissioned and compelled to preach Jesus Christ to a lost and dying world. If you haven't, you're still lost! If you have, thank Him, repent, and get out into the harvest.

COMPELLED

Paul tells us why the soul winner does what he does. The love of Christ Jesus compels him. Knowing what Christ has done and embracing the fact He died for us while we were still in sin truly does compel the believer to live for Him who died to be Lord over our lives: "For the love of Christ constraineth us; because we thus judge, that if one died for all, then were all dead: And that He died for all, that they which live should not henceforth live unto themselves, but unto Him which died for them, and rose again" (2 Corinthians 5:14-15). Once reflected and meditated upon, the compelling truth of Christ's love will cause anyone to lay down their life and receive the call to preach Jesus to the whole world. The Lamb of God suffered and bled for the souls of men, and we must let them know what He's come to do. Jesus lived, died, rose again, and lives forever more to be Lord over His people: "For to this end Christ both died, and rose, and revived, that He might be Lord both of the dead and living" (Romans 14:9). The Lord came to deploy all of His servants into the battle.

PREACH OR BE PREACHED TO

If you are still not persuaded about this truth that you should be preaching Jesus, you are in real eternal trouble. Because either you are a preacher of Jesus Christ or you desperately need a preacher sent by Him to rescue you from yourself. I tell you this in love. The culture in which we live preaches another Jesus. Listen to the Jesus of the Bible:

And when He had called the people unto Him with His disciples also, He said unto them, Whosoever will come after Me, let him deny himself, and take up his cross, and follow Me. For whosoever will save his life shall lose it; but whosoever shall lose his life for My sake and the gospel's, the same shall save it. For what shall it profit a man, if he shall gain the whole world, and lose his own soul? Or what shall a man give in exchange for his soul? Whosoever therefore shall be ashamed of Me and of My words in this adulterous and sinful generation; of him also shall the Son of Man be ashamed, when He cometh in the glory of His Father with the holy angels.

Mark 8:34-38

Jesus is talking about the effects of His salvation. If anyone has been saved by this message of the gospel, they'll live to share the gospel. Authentic disciples will enjoy going in Jesus' name to change lives for the sake of the gospel. Why do they enjoy going? It is because they know they have a life-changing message.

WE CAN KNOW

Let me illustrate this point by using the church at Thessalonica. They were a group of people who were interrupted by the Lord and invaded by His grace. Paul bears witness to this fact and helps us see how God works in the life of His elect:

Knowing, brethren beloved, your election of God. For our gospel came not unto you in word only, but also in power, and in the Holy Ghost, and in much assurance; as ye know what manner of men we were among you for your sake. And ye became followers of us, and of the Lord, having received the word in much affliction, with joy of the Holy Ghost: So that ye were ensamples to all that believe in Macedonia and Achaia. For from you sounded out the word of the Lord not only in Macedonia and Achaia, but also in every place your faith to God-ward is spread abroad; so that we need not to speak any thing. For they themselves shew of us what manner of entering in we had unto you, and how ye turned to God from idols to serve the living and true God; And to wait for His Son from heaven, whom He raised from the dead, even Jesus, which delivered us from the wrath to come.

1 Thessalonians 1:4-10

In the above passage, we see three specific marks that proved these men and women were the elect of God:

1. **How the Word of God Was Revealed -** Paul knew they were the elect of God because of how the gospel came to them. God used three things to reveal His message to His people. (1) His servants preached the gospel with power (2) He anointed the preaching with the Holy Spirit (3) He proved His power through the lives of the witnesses He changed as they demonstrated how the gospel effected their lives. In chapter two, he goes on to say they didn't have to entertain, flatter, or cheat them through craftiness of speech to believe the Word preached to them. God internally initiated and was intimately involved with the preaching of the Word.

2. **How the Word of God Was Received -** Not only was God involved in the preaching, but in the hearing of the Word. God opened their ears, eyes, and hearts to receive what was preached. They didn't accept the fact it was mere men speaking, but God Himself communicating His pleasure and purpose in delivering them from themselves: "For this cause also thank we God without ceasing, because, when ye received the word of God which ye heard of us, ye received it not as the word of men, but as it is in truth, the word of God, which effectually worketh also in you that believe" (1 Thessalonians 2:13). As with all believers, they received the Word with gladness of heart.[176] "Whosoever will come let him take of the water of life freely" and with a glad heart. All believers of the gospel receive it with great rejoicing.

3. How the Word of God Was Redemptive - They followed the Lord and His people because they turned from their idols to serve the living and true God. They also started living in the light of the return of Jesus Christ. But notice what Paul said about these people who are, without question, the elect of God. They sounded forth in every place the good news of their deliverance from self-centered living and their deliverance to unashamed and unadulterated service of the King of Kings and Lord of Lords and Deliverer of Deliverers. They preached the gospel of God to a lost and dying world while encouraging others to do the same.

MARKED BY THE TRUTH

These three marks will always distinguish God's anointed followers from imposters. Jesus Christ came to deploy us into His work. In Luke's account of the Great Commission, we see reason why all of God's "anointed followers of the Anointed One" will preach the gospel: "Jesus said unto them, "Thus it is written, and thus it behooved Christ to suffer, and to rise from the dead the third day, and that repentance and remission of sins should be preached in His name among all nations, beginning at Jerusalem. And ye are witnesses of these things" (Luke 24:46-48). We must all admit that the life, death, and resurrection of Jesus Christ is the most significant moment in time. The Bible describes the time of Jesus as the fullness of time: "But when the fullness of the time was come, God sent forth His Son, made of a woman, made under the law, to redeem them that were under the law, that we might receive the adoption of sons" (Galatians 4:4-5). It goes without question that this is speaking of the most significant moment in time. We must also admit it is the most significant message throughout time.

CARVED IN ETERNITY

When Jesus told His disciples the reason for His suffering, death, and resurrection, He said it was going to happen because it was written or engraved and therefore it was eternally decreed in heaven to be. Notice what else He said: He said not only was it written about Him, but it was also written about us. It was written in heaven that we would preach repentance and remission of sins in His name. Christ was quoting what was written; therefore, He was speaking in the third person concerning Himself. Wow! He was quoting what had been engraved in heaven from eternity past and would never be erased. It was God's saving plan of redemption. And He committed it to all of His creatures that had become "anointed followers of the Anointed One"—Christians. This was why those at Thessalonica preached the gospel and sounded forth their faith in the Lord. It has been written! He has come to deploy us into the mission fields!

PURPOSEFUL

Discipleship is always intentional and purposeful. Why is it intentional? Disciple-making is a direct and intentional act of obedience to the great commission. When disciples obey the Lord, it's always purposeful. We will never accidentally please or obey the Lord with eternal reward. Preaching the gospel is an act of obedience. Preaching the gospel of the kingdom will always include the gospel of the Lord Jesus Christ, just as discipleship must include evangelism. We are commissioned to make disciples of the kingdom. To do this, we must preach repentance.

TURNING FROM SIN TO TURN TO JESUS

Repentance is a gift from God and the effectual work of godly sorrow. We can think, act, love, look, and walk differently after godly sorrow effectually produces in us changed hearts and minds. When godly sorrow has moved us to deal with our sin, we will think differently about sin and the Lord afterward. This thinking differently is what is known as repentance. It is a gift of God and must be seen as such. When God is brought into view and the light of His ways shines upon our darkness, we must deal with our sinful condition through His grace.

THE NEGATIVE

When God leads us to repentance, there will always be two aspects involved. There is the negative aspect of repentance and the positive aspect of repentance. The negative aspect of repentance is the turning away from sin. God has granted us forgiveness in order for us to fear Him: "If Thou, Lord, shouldest mark iniquities, O Lord, who shall stand? But there is forgiveness with Thee, that thou mayest be feared" (Psalm 130:3-4). When we are forgiven of sin, we give place to God over the sin that once held us. When a man gives place to the Lord, he departs from sin. Why does he do this? He does it because he hates sin. "The fear of the Lord is to hate evil" (Proverbs 8:13a). "By mercy and truth iniquity is purged: and by the fear of the Lord men depart from evil" (Proverbs 16:6). When God grants forgiveness through the graceful gift of repentance, man sees sin in a negative way.

THE POSITIVE

The positive aspect of repentance is also found in the fear of the Lord, because the man who fears the Lord turns to Him to find refuge and confidence: "In the fear of the Lord is strong confidence: and His children shall have a place of refuge. The fear of the Lord is a fountain of life, to depart from the snares of death" (Proverbs 14:26-27). The positive side of repentance is that a man turns to the Lord and His ways. When a man fears the Lord, it will be manifested in a changed life. He'll enjoy the Lord more than sin. "God will hear, and afflict them... Because they have no changes, therefore they fear not God" (Psalm 55:19).[177]

HELP NEEDED

Preaching repentance and remission of sins in Jesus' name is not something we can do on our own. Jesus did come to deploy us, but not to deploy us without His power: "And, behold, I send the promise of My Father upon you: but tarry ye in the city of Jerusalem, until ye be endued with power from on high" (Luke 24:49). It is also eternally written that we have to be empowered to be a witness of Jesus. Luke's account in the book of Acts seals it as a necessity when He describes the ascension of the Lord: "But ye shall receive power, after that the Holy Ghost is come upon you: and ye shall be witnesses unto Me both in Jerusalem, and in all Judaea, and in Samaria, and unto the uttermost part of the earth" (Acts 1:8). Are you a witness of Jesus? Are you preaching the most significant message of the most significant moment in time? Do you need to give your life to the Lord now? Are you acting like a fool? Do you need to repent and ask the Lord for forgiveness? He lives to be Lord over your life today.

PRECIOUS PROMISES

The Bible gives us some wonderful promises about being a soul winner: "And they that be wise shall shine as the brightness of the firmament; and they that turn many to righteousness as the stars for ever and ever" (Daniel 12:3). "The fruit of the righteous is a tree of life; and he that winneth souls is wise" (Proverbs 11:30). Why are they wise? Why do they shine? God is at work in and through the life of the all His people.

> Wherefore, my beloved, as ye have always obeyed, not as in my presence only, but now much more in my absence, work out your own salvation with fear and trembling. For it is God which worketh in you both to will and to do of His good pleasure. Do all things without murmurings and disputings: That ye may be blameless and harmless, the sons of God, without rebuke, in the midst of a crooked and perverse nation, among whom ye shine as lights in the world; Holding forth the word of life; that I may rejoice in the day of Christ, that I have not run in vain, neither laboured in vain.
>
> Philippians 2:12-16

The heart of every authentic disciple is to make other disciple-makers. Paul understood the fact that if they at Philippi were not disciple-makers, his labor would have been in vain. This is at the heart of every champion of the truth.

THE AIM

Disciples who are dangerously strong for the truth on earth live to be in harmony with faith. The aim of faith is salvation of the souls. We see this even in Proverbs:

> If thou forbear to deliver them that are drawn unto death, and those that are ready to be slain; If thou sayest, Behold, we knew it not; doth not He that pondereth the heart consider it? and He that keepeth thy soul, doth not He know it? and shall not He render to every man according to his works?
>
> Proverbs 24:11-12

God delivers us to deploy us. He makes Himself known to us so we can be His witnesses:

> Ye are My witnesses, saith the Lord, and My servant whom I have chosen: that ye may know and believe Me, and understand that I am He: before Me there was no God formed, neither shall there be after Me. I, even I, am the Lord; and beside Me there is no Saviour. I have declared, and have saved, and I have shewed, when there was no strange god among you: therefore ye are my witnesses, saith the Lord, that I am God.
>
> Isaiah 43:10-12

Notice the order if you would. God chose them to know, believe, and understand He is God and there is no other. They were His witnesses, chosen by Him to know and to make known. This same order is revealed to Paul by Ananias in Damascus: And he said, "The God of our fathers hath chosen thee, that thou shouldest know His will, and see that Just One, and shouldest hear the voice of His mouth. For thou shalt be His witness unto all men of what thou hast seen and heard" (Acts 22:14-15). He was chosen to know, see, and hear so he could be a witness of God. It is through hearing that we see and in seeing that we know so we can be a witness of the Lord. We must be chosen to be a witness of the Lord. We must be chosen to deliver those who are drawn unto death. We must be chosen to hold back those stumbling to the slaughter. Are you chosen to declare the praises of Him who called you out of darkness into His marvelous light? "But ye are a chosen generation, a royal priesthood, an holy nation, a peculiar people; that ye should shew forth the praises of Him who hath called you out of darkness into His marvelous light: Which in time past were not a people, but are now the people of God: which had not obtained mercy, but now have obtained mercy" (1 Peter 2:9-10).

WHOSOEVER COME

Paul didn't know who the elect were until God worked His grace in their lives, as He did with Paul. Yet he knew God had an elect, and he knew he was deployed to go and let them know they belonged to the Lord Jesus. He knew he had a commission to represent Him as a public servant and had the sacred duty of preaching the gospel to the nations. He also knew they could not offer up a sacrifice acceptable unto the Lord until they were made new creatures by God: "That I should be the minister of Jesus Christ to the Gentiles, ministering the gospel of God, that the offering up of the Gentiles might be acceptable, being sanctified by the Holy Ghost" (Romans 15:16). Paul knew they could not glorify God the way they should because they were dead in sin. They needed to be regenerated and renewed by the Holy Spirit to heavily promote the Lord and His ways. This is why Paul told Timothy he endured all He had endured: "Therefore I endure all things for the elect's sakes, that they may also obtain the salvation which is in Christ Jesus with eternal glory" (2 Timothy 2:10).

FOR HIS GLORY

We are deployed by the Lord for His glory, not ours. It is not so men can be better men. It is not so women can have peace and joy.

It is not so people can escape hell and go to heaven. Yes, all these things will be byproducts of salvation in Christ, but they are not the aim of salvation. The aim of salvation is for God to be glorified through the life sacrifice of His Son, Jesus Christ. The only way a man can take part in glorifying the Lord is through being saved by the grace of God. Salvation is for God's glory and so that we can rejoice from its matchless benefits.

TAKING HOLD

Peter described the aim of the faith as the salvation of souls: "Receiving the end of your faith, even the salvation of your souls" (1 Peter 1:9). The meaning of this verse refers to an individual who is willing to lose their life for the sake of others. They are living in persecution because they are calling on men everywhere to repent of their sin and turn to Jesus. The reason they are doing this is because they have taken hold of salvation to tend to the aim of the faith, which is the salvation of souls. Have you received (taken hold of/ tended to) the end of your faith (the salvation of souls)? Isn't this exactly what Christ came to accomplish. He came to seek and save that which is lost. It's not enough to desire to go; you must lose your life for Jesus' sake and the gospel.[178] "The soul of the sluggard desireth, and hath nothing: but the soul of the diligent shall be made fat" (Proverbs 13:4). You must be diligent to act on what you know to be true and trust that it is of God.

TO PERSUADE

Jesus Christ did not deliver us to make claims of how we desire to do His work. No! He disciples us so we can be deployed in the work in which God's people have always been involved. His providential redemption has always been the priority of all His Spirit-filled saints. Paul told Titus he was a slave of God and an apostle of the Lord Jesus Christ for the persuasion of God's elect in order for them to know and recognize the truth, which would always be in line with godliness.[179] He told the church at Rome the same thing in regards to making the Gentiles obey the gospel: "For I will not dare to speak of any of those things which Christ hath not wrought by me, to make the Gentiles obedient, by word and deed..." (Romans 15:18). Paul tended to the aim of the faith—the salvation of souls. He put thought into it. He gave all his resources to it. He acted on what he knew. He was once lost, but now he had been found. He was once blind and in darkness, but now he could see. He had to go tell the Good News because he was compelled by the love of Christ. Oh, how beautiful are the feet of those who bring glad tidings.

POWER TO PREACH

There are many different methods to preaching the gospel. But there is only one way to preach the gospel, and that is God's way. Anyone can preach the gospel in word only. But the kingdom is not only in word, but also in power. We need power when we preach the gospel. We need the Holy Spirit when we bear witness to the life of Christ. We also need a personal witness that gives evidence the gospel is the power of God unto salvation for them who believe.[180] Paul asked the church at Colossae to pray for him and for a door to be opened for the Word. He asked them to pray for him as he spoke the mystery of Christ:

> Continue in prayer, and watch in the same with thanksgiving; Withal praying also for us, that God would open unto us a door of utterance, to speak the mystery of Christ, for which I am also in bonds: That I may make it manifest, as I ought to speak. Walk in wisdom toward them that are without, redeeming the time. Let your speech be alway with grace, seasoned with salt, that ye may know how ye ought to answer every man.
> Colossians 4:2-6

He wanted to preach with authority and accuracy.[181] He instructed the church to walk in wisdom and to take advantage of every opportunity they had to share the gospel. How were they to do this? He told them to speak truth and cast their life witness alongside it. They were to take the grace truths of God and season them with their personal testimony.

Tell the truth and show how the truth has affected your personal life. This is what it means to be a witness. We can't witness what we don't know. Tell the world what you know about Jesus and how He transformed your life.

ACCURACY AND AUTHORITY

Paul knew just how powerful this way was. It was God's way! Truth had to be spoken accurately and with authority. Yet Paul also knew we all needed people interceding for us. Just think about how long Paul had been preaching the gospel at this point. For twenty-five-plus years he had preached the gospel. He was currently in jail for preaching the gospel as he wrote this letter. Yet he asked them to pray for more doors to be opened for the Word, and he asked them to pray for him to accurately share the mystery. Wow! Here's the man who taught us so much about the message of the cross, and he's asking for prayer to preach the same message. Praise God for this revelation. We need people praying for us when we witness. We need to pray for others as they live to be a witness of the Lord. We are dealing with life or death. We must be convinced and convicted about these things and confident in the message we preach.

IT MATTERS

What really matters is that you witness! What matters most is that you witness God's way. "And Paul, as his manner was, went in unto them, and three sabbath days reasoned with them out of the Scriptures, opening and alleging, that Christ must needs have suffered, and risen again from the dead; and that this Jesus, whom I preach unto you, is Christ" (Acts 17:2-3). Paul's speech was given with grace. He took the Scriptures and opened them up thoroughly by teaching the truth within. He then seasoned the truth with salt by placing himself alongside the truth. He was demonstrating how Christ changed his life so powerfully and radically.

CAST IT ALONGSIDE

He showed Philemon how to do the exact same thing. He told Philemon his partnership with God could be powerful and effective, providing that Philemon would recognize and acknowledge there was something beneficial in him that could be used for Christ's sake.[182] This is what it means to speak the truth in love. Sharing God's redemption, and sharing it His way. This leads to an effective partnership. We are co-laborers with God in this work:

> Who then is Paul, and who is Apollos, but ministers by whom ye believed, even as the Lord gave to every man? I have planted, Apollos watered; but God gave the increase. So then neither is he that planteth any thing, neither he that watereth; but God that giveth the increase. Now he that planteth and he that watereth are one: and every man shall receive his own reward according to his own labour. For we are labourers together with God: ye are God's husbandry, ye are God's building. According to the grace of God which is given unto me, as a wise masterbuilder, I have laid the foundation, and another buildeth thereon. But let every man take heed how he buildeth thereupon. For other foundation can no man lay than that is laid, which is Jesus Christ.
>
> 1 Corinthians 3:5-11

It's never about us, but it's always about Him. He has delivered you to disciple you. He disciples you so He can defend you. He defends you to deploy you. He deploys you to gather His sheep. What a Master! What a Savior! What a Friend! Trust Him and His ways today and He'll use you to impact the world for His glory.

IT'S NOT HARD

Do not look for the most popular way to witness. Just tell people about the Redeemer who delivered your life. Tell them how you have fallen in love with Jesus and how much you like Him. Let them know how God interrupted you with Jesus and invaded your life with His grace. Open up the Scriptures and show how God planned and purposed to rescue sinners. Demonstrate how He has forgiven and reconciled your life as a witness to them. Just go tell somebody, somewhere, and do it soon. Go do this every day.

DO IT

Jude exhorts us to do the following:

...building up yourselves on your most holy faith, praying in the Holy Ghost, Keep yourselves in the love of God, looking for the mercy of our Lord Jesus Christ unto eternal life. And of some have compassion, making a difference: And others save with fear, pulling them out of the fire; hating even the garment spotted by the flesh. Now unto Him that is able to keep you from falling, and to present you faultless before the presence of His glory with exceeding joy, To the only wise God our Saviour, be glory and majesty, dominion and power, both now and ever. Amen.

Jude 1:20-25

The fields are ready. Get right and stay right with the Lord. Stay focused on Him while you walk steadfastly with Him. He's promised to use you in these last days. Pray that in these last days, God, the Lord of the harvest, will thrust laborers out into His harvest. Have fun, fear God, and always be faith-filled. Magnify the Lord! Jesus did come to deploy all of us into His harvest.

NOT FISHING, NOT FOLLOWING

Take your left hand and use your thumb and fingers to remember what I call the five-fold effect of the gospel. When it is preached in the power of the Holy Spirit, it is eternally effective: First, the gospel will always wound the sinner before it heals him; second, the gospel will always warn the sinner of a sure judgment of sin; third, the gospel will always wow the sinner with the fact that God gave His Son as His Substitute to take sins and impart His righteousness on us; fourth, the gospel will always work the sinner to surrender his sin and life over to Jesus; and fifth, the gospel will always win the sinner over to go preach repentance to a lost and dying world so others, too, can be delivered from darkness and transferred into the kingdom of God's Son.

THE FIVE-FOLD EFFECT OF THE GOSPEL

1. **Wounds** the sinner before it can heal him.
2. **Warns** the sinner of a sure judgment.
3. **Wows** the sinner with the fact that God gave us His Son.
4. **Works** the sinner to surrender his sin and life over to Jesus.
5. **Wins** the sinner over so he can see others delivered from darkness unto the light of God's Son.

The world needs to hear the true Gospel that magnifies the Lord. Go tell them why Jesus came and what He came to do. "He came to seek and save that which is lost." (Luke 19:10) Go tell them how and why He came to die for the lives of men, women, boys, and girls. **Go tell them He came to:**

1. **Defer** His rights, results, and rewards to His Father.
2. **Define** for us what is truth, who is truth, and what truth does.
3. **Declare** the heart and holiness of the God the Father
4. **Demonstrate** the love of God, His loyalty, and His line of judgment.
5. **Destroy** the works of the devil and the power of darkness.
6. **Deliver** us from something to something.
7. **Disciple** us all the days of our lives.
8. **Divide** us from the world.
9. **Defend** us from ourselves, the world and the devil.
10. **Deploy** us in the harvest

God bless you as you *Magnify the Lord!*

End Notes

1. Proverbs 25:2
2. John 14:6
3. Romans 8:29
4. Hebrews 12:1-3, Acts 20:24
5. 1 Corinthians 1:30
6. Lamentations 3:19-24
7. Matthew 6:33
8. Proverbs 11:25, 2 Timothy 3:16-17
9. Isaiah 7:14 ; 9:6-7
10. 2 Peter 3:18
11. Hebrews 11:6-7; Psalm 25:12-14, 81:10-16, 119:49
12. Luke 6:38
13. Matthew 6:6
14. Mark 8:34-38
15. Isaiah 55:10:11
16. Matthew 7:29
17. Romans 8:28-29
18. Joshua 6
19. Judges 7
20. 1 Corinthians 2:14
21. 2 Chronicles 20
22. Acts 3:11-26
23. Luke 9:22
24. 1 Corinthians 15:20-28
25. Proverbs 10:3
26. Matthew 5:3-11

27. Hebrews 11
28. 2 Corinthians 1:20
29. John 8:44, 2 Corinthians 11:14-15, 1 John 3:8, Revelation 12:9
30. John 18:37
31. 2 Corinthians 10:1-6; Psalm 119:11, 119:105; Proverbs 2, 3:5-6, 16:3
32. Genesis 6:5; 8:21; Isaiah 64:6; Jeremiah 17:5; Romans 3:10-18, 23
33. Romans 1:18-32
34. Genesis 1-3
35. Ephesians 2:1-5
36. 2 Corinthians 5:17-21
37. John 18:37, 7:7
38. 1 John 2:15-17, 4:1-6; James 3:13-18, 4:1-10; John 7:7, 17:14-19, 18:36; Titus 3:9-11; 1 Corinthians 6:1-11; John 20:21
39. James 4:4
40. Proverbs 24:11-12
41. Micah 3:1-12
42. Romans 8:5-11, 2 Peter 2
43. Acts 20:26-32
44. Jeremiah 23
45. Amos 6:1
46. Romans 3:4
47. John 8:31-59
48. 2 Corinthians 3, 4; Matthew 13:10-17
49. John 10
50. Ephesians 2:8-10, 2 Corinthians 5:17-21
51. Colossians 1:24-27
52. 1 Timothy 3:16
53. 1 Corinthians 16:22
54. 1 John 1:1-9
55. Hebrews 6:3
56. Luke 27:1-35
57. John 1:1-3
58. Colossians 1:15-18

59. Deuteronomy 29:29
60. Romans 16:25-27
61. John 1:1-18
62. Ephesians 1:3-12, 1 John 2:1-2
63. Romans 9:22-23
64. Genesis 5:22
65. Romans 15:4, Isaiah 66:1-2
66. 1 Corinthians 1:18-21
67. Galatians 5:17
68. Matthew 6:31-34
69. Exodus 3:14
70. Romans 9:23
71. Ephesians 1
72. 2 Timothy 1:8-10, Titus 3:4-7
73. 2 Corinthians 5:14-21
74. Hebrews 10:10
75. Matthew 24:14
76. Acts 28:23, 30-31
77. John 15:22
78. John 19:39
79. Jeremiah 32:38-44
80. Exodus 32:11-14, Deuteronomy 32:19-27
81. 2 Samuel 12
82. Galatians 6; Hebrews 12
83. Hebrews 12
84. Genesis 1-2
85. Genesis 3
86. Romans 5
87. Psalm 1:1-6, 119:155; Romans 2:6-10, Ephesians 2:8-10, Titus 3:3-8
88. 2 Corinthians 5:17-21
89. Ephesians 4:7-8, Colossians 1:12-13, 1 Corinthians 6:20, 2 Corinthians 5:14-15
90. 1 Corinthians 16:22
91. Psalm 3:7
92. Isaiah 55:10-11
93. John 14:12

94. Revelation 3:1
95. 2 Chronicles 34-35
96. Matthew 6:25-34
97. Psalm 91
98. 1 Kings 12:26-33
99. 2 Kings 17:28-29, 17:32, 17:41
100. Matthew 15:8-9
101. Hebrews 3:6, 14; 5:9; 11:14-16
102. Jeremiah 17:9
103. Romans 3:4
104. 1 Timothy 2:5-6
105. Colossians 3:3-4
106. Romans 7:1-6
107. Proverbs 23:7
108. Psalm 49:5-15
109. Hebrews 11:1
110. Romans 10:17
111. Ecclesiastes 4:12
112. 2 Peter 3, 2 Thessalonians 1:8-10
113. Romans 1:18-32
114. Titus 2:11-14
115. Colossians 1:13
116. John 17, Romans 12:1-2, Ephesians 5:9-15
117. 2 Corinthians 13:5, Hebrews 3, 1 Peter 3:15-17
118. 1 Corinthians 15:56
119. Hebrews 2:14-15, 1 John 4:17-19
120. 1 John 5:18
121. Ephesians 2:8-10, 2 Peter 1:1-11, Philippians 2:11-14
122. Mark 8:34-38
123. Romans 6:16-22
124. 1 Timothy 3:14-16
125. 1 Peter 1:1-12
126. Philippians 2:5-11
127. 1 Peter 1:6-10
128. Psalm 34:18
129. Matthew 5:6; Is. 61:1-3, 11

130. Psalm 16:3; 142:7; 32:10, 7; 33:1; 34:1-3; 2 John 1:1-3; Luke 17:1-10; Ephesians 5:32; Psalm 133
131. 1 Peter 2:9-11 ; 3:15
132. Ephesians 5:30-33
133. 2 Corinthians 5:14-15
134. Galatians 3, Romans 9
135. Psalm 89:19-23
136. Matthew 22:32
137. Psalm 31:19
138. Matthew 10:24-25
139. Luke 14:33-35
140. Philippians 3:7-21
141. Romans 8:28
142. 2 Corinthians 4:10-12
143. 1 Peter 1:13-25
144. I was actively serving in the Navy when Jesus interrupted my life and invaded me with grace and truth.
145. Matthew 18:15-20, 1 Corinthians 5
146. 2 Corinthians 5:17-21
147. 1 Corinthians 4:1-2
148. 1 Timothy. 5
149. Cain wanted to be accepted and noticed for what he did (Genesis 4, Jude v.11).
150. 3:1-3
151. Matthew 24:4, 11, 24
152. Matthew 24:45
153. John 14:6
154. Psalm 66
155. Psalm 55:21
156. Deuteronomy 32:10-12
157. Proverbs 2
158. Psalm 17:13-15, Psalm 49:11-13, Philippians 3:17-21
159. John 10:16
160. Psalm 23
161. 2 Corinthians 4:10-13
162. 2 Corinthians 5:17
163. Hebrews 2:14-18

164. Ephesians 6:10-20
165. 1 Peter 8-11
166. 1 Corinthians 10:1-13
167. Ephesians 6:10-18
168. James 4:5-10
169. Deuteronomy 20
170. 2 Corinthians 10:1-6
171. Praying under the influence of the Spirit and instruction of the Scripture is the *safest* and *surest* way to touch the heart of God. We are exhorted by the Scriptures to be filled with the Spirit and to allow the Word of Christ to dwell richly in us (Ephesians 5:18; Colossians 3:16). Talking can be used to help someone organize their thoughts as they enter into the presence of the Lord in prayer. This acrostic flows with the prayer that Jesus used to teach His disciples how to pray in Matthew 6:9-13. Each letter in the word *talking* represents something you can do with the Lord. It stands for: **Telling, affirming, listening, knowing, inviting, naming, giving.** *T* means **telling** God what you know about Him ("Our Father, Hallowed be Thy name."). *A* means **affirming** God's kingdom and His will and ways ("Thy kingdom come, Thy will be done..."). *L* means **listening** for God's voice and will while you pray for His "...will to be done on earth as it is in heaven." *K* means **knowing** with all confidence God hears available seekers ("Our," "us," "we"). *I* means **inviting** God to take over your life now by invading you with His eternal will ("...on earth as it is in heaven."). *N* means **naming** your need to rest your life in His promises and your dependence upon Him to meet your daily needs ("Give us...," "And forgive us...," "...do not lead us into temptation, but deliver us..."). *G* means **giving** God your trust and the glory He deserves ("For Thine is the kingdom and the power and the glory forever. Amen.").
172. Psalm 34:1-3
173. *Promote/honor* means "to promote with weight."
174. Romans 8:18-22

175. Acts 28:23, 31
176. Luke 19:6, Acts 2:41, Acts 13:48
177. Refer to chapter three for a more detailed look at repentance.
178. Mark 8:34-38
179. Titus 1:1-2
180. Romans 1:16, 1 Corinthians 1:18
181. Ephesians 6:18-20
182. Philemon 1:6

About the Author

Nick Holden grew up in Covington, Louisiana, where he met his bride of nineteen years, Stephanie. Nick, Stephanie, and their three daughters live in Meridian, Mississippi. Prior to his calling into the ministry, Nick served in the US Navy. His entire life centered around pleasing himself. He was a lost sinner living out the carnal pleasures of his depraved nature until the kindness and the love of God his Savior toward man was made known to him through the gospel. (Titus 3:3-7) He was interrupted by Jesus and invaded by His grace to deny himself, take up his cross, and follow his Deliverer in July of 1997. He heard God calling him into full-time ministry and surrendered in obedience to His call in September of 1998. The church ordained him as a deacon in January of 1999 and ordained him into the gospel ministry in October of the same year.

He accepted his first and only church position in September of 1999 in the Meridian area, where he served as pastor for seven-plus years. In June of 2006, he and his family surrendered to be missionaries to the body of Christ in America, and they started Truth Impacts Ministries. He left pastoral work in January, and his first month as a full-time evangelist was in February of 2007. He and his family are members of and serve the glorious kingdom of God from Faith Baptist Church in Meridian, Mississippi.

Nick has written several studies and other materials for the purpose of seeing Jesus heavily promoted in our day. He has a study that deals with sixteen indicators of a backslider in heart that are very useful for pre-revival preparation. It is a character study of King Saul. The heart of the material is teaching God's people how to recognize and respond properly to the God-given indicators of a wayward heart. It is designed to be used **six to three** weeks prior to revival for the purpose of undergirding the pastor to lead his flock to repentance. *Magnify the Lord* is his first book. Pray for him as God prepares his heart and mind to follow the leadership of the Lord in a writing ministry.

On the Web: www.truthimpacts.org
By e-mail: truthimpacts@comcast.net

Truth Impacts Ministries

"Dedicated and determined to teach God's people how to discern truth for themselves for the glory of God."

Truth Impacts Ministries (**T.I.M**) is the family ministry of Nick and Stephanie Holden. They and their three daughters have given themselves to the Lord Jesus Christ and the advancement of His kingdom's glory. After seven years as a pastor and being involved in nearly fifty revivals, the Holdens have seen the need to help God's people learn how to discern truth for themselves.

The church in America must recover the ability to supernaturally discern truth. The Holdens are missionaries with a message for this generation, which is in desperate need of revival. They know that truth, when accepted in humility and acted upon passionately, will impact ministries in any age and in all cultures. Jesus, who is the Truth, was born and sent into this world to bear witness to what truth really is and expose the lie (John 1:37, 14:6, 8:32).

T.I.M. exists to glorify the Lord Jesus and to help His people become dangerously strong for the truth on the earth. Champions for the truth are what America needs in this hour. **T.I.M.** understands the thoughts, emotions, and lifestyles of most people are a reality, even undeniable facts, but they are not rooted in or the result of truth. The Holdens live to help others discern the difference.

As servant slaves of Jesus, the Holdens desire to wash the feet of the disciples with living water. They know the Father has dug life-producing wells, yet the enemy has covered some of them up with the dirt of this world. They want the water to be restored and released again (Genesis 26, Isaiah 12:3, John 7:38).

They are your servants for revivals, conferences, Bible studies, retreats, and music through the leading of the Lord. For more information and availability, you can reach **T.I.M.** at one of the following:

On the Web at: <u>www.truthimpacts.org</u>
By e-mail: <u>truthimpacts@comcast.net</u>

"Uncovering the wells of salvation so God's people can drink from them once again with joy."

Printed in the United States
200346BV00003B/103-525/A